MANAGEMENT PROBLEMS OF CORPORATE ACQUISITIONS

Management Problems
of
Corporate Acquisitions

MYLES L. MACE
Professor of Business Administration

GEORGE G. MONTGOMERY, JR.
Formerly Research Associate in Business Administration

DIVISION OF RESEARCH
GRADUATE SCHOOL OF BUSINESS ADMINISTRATION
HARVARD UNIVERSITY
BOSTON · 1962

Foreword

IN VIEW of the almost universal appearance of acquisitions and mergers in the history of our larger companies, it is not surprising that the process and its consequences have received considerable attention from business regulatory agencies. Nor is it surprising that there has been legislation to limit and control these activities. The legal and economic aspects of mergers and acquisitions have been explored at length with a large output of reports and articles dealing with these topics. What *is* surprising, on the other hand, is the small amount of attention that has apparently been paid to the *management problems* associated with mergers and acquisitions. The thorough study of these problems reported in this volume by Professor Mace and Mr. Montgomery thus provides information which has long been needed and which should be of great value to the managements of growing enterprises.

The study considers and looks at the acquisition process as a whole from the initial decision to acquire (or be acquired) to the end result when the acquired organization has become an integral functioning part of the combined company. Its focus is upon the management problems arising at each stage of the process. The study brings out the major questions to be considered both from the point of view of the management of a company contemplating entering upon an acquisition program and from the point of view of managers or owners considering an offer to merge or sell. In addition, the study reports on the ways in which a number of companies have successfully met the many problems encountered in the course of acquiring other companies. Each major step is described and the attendant problems and pertinent issues are examined in detail. These are illustrated in each case by examples based upon the experiences of a variety of manufacturing concerns.

Financial support for this study was provided by an allocation from research funds made available to the School by The Associates of the Harvard Business School. We are deeply grateful to the many companies whose contributions to The Associates have made this and other research studies possible.

Lewis B. Ward
Professor of Business Research

Soldiers Field
Boston, Massachusetts
March 1962

Preface

As MEMBERS of a faculty interested in today's and tomorrow's management problems, the authors undertook a research study of the problems involved in the acquisition of one company by another. One of the authors, Professor Mace, was vice president, director, and general manager of the Electronics Equipment Division of Litton Industries, Beverly Hills, California, from 1955 until 1958. During this period he participated in the early growth of Litton, both through acquisition and through internal developments. This experience together with the increasing rate of acquisitions in other companies and industries stimulated his interest in making a study broader than the experience of one company.

The other author, Mr. Montgomery, after graduating from the Harvard Business School and interested primarily in a career in business, stayed on at the School as a research associate and devoted two years to this project. At the present time, Mr. Montgomery is with the investment banking firm of White, Weld & Company, New York City.

In this report will be found both disguised and undisguised names of executives, companies, industries, and geographical locations. Field research efforts, such as this, depend upon candid and open discussion of the real problems involved, and the publication of intimate discussions must observe these confidences. The material has not been disguised when there is no possibility of embarrassment to the executives and companies involved. But when the data might in any way have caused the cooperating executives to regret having provided the essential information, every effort has been made to disguise the sources of this information. Our purpose is not to show how managements erred, but rather to distill from their experiences lessons which might be of help to others. We are greatly indebted to the many busy executives who shared their time and experience so that others might gain from this knowledge. Acknowledgment by name is precluded, but the debt is real.

The case examples which have been chosen and presented as supporting evidence for our conclusions were greatly simplified, of course. We made every effort to maintain the integrity of the facts given to us, to report the circumstances faithfully, and to derive whatever useful generalizations seemed logical and appropriate. All descriptions of company situations represent the experiences of operating managements. We believe this basic and primary source of data to be essential.

We have endeavored to extract from the extensive field studies what Dean Stanley F. Teele of the Harvard Business School once described as currently useful generalizations. We hope these will be of value to line and staff management executives. But, in addition, we believe that the abbreviated case material presented herein from which these generalizations are derived will enable executives to find situations substantially similar to their own. One value of case material is that it permits readers to think about their own problems with the recorded experience of others as background. We believe that there is usefulness in reporting the details of some recent acquisition management problems so that line and staff executives can share vicariously the experience of others and, with this knowledge, can shape, cut, qualify, and adapt these lessons to their own situations. The findings of this research effort are intended primarily for top management executives interested in acquisition as an approach to achieving corporate objectives and for owners and managers contemplating sale of their enterprises.

We are grateful to many of our colleagues for their suggestions, wise counsel, and critical comments. Among these are Associate Dean Russell H. Hassler, Professors Kenneth R.

Andrews, Walter F. Frese, and Lewis B. Ward. Mrs. Laura Snow contributed greatly in typing and in constructive suggestions.

We are especially appreciative to Miss Ruth Norton, Editor and Executive Secretary of the Division of Research. Her interest, sharp editorial eye, and judgment vastly improved the manuscript.

The responsibility for the conduct of the study and for the report rests, inevitably, on the authors.

MYLES L. MACE
GEORGE G. MONTGOMERY JR.

Soldiers Field
Boston, Massachusetts
March 1962

Contents

x

Contents

CHAPTER I

Introduction

THIS study was initiated as the result of suggestions by a number of business executives who were interested in learning more about the practical management problems involved in the purchase of the stock or assets of other companies. These members of top management noted that the number of corporate acquisitions had risen sharply since the end of World War II, and that some of their competitors had been buying other enterprises, and they wondered whether the acquisition of going concerns could contribute to their corporate plans for growth. Their desire for the achievement of growth objectives through the purchase of other companies was tempered by the knowledge that some companies had been quite unsuccessful either in finding desirable organizations to acquire or in operating them profitably after they were purchased. They raised such questions as: What is there about the process of acquisition that is different from the usual day-to-day operations of a business? What are the pitfalls? What are the problems?

We were also encouraged to study the management problems of acquisition by the interest expressed by owners and managers of companies who were being approached frequently by representatives of potential acquirers, business brokers, and others. The kinds of questions they asked were: What are the considerations to be taken into account when offers to purchase our companies are received? How should the decision to sell out be made? What responsibilities do we have to our employees, stockholders, communities, and ourselves?

And very soon after our study was undertaken, it became clear that many company managements who were themselves active in the acquisition process were without training, without experience, and without access to competent consulting advice, and they evidenced much concern about what they were doing in the field of acquisitions. Our discussions with these executives were extensive because of their interest in learning what other companies were doing that might provide guidance to them in their own activities.

NUMBER OF ACQUISITIONS

There is no accurate statistical or meaningful summary of the number and kinds of mergers and acquisitions that take place annually. Two agencies, the Federal Trade Commission and the National Industrial Conference Board, prepare periodic reports but on slightly different bases, hence with different results. For example, the Federal Trade Commission's total recordings of mergers and acquisitions for 1958 was 899.[1] The Conference Board's recorded total was 24.1% higher or 1,116 acquisitions for the year January 11, 1958, to January 10, 1959. The large difference here is attributable to (1) different sources used by the compiling agencies, (2) slightly dissimilar recording periods, and (3) a definition of partial acquisitions that does not cover the same specifications.[2]

But even the existence of accurate and complete reports of *all* acquisitions would provide only a partial indication of the current management involvement in the acquisition process. In addition to the purchases of companies that are consummated in any year, there are numberless unrecorded discus-

[1] Federal Trade Commission, *1958 Staff Report on Mergers,* January 14, 1959, Table I, "Mergers and Acquisitions of Manufacturing and Mining, Wholesale and Retail, Service and Other Concerns by Months: 1958."

[2] National Industrial Conference Board, *Business Record,* May 1959, p. 239.

sions and negotiations with acquisition as the objective. We found that the owners of some companies were approached as frequently as three or four times a week. And to illustrate the activity of companies interested in acquiring others, one executive stated that during the last three years he had evaluated 200 companies, approached the managements of 39, negotiated seriously with 13, and acquired 5. We found other companies with active acquisition programs that had not purchased a single company after three to five years of effort.

The statistical reports of acquisitions, the unrecorded discussions by executives interested in the purchase of other companies, and the growing recognition by managements that the acquisition of companies is an important alternative to consider in achieving corporate growth plans, combined to indicate a need for a study of some of the practical management problems involved.

DEFINITIONS

During the course of our field study, we found considerable looseness of expression when there were discussions of terms. In some cases the words merger, acquisition, and consolidation were used interchangeably. It was noted that when management representatives of an acquiring company talked with executives of a potential acquisition, the conversation was always in terms of "merger" although it was implicit and apparent that Company A proposed to "acquire" Company B. In these situations the negotiating executive of the acquiring company would discuss "merger" with the management of the company to be acquired, but when he discussed the opportunity with his board of directors, he referred invariably to the possibility of "acquisition." There seemed to be an inoffensive quality in the word "merge" not found in the word "acquire." As one executive stated, "The reasons for the difference are unclear but managements find comfort in the merging of mutual interests.   Being acquired connotes being had!"

In other situations the word merger was used to mean the union of two companies of substantially equal size while the word acquisition described the combination of a large company with a much smaller one.

This confusion of terms arises in part from tax and legal technicalities governing the form of joining two enterprises. When Corporation A acquires the stock or assets of another company, legal, tax, and financial factors determine whether the *form* of bringing together the two enterprises is a merger, a consolidation, a purchase of assets, a purchase of stock, or an exchange of stock.   Although the form selected to unite two entities is extremely important to both parties of the transaction, we are not primarily concerned here with tax, legal, and accounting considerations which are involved in a decision as to the form of a combination.   We are concerned with the *management problems* involved in the process by which companies acquire stock or assets of other enterprises. In this report, the word acquisition is used to describe this process — bringing additional economic activities or assets under a company's control, whatever legal form is used to achieve the result.

PROBLEM AREAS COVERED

Announcements substantially like the following appear in the daily press:

> The Johnson Manufacturing Company announced today it had acquired the McNamara Company of Boston, Massachusetts.
>
> The McNamara Company was organized in 1947 and has its offices and plant at 5800 South Washburn, East Boston. The company compounds, sells, and provides technical service in the field of polyester resins, used primarily in the man-

ufacture of boats. It provides related plastic products to other industries, but the plastic boat business is the primary market. It now employs slightly more than 250 persons at the East Boston plant and has technical sales and services offices in the principal boat manufacturing cities.

Johnson executives said that there would be no changes in the fundamental policies and programs created by the McNamara management and that no changes would be made in personnel or operating procedures. The McNamara Company will operate as an autonomous subsidiary of Johnson.

With the acquisition of the McNamara Company, the Johnson Manufacturing Company will have a controlled market for part of its basic resin supply. This is Johnson's initial entry into the compounding of resins for specific uses. Johnson plans to expand and accelerate the use of polyester resins in boats, construction, and other applications.

Research, development, manufacturing, and technical sales and service efforts of Johnson and McNamara will be operated together, it was stated.

The appearance of the press announcement that the Johnson Manufacturing Company had acquired the McNamara Company, that it planned to continue the fundamental policies established by McNamara management, that no major changes in personnel or operating procedures were expected, that finished product fabrication was a new field for the Johnson Company, and that research, development, fabrication, and sales efforts would be operated together, raises a large number of questions.

Why did the Johnson Company decide to grow through acquisition rather than through internal efforts? Did the Johnson Company board of directors participate in the policy decision? How did the Johnson Company organize its acquisition efforts? Who performed the function: the president? Is this a line or a staff responsibility? Why was the McNamara Company acquired? How was it found? Were brokers, commercial bankers, investment bankers, or consultants used to locate prospective companies? Who made the approach to whom in McNamara? Why did the owners of McNamara sell? What were the financial considerations? How was the value of McNamara determined? What obstacles arose during negotiations and how were these overcome? How did the Johnson Company evaluate the management of McNamara? Will the fundamental policies established by McNamara be continued? Will there be no changes in personnel and operating procedures? What is meant by the statement that research, development, fabrication, and sales will be operated together? Will McNamara operate as a decentralized division or be integrated into the Johnson Company? These questions and many others occur in any discussion of acquisitions, and answers or partial answers to such questions will be discussed in the succeeding chapters.

SOME PROBLEM AREAS NOT COVERED

Our study was not concerned with antitrust problems or the economic goodness or badness of acquisition as a method of company growth. While possible violation of antitrust laws is an important factor to be taken into account by the managements of the acquirer as well as the acquired, the relevant laws governing acquisition constitute an extremely complex field and require specialized study. Accordingly, when any acquisition has possible antitrust implications, parties to the negotiation should seek the service of professional legal counsel.

Nor were we concerned with the economic implications of acquisitions. We have not attempted to make an industry-by-industry statistical analysis of the effects of acquisitions on competition or on the resulting share of the market.

Research Method

Our research approach was to interview in depth the executives of a number of companies actively engaged in the acquisition process, either in the acquisition of others or in the process of being acquired. Included were management personnel involved in all phases of the process — some were in the early stages of thinking about buying other enterprises, some were considering selling their companies to others, a number were evaluating and negotiating, while still others were experiencing the problems of integration of the acquired organization with the acquirers.

During the year and a half of field study, we interviewed over 275 executives identified with 75 domestic manufacturing companies. One of our problems was in the selection of companies to approach. In almost every interview there were suggestions that we talk with executives from, say, the Olson Company or the Eastern Supply Corporation. And the daily press continues to report acquisitions by well-known and less well-known companies, many of which appeared to be candidates for fruitful research.

We believe that the managements we interviewed constitute a representative sample, and although there will be growing sophistication as the acquisition function matures, we hope that our findings to date are worthy of managements' attention today. More data could have been added through larger samples, but an interview termination date is required if current conclusions are to be published. Although we do not have case examples from all industry groups, the field research suggests that while every industry, and in fact every company, thinks of itself as unique, procedures in one industry apply equally well in others.

Our sample was limited to manufacturing companies involved in the acquisition process in the United States. Discussions held early in the study concerned with the acquisition of companies abroad indicated that although there are many management problems common to both foreign and domestic acquisitions, substantive differences were found that indicated a separate treatment of the problems abroad would be justified. Thus our study included only situations within the United States.

We have attempted to reproduce the actual circumstances of each illustrative situation faithfully and without undue length and detail. Many more case examples could have been used to illustrate the specific problems and solutions we found. The material selected for publication represents, we believe, typical situations from the complete sample and the addition of further examples would have resulted in redundancy.

The process of acquisition, like the process of administration, is not a mechanical, sequential performance of essential steps. Rather, the elements of acquisition are intertwined — evaluation goes on during negotiations and the problems of integration are profoundly affected by what is said by representatives of the acquirer and the acquired during business discussions. But for clarity of analysis and presentation we have arbitrarily broken our report on the process of acquisition into what seem to be workable parts, starting with the reasons for buying or selling the companies and ending with the problems of integration.

Much more will be learned over the years about management problems of acquisitions, and this report should be regarded not as final but as an analysis of the management problems of acquisition *circa* 1962.

CHAPTER II

Some Reasons for the Acquisition of One Company by Another

ACQUISITION AS A MEANS OF ACHIEVING A COMPANY'S PLAN FOR GROWTH

DURING the last few years there has been considerable discussion among professional management groups and business associations about the importance of top management planning. Planning of course includes all the major functions in a business — finance, marketing, production, personnel, plus the many subplans required under each of these headings. The methods by which any corporation's plans are achieved can take many different forms. But *one method,* which more and more managements are recognizing, is the process of acquisition.

An investment banker with extensive experience in acquisitions stated that it is a mistake to consider the acquisition alternative in a vacuum. Acquisition is *a* way to achieve corporate objectives, but there are always many other possible methods. To achieve the basic objective of making the company larger, more successful, and more profitable, many possible alternatives should be taken into account. He added that effective business strategy consists of being aware of all the variables so as to get the optimum interplay. This requires not only a clear definition of the variables but also a careful analysis of them. The completion of such an analysis then can lead to a decision whether acquisition seems to be the best answer. He reported that in some companies this careful consideration of alternatives is not done and concluded, "The main objective of growth through acquisition in a few cases seems to be to permit the executives to fly bigger DC–3s."

Too often managements think primarily of acquisitions as a method of adding products to the existing product line. It is often said that there are only two ways to grow: through the internal development of products and through the acquisition of enterprises with similar or different products.

The concept that the acquisition process is limited to broadening the product line, however, is erroneous. Many other business goals can be fulfilled by acquisition. These include strengthening the company's financial position, procuring the services of one or more key personnel or new executive talent, obtaining land, buildings, and equipment for expansion, stabilizing cyclical or seasonal types of business, avoiding concentration in a government-regulated area of industry, acquiring the technical skills of highly trained scientists, and many other critical elements in business which determine growth and success. The process of acquisition, then, is one that ought to be considered by the management of any enterprise as its plans for growth are executed. Acquisition is one way to be considered in achieving the complete set of defined objectives. And many companies have found it a very satisfactory way.

In some situations executives, having learned of unfortunate experiences in other companies as a result of acquisition, intuitively refused to consider acquisition as an element of their companies' growth programs. Such decisions are unfortunate for they deny their organizations the potential benefits of many acquisition opportunities. On the other hand, there were many executives who were pursuing active acquisition programs because in 1960 it seemed to be the fad, much as having an executive development program was in 1950. One president stated that he was determined to acquire other companies and to publicize their acquisitions in order to create a corporate image of a dynamic, aggressive, and successful company.

Like all approaches to the solution of management problems, acquisition may for any particular company provide a profitable and satisfactory alternative to other ways of expanding company activities. Acquisition *per se* does not automatically solve all problems for all companies. It is short-sighted for management to refuse to consider any acquisition, and it is foolish for management to operate on the assumption that acquisition will guarantee sound growth and increased profits. The acquisition of other companies or parts of companies is just one of many possible ways of achieving an organization's goals.

When acquisition is contemplated as one method for corporate growth, it must be remembered that it includes a large bundle of problems quite different from those involved in the day-to-day operations of a business. Failure to recognize these differences has led many managements into unfortunate and unprofitable acquisition experiences.

BIGNESS FOR BIGNESS' SAKE

Frequently during the study we encountered the expression that "We do not want to grow big through acquisition just for bigness' sake." Bigness, as such, probably has no intrinsic value if earnings per share or return on investment are not increased. We did find a few instances, however, where the purpose of the acquisition was bigness for bigness' sake and was logical. In one such situation this resulted from the policy of the Armed Services to evaluate a company's productive capability in terms of its existing production facilities, plus the financial strength indicated by substantial working capital. In this instance, where a government research and development contract had resulted in the need for a newly designed piece of equipment to be produced in volume, the company, strong in research engineers, was denied the subsequent production contract because "it was not big enough." The president indicated that the decision subsequently to acquire another organization was motivated almost completely by the need to appear more substantial and therefore to be able to qualify for production contracts. The military approach to evaluating production capability, relying almost completely on quantitative factors, discounts the ability of management to do as good a job in organizing production as it did in organizing the research effort. Acquisitions to fulfill the standards of size in order to qualify for certain production contracts have been a motivation factor in a few situations, but bigness for bigness' sake generally remains an invalid reason.

Acquisition for Investment

Perhaps the simplest reason given for an acquisition was that it was a good investment. This was given as the reason for the acquisition of a medium-sized chemical company by a nonchemical purchaser, the Trask Company. Trask was headed by what was described as a "free wheeling opportunistic entrepreneur" who, contrary to most encountered in our field research, rarely developed a plan and even if one was developed never followed it. A Trask Company director knew that the Chemco Company, located in the Middle West, was about to realize substantial profits from several years of costly research and development expenditures. Chemco had been earning slightly less than $2 a share, and its excellent nonowner management expected earnings to rise to $9 per share within five years. The principal owners of Chemco were approached by the Trask management who pointed out the large additional sales which Trask could send their way, the substantial capital available to finance Chemco's continued expansion, and the many administrative economies which could be achieved.

After the acquisition was completed, it became clear that none of the so-called business reasons cited earlier was valid. No new business was sent to Chemco, no additional capital was provided, and there were no administrative economies realized. Nevertheless, from the point of view of the Trask Company, the acquisition did provide the higher earnings anticipated by Chemco and while the reason for acquisition was described later with high-sounding words, the basic, fundamental, and single reason for the acquisition was the prospect of very substantial earnings — a good investment indeed for the Trask Company. The stockholders of the Chemco Company, however, probably would have realized more financially if they had not agreed to the sale of their company.

ACQUISITION TO SERVE A MARKET NEED

A very different reason for acquisition may be illustrated by the program of the Thompson Ramo Wooldridge Company. Here an opportunity to grow in the electronic components industry was recognized by the TRW management, an industry in which TRW had already participated profitably through its subsidiary, Pacific Semiconductors, Inc. An analysis was made of further opportunities in the electronics industry, and the passive component segment appeared appealing for the following cited reasons:

1. Component business rides the trend of the electronics industry which is expanding rapidly;
2. A well-established component business has a stability not found in do-or-die systems companies;
3. The component segment of the electronics industry is made up of many small and medium-sized companies rather than large, deeply entrenched companies — thus it is easier to enter;

4. The component market — especially the passive component market —is a large, attractive market;

5. Industrial marketing capability is required, and development of consumer distribution channels is unnecessary;

6. In general, component companies are only marginally effective in marketing their products;

7. Component companies, organized to serve the radio-T.V. industry are typically inexperienced and ill-equipped in the field of sophisticated quality control;

8. Component companies, for the most part, lack the technical insight and capability to improve and advance their product line;

9. Component companies generally have limited financial resources; and

10. Growing predominance of the military electronics equipment market, with its intense concern about reliability, creates applications, quality, and marketing problems which component companies are for the most part poorly equipped to meet.

With this situation existing in the passive component industry, TRW management decided to enter the industry through the acquisition of going businesses to obtain product position and manufacturing capabilities. With this start the plan was to build distribution effectiveness, integrate marketing management and field engineering support, gradually modify and integrate field selling, and merchandise quality, performance and reliability.

It is significant that a situation in the electronics industry was recognized which to the management of TRW represented an opportunity to apply profitably the results of their experience in electronics, both as a buyer of components for complex systems, and as a supplier of semiconductor devices to others. The acquisitions which have taken place and are still taking place to implement this program are for the purpose of serving a recognized need in the components market.

ACQUISITION TO BUY TIME

Still another reason for acquisition is to be found in the case of a newly organized company. When Litton Industries was organized in December 1953, its top management prepared a carefully thought-out five-year plan for its growth internally and through acquisition. First the San Carlos, California, Micro-Wave Tube Division was acquired, and at the same time the Electronics Equipment Division in Beverly Hills was started by the employment of engineers skilled in digital computers, data processing, inertial navigation, and radar systems. The 1953 growth program included a plan to enter the office equipment business, among others, after a research, development, and manufacturing position had been established through internal growth. This position was reached in a few years, and the alternatives were then considered for establishing a market position in the office equipment industry.

It would have been possible to create a national sales and service organization to market commercial products resulting from company-sponsored data processing technical developments. This alternative was considered at length and it was concluded that while it would be possible to create a national sales and service organization, the effort would probably require eight to ten years. The loss of time implications were clear, and thus this alternative was discarded. The acquisition of a concern already established in the market was then considered, and negotiations were initiated with the Monroe Calculating Machine Company, which had 350 company-owned sales and service branches within the United States. The acquisition of Monroe was completed in late 1957 and a market position in the office equipment business was established then rather than eight years later. Since its acquisition the Monroe business machines sales have almost doubled.

It should be noted in the Litton situation that the acquisition approach to growth complemented and strengthened the company's program for growth through internal research and development methods. Growth by acquisition and growth through internal developments are not either/or alternatives. Both approaches are and can be used.

Many other examples of companies buying time through acquisition were found. A chemical company that had developed a new product as the result of research in organic chemicals needed a manufacturing and marketing organization in order to reach the market. This was achieved through acquisition after the management concluded that the product would be copied by others and the profits lost if it took the time to develop its own manufacturing and marketing groups.

ACQUISITION TO ACQUIRE TECHNICAL KNOW-HOW

Another reason, not to be overlooked, is shown by the following experience. The Acme Construction Company was engaged in the engineering, design fabrication, and assembly of continuous process chemical plants. Although a substantial proportion of the assemblies for each plant was purchased from outside suppliers, there were a few critical elements which, since they determined a plant's efficiency, were engineered and manufactured by Acme. Among these were compressors. One of the important sections of Acme's engineering department devoted its time exclusively to the development of reliable and superior compressors. It was believed that these engineers were as competent as any in the industry and that they were aware of the most advanced state of developments in the compressor field.

In 1958 an engineer and owner-manager of a 10-man company approached Acme with a substantially completed prototype of a new approach to producing compressors. The owner had spent several years in bringing the product to its then state of performance and was unable to raise or put any more money into its development. Management and technical personnel of Acme studied the prototype and concluded that a significant technical breakthrough had been achieved and further work on the idea by Acme engineers would perfect it for inclusion in plants then under design and construction. After brief negotiations, Acme acquired the 10-man company and shortly thereafter the needed additional engineering work resulted in products superior to any then in use. Acme thereby strengthened its position in the industry by acquiring the results of technical work performed outside its own design group.

There is an important point to be noted here. Many companies today are engaged in substantial expenditures of money for research and development. Each management tries to attract and motivate the best technical brains it can to work in its areas of operations. The management of company research and development laboratories is described constantly by executives as one of the more difficult problems of the 1960's. How much should we spend on research? What projects should be worked on? When should a project be terminated? Considerable reliance for answers to these and many other related questions is put on the heads of technical laboratories, particularly in organizations where the top executives do not have technical training or experience.

During our field study we observed that in many cases directors of laboratories were completely disinterested in considering the technical accomplishments of other companies or individuals in the same industry. Only lip service was given to keeping abreast of technical work by others. When company managements asked their opinions on the possible purchase of a company that had made substantial, creative achievements or on taking a license under patents established elsewhere, laboratory directors frequently scoffed at the suggestion and refused to consider the possibility that someone outside their laboratories could come up with a more advanced development. This phenomenon was described by one president as the Not-Invented-Here, the NIH concept. "If we didn't think of the idea, it isn't any good."

Top management of technically oriented companies must be alert constantly to the risk of NIH. To neglect the developments of others through an unwillingness to consider the acquisition of technical know-how created in other laboratories is to deprive the company of a significant opportunity to strengthen its own position. To rely completely upon one's own research and development team is to assume that this is the only source of ideas on the subject. In many instances material and important results are attained in the laboratories of individuals and small companies. New approaches, new techniques, and new contributions are constantly coming out of these relatively small groups.

Most larger companies can augment their own research and development programs by searching out and acquiring the know-how developed elsewhere. The smaller organizations may need and want the resources of a larger, financially capable, and established company. The willingness to acquire technical know-how, as the Acme company did, enables both the seller and the buyer to profit from commercial realization on the idea or product.

Acquisition to Achieve Product Diversification

Professor Kenneth R. Andrews [1] described product diversification as the:

> . . . manufacture or distribution by a single company of more than one commodity. . . . The degree of diversification is established by the lack of relationship among prod-

[1] "Product Diversification and the Public Interest," *Harvard Business Review*, July 1951, pp. 91–92.

ucts. A medium-sized ice company in the laundry business is, for our purposes, more diversified than a much larger tobacco company selling a dozen forms of tobacco. . . .

But in general terms the range of diversification can be established at sight. For example:

The Coca-Cola Company is a one-product firm.[2]

The Cream of Wheat Corporation, which with five-minute Cream of Wheat as well as the old-fashioned kind is now a two-product firm, is only a little farther along the road to variety.

Progressive diversification like that of the Scott Paper Company, although still conservative, is further advanced in degree. When this company added a new kitchen towel to its line of toilet tissues in 1931, then face tissues in 1941 and wax paper in 1945, it diversified, but among products inescapably and visibly bound to paper.

A more diverse range is represented by the movement of Cargill, Inc., from the merchandising and storage of grain into the manufacture of feed, vegetable oils, seeds, and other products divisible into a large common denominator, namely, service to agriculture.

Still more diverse is General Mills, with not only vegetable oils but also pharmaceutical products and household appliances to vary its grain milling and cereal business, and to use fully its executive and material resources.

An extreme of diversity is represented by the Avco Manufacturing Corporation, particularly after purchase of its Crosley Division. With equal aplomb, it thenceforth made home appliances (ranges, water heaters, freezers, refrigerators, radio and television receivers), agricultural implements, sinks and cabinets, precision parts for aircraft engines; and besides that and other activities operated a motor coach business and broadcasting station.

The highest level of diversification is represented by a collection of separate products which are not closely bound together either by fairly obvious similarities in physical spe-

[2] No longer. In December 1960 Coca-Cola acquired the Minute Maid Corporation, processor and distributor of frozen orange and other fruit juices.

cifications, or by other affinities, like production techniques which are harder to see. An example of extreme diversification (which the Federal Trade Commission is fond of citing) is American Home Products, a composite of half a hundred companies making thousands of products including ethical and proprietary drugs, veterinary medicines, grocery products, and items as apparently diverse as waxes, polishes, pigments, insecticides, and Three-in-One Oil.

Product diversification as outlined by Professor Andrews and as found in our field work can be achieved through the internal development of new products and the acquisition of other companies. And the diversification may be narrow if the new products added are closely allied to the existing product line or broad if the new products added have no relationship to the present product line.

But top management attitudes toward product diversification through acquisition vary widely. Some executives enthusiastically endorse the idea of moving into new product areas. They know well the sharp and difficult competitive conditions in their own industries, a point of view which seems to be characteristic of *all* industries, and look admiringly across the business street at what appears to be greener competitive pastures. Lack of knowledge about life in other product fields gives them a spirit of optimism and they eagerly seek opportunities to venture into different product areas.

In other organizations top executives are most reluctant to enter fields in which they have not had experience, and when discussing growth opportunities, they make very clear their exclusive interest in confining product growth to areas identical with or closely similar to their current lines. To support this point of view, they quote the inauspicious and abortive expeditions of some companies into new and unknown product areas through acquisitions.

Our field case studies indicate that several essential conditions need to be present in the acquiring company which permit entry into unrelated product line fields.

1. The existence of a venturesome, risk-taking management point of view.
2. Competent management in the acquiring organization who are motivated to perform well in the new product field.
3. Competent management in the acquiring organization who can quickly adjust to being responsible for doing business in new industries, or the employment of executives from other companies who have had experience in the new field.
4. Recognition by the acquiring management of the differing requirements for success in different industries; and
5. A willingness by the acquiring management to include newly acquired top management executives in company policy-making.

When these conditions exist in the management of the acquirer, ventures into unknown fields generally seem to be successful. The willingness of executives to consider new and different fields of activity was also related to the profitability of their existing business. When their current operations were going smoothly, top managements were less willing to consider expanding into other fields. But when their established operations were not profitable, the gamut of solutions suggested was widened to include almost any type of new venture. In a few instances the chief executives waited too long before recognizing, for example, that their product lines were becoming obsolete.[3]

3 *Environmental Change and Corporate Strategy,* Stanford Research Institute, Menlo Park, California, 1960. The Stanford Research Institute made a six-year research study of the causes of company success and failure in an effort to discover methods whereby managements can enable their companies to make more money. It was reported, "There are many ways in which companies can respond to opportunities in the changing environment. All involve planning and positive action. Diversification is one strategic step which companies can take to increase their exposure to environmental opportunities.

The managements of many small companies, organized initially to perform military contracts, became aware of the risks of total dependence on a single customer, the United States Government. Even with rising military budgets and the possibility of sharing in this growing market, some managements recognized the values of a balanced product line and acquired other companies in nonmilitary businesses to reduce the risks of selling to only one customer.

The managements of many large companies with substantial government contracts also sought to diversify their market by acquiring companies in civilian businesses. General Dynamics, for example, announced its objective to broaden its product base. Mr. Earl D. Johnson, president of the company, stated:

> . . . At General Dynamics more than three-quarters of our activities are still in the defense business; and although our nondefense business has been growing very rapidly, our defense business has been growing just as fast. As a result, the ratio between the two remains approximately the same.
>
> .   .   .   .   .
>
> . . . We all hope that the nation's armament bill can be reduced, even though it may not be possible until some distant date. Therefore, as trustees of stockholders' money it is only sound that we achieve a broader diversification in the commercial field. Hence, an understanding of the nature of our business provides direct clues as to our future plan-

"The high growth companies studied showed a substantial awareness of the necessity for keeping up with changing times by shifting product emphasis. Many more high growth than low growth companies diversified into different industries in this ten-year period (1949–1958).

"Not only did over 60% of the high growth companies take a diversification step, but their shifts were much more extensive than were those of the companies in the low growth group. In fact, over half of the low growth companies that did diversify, did so to an extent of only 10% or less of their current product mix.

"When a diversification step was taken, more high growth companies than low growth companies chose the acquisition route as a means of gaining initial entry into a new industry. The low growth companies moved more slowly, usually relying on their own internal development."

ning in the merger field. The need for greater balance between defense and commercial business is one of our unique characteristics. That is one of our first priorities in assessing the question of whether to merge or not to merge.

This "urge to merge" does not mean that we don't like the defense business; our studies show that it is likely to be more stable than regular commercial business for years to come. Rather, it means that, as prudent trustees of stockholders' money, we must provide the broadest supporting foundation we can devise.[4]

In another instance, at the annual meeting in May 1961 of the Seagrave Corporation, primarily a manufacturer of fire fighting equipment, Mr. Arnold A. Saltzman, president, after reporting that 1960 earnings were substantially better than in the preceding year stated:

Seagrave cannot look to its existing business alone for large-scale growth. . . . Over the next two or three years you may expect to see the company engaged in many new fields of endeavor and industries with capabilities of more than normal growth, and with subsidiaries or divisions doing a substantially larger volume of business and with markedly increased record of earnings.[5]

ACQUISITION TO ACHIEVE INTEGRATION

Another reason for acquisitions is for the purpose of integration. An interesting example of this is found in the paper box and corrugated paper container fields. There are essentially three broad production steps in the manufacture of products for these two major fields of business, paper boxes and corrugated paper containers. First is growing timber; second is breaking down timber into various pulps which are then manufactured into several grades of paper such as kraft

4 Earl D. Johnson, "To Merge or Not to Merge," *Corporate Mergers and Acquisitions,* American Management Association Management Report No. 4, 1958, pp. 8–9.

5 *Wall Street Journal,* May 24, 1961, p. 7.

liner and box board; and third is converting these various grades of paper into final products including labels, bags, folding boxes, corrugated containers, and others. The kraft liner that goes into the manufacture of corrugated containers, for example, can be shipped economically long distances, but the corrugated containers must be produced close to the users' plants because first, they are bulky, difficult, and expensive to ship; second, they are designed specifically for individual customers; and third, they must be delivered quickly to the end user who does not maintain warehouse storage space for large inventories. The conversion stage is basically a service industry dictated by the needs and demands of the customer.

In 1939, 70% of all boxes were made by independent converters, a few of which were publicly held but most of which were small or medium-sized companies. After World War II, several paper mills, which until then had had no or only limited company-owned corrugated container manufacturing plants, began to purchase container companies in order to profit from the complete manufacturing, sales, and service distribution process. A second purpose was to protect the mill market for the sale of kraft liner. A mill typically required a capital investment of over $20,000,000, while investment in a converting plant required only $1,000,000 or $2,000,000. Profits at the conversion stage were most attractive to the paper mill managements; and as one basic paper mill after another became engaged in acquiring corrugated container manufacturing plants, it became clear that the real characteristics of the industry were changing. By the late 1950's, 80% of all corrugated containers were manufactured by integrated companies, and one industry executive stated that substantially all the remaining 20% would be absorbed by integrated companies in a few years.[6]

[6] Acquisitions in the Pulp and Paper Field, 1953–1958 and 1958–1960, "Urge to Merge: Story of 50's," *Pulp and Paper,* June 1960.

Once the trend to reshape this segment of the paper industry started, it became imperative for other mills in the industry to acquire independent converters quickly. Changes such as this are ever present in business, and managements of companies in virtually all industries must be aware of such evolving patterns and must be ready to use acquisitions as one means for their survival.

OTHER REASONS FOR ACQUISITION

There are many other valid business reasons for acquisition. One company, for instance, which had reached the limit of its borrowing capacity, used its stock to acquire another with no debt and the combination resulted in a considerable increase in borrowing capacity which was needed to finance an internally developed product line. Other situations, of course, were found where the acquiring company had excess cash. Rather than adjusting the pattern of dividends, and believing that there were market opportunities for the profitable use of the money, the managements searched for and found attractive acquisitions, sometimes in the same product area and sometimes in operations quite foreign to the old line. Other companies with high price-earnings ratios acquired enterprises for the purpose of increasing their earnings per share and hence the market price of their stock. This action, said one president, permitted the acquisition of additional companies with the currency of stock, or "Chinese money" as it is known in some organizations.

In other situations, one company acquired an organization with a substantial operating tax loss carry-forward in order to reduce its own federal income tax; another company located in the East purchased the stock of a large midwestern corporation in order to increase its book value per share for greater acceptability in financial circles.

In some companies acquisitions were made in order to expand their sales territory coverage to more than a regional market. Other companies added marketing groups through acquisition to better control the distribution of the growing volume to be expected from their manufacturing capabilities. Several oil companies, for example, long in production and refining capacity, have acquired independent marketing organizations which serve adjacent territories. The management of one company with a need for a young, proven, and dynamic chief marketing executive acquired another company for this single purpose. Others have acquired companies to assure a source of supply of a critical item used in their products, to gain a patent position, to avoid litigation, and to avoid competition by a supplier.

These are some of what seem to be the principal reasons for the acquisition of one company by another. It should be noted again that a company's acquisition of another company should be thought of as more than just an attempt to strengthen its product lines. Corporate plans include the whole range of a business's operations and the acquisition of other companies is one of the many alternatives available for managements to consider in accomplishing a great variety of long and short-term goals.

CHAPTER III

Some Reasons for Selling One Company to Another

In the previous chapter we discussed some of the reasons why company managements are interested in acquiring others in the continuing process of corporate growth. The other side of the coin, of course, is why owners of some companies conclude that there is management merit in selling to another owner.[1]

Some owners and managers with whom this subject was discussed stated strongly that too many managements today have been caught up in the acquisition fad and through lack of experience have let themselves be persuaded by fast talking and misleading representations of acquiring organizations. We encountered a few owners who had sold their companies two or three times in their careers, but this was unusual. For most, participation in the decision to sell was the first and only time in their business experience when this particular question was faced. Sellers, accustomed to dealing with the day-to-day problems of their businesses, found themselves ill-equipped to evaluate the risks, problems, and rewards of becoming a part of another group.

Very early in our field study we talked with the president of an unlisted midwestern company. On the previous day he had been in the office of the president of a large, New York based, well-known company, and had received what seemed to be a very attractive financial offer to buy the corporation, of which he owned about 20% of the common stock. He asked,

[1] In this chapter we are concerned with the general reasons for selling a company. Chapter VII on Nonfinancial Evaluation Problems will cover why particular owners decided to sell or not to sell to specific prespective buyers.

"How do I know whether I should encourage selling out? Would the proposed offer to buy our company be better for the employees, stockholders, customers? To what extent am I having trouble in being objective? I really like my job as president and do not particularly care to work for these New York people. But maybe it would be better for our other interests if we did agree to sell. Just how do you make this kind of decision?"

Some thoughtful observers are concerned with the rising rate of sales of small and medium-sized companies. Mr. Robert L. Chambers, formerly president of Magna Engineering Company, stated:

> The man I am most envious of is the president of a profitable growing company who:
> 1. Owns his company or has completely compatible co-owners.
> 2. Has adequate capital not only for current operations but also to finance a growth program that will challenge his young and capable executive team.
> 3. Has resolved all his personal estate problems as well as those of other principal stockholders.
>
> Undoubtedly such a man averages no more than four hours a day at his office, the balance spent either on the golf course, with his family, or traveling in foreign lands. His brow is unfurrowed, his shoulders erect, his hair jet black. Such a man should consult a psychiatrist if he entertains the slightest thought of selling his company.[2]

The president of a West Coast company, a successful pioneer in a highly technical field, is approached three to four times a week by prospective acquirers. He and his board of directors have concluded that there are no valid business reasons for selling — the company has competent management, there are successors for all top management positions, the

[2] Robert L. Chambers, "How Not to Sell Your Company," *Harvard Business Review*, May–June 1961, p. 105.

market is varied without undue reliance on any single customer or type of customer, manufacturing facilities are adequate for present production requirements, there is sufficient
capital or the opportunity to get additional low-cost capital,
there is no threat of product obsolescence, research and development have produced commercially exploitable new
products, and "Besides, the key management and technical
personnel are young and want to go it on their own." The
president added that "all too often the reason for selling a
company, at least in this industry, is that Santa Claus is not
coming next year."

The president and majority owner of Easton Products,
Inc., a plastic company in the Middle West, studied carefully
a purchase proposal made by the management of a large eastern company seeking an entreé to the plastics industry. A
letter to the president of the prospective acquiring company
summarized his conclusions:

> In this period I've taken the time, as you suggested, to
> gather some factual data, weigh many of the answers that
> you gave to my questions, and thus apply more objective
> thinking than heretofore. Let me give you some of the
> background upon which my conclusions are drawn.
>
> When I came here some five years ago, I think you know
> that Easton Products was a company with a bright future
> but was in serious financial condition, had a noncomple-
> mentary product line, and had some serious organizational
> weaknesses. While we made good progress saleswise and
> improved ourselves financially and organizationally, this
> took some time. Frankly, it hasn't been until 1959 that
> we've felt we were really "set" to make a real forward push.
>
> Within the past year we've added a significant number of
> really good men in key spots. This year with a capital
> budget of over one-quarter of a million dollars, we will have
> provided important facilities — sizable additions in the
> office, laboratory, and plant.
>
> I don't mean to state these things in a way that infers our

record hasn't been good, because it has and I don't think we need to apologize for it. Our five-year average increase in sales has been over 30% per year. Our five-year return on investment average has been over 20% on year-end net worth. It would be close to double that of your company if figured on the beginning and end-of-the-year net worth average.

I believe, and a number of experiences within the past year seem to justify the feeling on our part, that we've just arrived at a position of size and reputation where major customers and suppliers recognize our efforts to date. As a result, our future never looked brighter than it does today.

A considerable part of our research effort has been and continues to be directed to the development of new products which are more adaptable to mass production usage, all quite new but now being offered commercially. Longer range research under Dr. Johnson's direction has been under way less than two years, and these efforts are proving to be most fruitful and will, without a doubt, enable us to supply better, low-cost systems which will broaden our markets and secure our position.

I mentioned one other point in our last meeting which I'd like to reiterate. We have on file over two dozen recent prospectuses of small companies about our size which have recently made public offerings of their securities. On the whole, our record at least equals that of any of them and really is far sounder than many. Investment bankers have been after us to consider such an offering but we have put them off simply because we have no important needs for funds at the present time which have not been more easily met by our major stockholders. We expect to do something in this direction, however, within the next couple of years.

You know that we've frequently turned down considerations of merger over the years and the only reason we've gone this far with you is that we have such a high regard for you through the personal contact over the years and our joint efforts suggested good reasons for exploration of a closer relationship.

What I've said so far in this letter I know sounds less than modest, but I'm confident it reflects the true feelings of our management group. We've got to see and feel the direct results of our build-up to a big move forward. To eclipse this now would leave us all with the feeling in the future that we should have waited a couple of years before considering a merger with a larger company.

In the case of the Easton Products Company and the West Coast company, the top managements believed that there were in fact no *business reasons* for selling to others. Their situations were entirely consistent with the standards prescribed by Mr. Chambers for going it alone.

Confirming the validity of these individual company conclusions but illustrating the concept by an example in the electronics industry, Mr. David Packard, president of Hewlett-Packard, stated in part:

> The vast majority of firms showing their products here at Wescon this week were started as independent business ventures by one or a few individuals who felt that working on their own for a small independent firm would give them the opportunity to do a better job. This week's show presents a magnificent display of the ingenious ideas which came from a dynamic free enterprise industry. One notes as he goes through the exhibits that very large and also very small firms are represented. A close examination of the products of each reveals that some of the best products and some of the most ingenious ideas came from the smallest firms. In other words, although the large enterprises are doing an outstanding job in our industry, great size and financial strength are not a prerequisite to top quality performance in the American electronics industry — and I hope they never will be.

.   .   .   .   .

I think we have a serious problem to preserve these important strengths of our industry. There is a growing trend toward mergers and acquisitions — spurred by the attraction

of the exorbitant price-to-earnings ratios which the investment community has generated out of this enthusiasm for
our performance.   There is no evidence which will stand
critical examination to indicate our industry is any stronger
as a result of these mergers and acquisitions.   I have seen
many cases where, when the pride of ownership and the
opportunity for truly free unlimited decision were lost, the
enterprise which was acquired lost, rather than gained, in
true productive compatibility.[3]

What Mr. Packard, Mr. Chambers, and the presidents of
the Easton Products Company and the Middle West company
are saying is that unless the owners have a *real business reason* for selling their enterprises, the risks, problems, and dis-
appointments of selling are likely to far overbalance the so-
called benefits of joining forces with another.   Accordingly,
it is of the utmost importance that the owners and managers
of companies contemplating an offer to purchase their concerns examine with great care what business benefits will
accrue through sale.   This requires time and thoughtfulness.
Many business executives feel overburdened by the many
daily problems facing them.   The appearance of a prospective buyer has a great immediate appeal and the temptation is
to accept his offer with pious hopes that all present and future
problems will be thereby solved.   Selling does not automatically solve any problems for the company, and there is a great
possibility that these problems may be compounded by having the company owned by less experienced owners.
    Owners of companies should be cautious about the
"Golden Gate approach."   Careful, clinical attention should
be given to the basic question: "What can the prospective buyer do for our company?"   Unless there is clear evidence that substantial contributions can be made, there is

[3] An address to the Western Electronics Manufacturers Association, Los
Angeles, August 24, 1960.

no real reason for adding the complicating participation of new owners to the already perplexing problems of management.

It is important for acquiring managements to determine the real reasons why Company A can be purchased. A common element of intercompany negotiations is the practice of sellers to dress up or otherwise disguise the true nature of their motivations for considering divestment. Some owners, for instance, recognizing that rapid technological changes are about to make their product lines obsolete, will offer such reasons as that they feel they would like to retire; that they want to write business books; that they want to go into teaching; that with their children out of school, their wives are urging relaxation and travel; that the company needs additional capital for its imminent growth; that — and so on. These and many other reasons may be proferred as explanations for giving up control of a company that is on the "threshold of new and higher earnings rates, a new plateau of continued success."

In most, but not all, of the cases studied, the one single factor which characterized the decisions to sell was fear: fear about the future; fear that the product line was outmoded; fear that while company-rich although cash-poor, the capital accumulated in a lifetime would be lost; fear that technology, once reasonably simple, was beyond the management's capacity to cope with; and fear that key people were becoming dissatisfied with salary compensation and would leave to join enterprises where capital participation was possible. These and other fears were rarely expressed as such, but were carefully disguised by stressing other reasons. Negotiation discussions usually did not include explicit acknowledgment as to the *real* reasons for sale, but this seems to be an accepted part of bargaining. Our conclusion, however, does underline again the importance of the buyer ferreting out why Company A can be purchased.

There is nothing basically or fatally wrong with such fears of sellers; in many cases they are real and valid. But they must be isolated and defined before a buyer can sensibly determine whether he has the capability to face these fears and to profit from their solution.[4] Sometimes the seller will disclose the basic reason for sale, but in many situations the motives are carefully concealed.

Thus, it is critically important for an acquiring management to determine the real reasons and motivations for owners to sell. For unless these reasons are isolated and identified, the buyer has no basis for concluding whether he can solve the problems confronting the management of the company to be acquired. Many managements have been misled by their own wishful thinking, supported by the representations of the sellers as to what is really going on within the companies they wish to sell. And wishful thinking can be particularly treacherous for the inexperienced acquirer who wants to purchase *something*.

Alertness in getting at the real reasons for an owner's desire to sell his company was exemplified in the case of an east coast manufacturing company. Mr. Brown, the president, learned of the Ramsey Company in St. Louis which was owned by two brothers, both of whom were over 65 years of age. Preliminary investigation by Mr. Brown indicated that the Ramsey Company operated in an area of Mr. Brown's interest, that sales and profits had grown steadily during the last ten years, and that the steady growth was attributable in large part to research and development achievements in the laboratory. Mr. Brown approached the two brothers who told him that they would be willing to sell their company for $4,000,000, approximately 17 times the previous year's earnings. They stated that they both were ready to retire but that they would stay on for six months during which time

4 Detailed consideration of the problems of evaluation by both sellers and buyers is presented in Chapter VII.

Mr. Brown could put his own management into the St. Louis organization. The reason expressed for being willing to sell seemed plausible. Mr. Brown's company stock was traded on the New York Stock Exchange at about 19 times earnings; thus there would be no dilution of earnings per share if the company were purchased with stock.

Negotiations proceeded smoothly until Mr. Brown, as part of his evaluation, chatted with the president of the Ramsey Company's largest customer. He learned that the Ramsey Company vice president of research had resigned six months earlier to organize his own enterprise, that competitors of the Ramsey Company had developed better and cheaper products, and that the Ramsey Company was substantially behind in industry technical developments. These findings were confirmed by additional investigation and the negotiations were terminated shortly thereafter. What seemed to Mr. Brown to be a logical and plausible reason for selling turned out to be false and misleading.

"Good" Business Reasons for Selling

There are, however, good business reasons for the owners to sell their enterprises. Business reasons include, for our purposes, what could be described as the personal and career reasons of the owners, such as the desire to convert one's holdings in a closely held corporation to the more liquid stock of a listed company.

We found that typically the decision to sell was based on several valid business reasons — one may have been controlling but it was usually the existence of several that led to the sale. A good example of the intertwined but related motivations leading to sale was that of the president, Mr. Charles, of the Craven Products Company, a manufacturer on the West Coast.

When the Craven Products Company was established in

1948, it had about a dozen competitors. The company moved rapidly and did well without too much new rivalry. Starting in the mid-1950's, however, the number of competitors increased sharply so that by 1959 there were 350 companies in the industry, most of which were small concerns. The Craven profits held up through 1958, but according to Mr. Charles, "the handwriting was on the wall, the honeymoon was over." The Craven management believed that the problem could be corrected, but only through additional financial help. Mr. Charles stated that even at the existing rate of sales, working capital was always scarce and one bad year could have been serious.

The large number of firms coming into the field did not concern the Craven management, provided capital could be raised to automate the production processes. With new and more efficient production equipment, they believed that the next ten years would show a better earnings rate than the last ten years. Most of the small competitors were inadequately financed and had an extremely high ratio of labor to selling price. Automation of the Craven process could reduce its labor component substantially.

Late in 1958 representatives of the Traverse Company approached Mr. Charles and indicated they had decided to enter the field as an end product manufacturer. Traverse Company executives had studied the companies in the end product area and decided that the only one they wanted was Craven. They hoped that Craven's owners would entertain an offer, but if they were not interested the Traverse Company planned to build its own plant and organization to enter the market on a modest scale. Traverse Company executives stated that if Craven joined them, the organization would be operated as an autonomous division and key personnel would not be replaced as long as they did a good job.

The Craven management and the other owners considered the opportunity to sell out; they concluded that they should and that the best possible purchaser would be the Traverse Company.

Summarizing the reasons for the decision to sell, Mr. Charles listed the following:

1. The offer was very attractive from a capital gains point of view and the stockholders strongly supported a sale.
2. Craven lacked additional capital sufficient to expand and automate without which a sharp decline in profits was anticipated.
3. Craven earnings' record was at a peak.
4. The arrangement of continuing the present management meant a great deal, especially since Mr. Charles' experience provided assurance that the management would keep its word.
5. After 14 good years, this segment of the industry could slump, causing a financial problem and the loss of an opportunity for the Craven Company to sell at the top price.
6. The Craven management wanted greater financial backing to do a bigger and better job in the industry.

PREDOMINANT REASONS FOR SELLING

In each of the situations which we studied, several reasons were given by the owners and management for selling the business, as in the Craven Company. Rarely did we find that one single, exclusive reason accounted for the sale of an enterprise. But for purposes of discussion we have divided some of the principal reasons into the following categories:

Management Succession

Two situations we found illustrate concern by management about the ability of younger men in the organization to carry on profitable operations in the future. In the first, the president was 70 years old and the senior vice president was 69. These two men had organized the company in 1936 to design, manufacture, and sell industrial process control instruments. The company had been successful and by 1961 was regarded as a leader in the industry. Some common and nonvoting preferred stock had been issued during the 25 years since the company was founded which was quoted daily on the over-the-counter market, but in January 1961 the president and senior vice president each still owned about 40% of the voting common stock.

During the company's growth a careful policy to promote from within had been followed; young men had been employed when they graduated from college; and all of the second-level top executive positions were filled by men who had been in the employ of the company for many years. The president and the senior vice president worked together effectively as a top management team, the former concentrating on marketing and financial problems and the latter concerning himself with the production area. Because they were so effective, they made all major and many minor decisions jointly, and the younger men rarely had the opportunity to fulfill top job responsibilities, even when the company's employment peaked at just over 1,800 employees.

Late in 1960 the senior vice president became ill and it was clear that at best he could not work more than half-time. The president's wife, concerned by the senior vice president's heart attack, increased her efforts to persuade her husband to take it easier. The president and senior vice president discussed at length what organizational changes might be made to accommodate their possible less active roles and concluded that key personnel within the organization had not had the experience to take over the top positions, nor did they seem to have the potential to grow to meet the requirements if a transition period program of two years was scheduled. Accordingly, they negotiated the sale of the enterprise and described their reasons for selling as ill health and a desire to travel and take it easy. The real reason, however, was their basic concern about the capacity of younger men in the company to carry on profitable operations in the future. The two owners did not have the potential estate tax valuation problems so common in companies with no market for their securities and they would have continued the company as an independent operation if they had felt that competent executives were available to succeed them.

In the second case, the company was owned by three families, none of whom was active in the management in 1959. The Blake Company had been established in the middle 1920's in Cleveland to manufacture and distribute a specialized food product and from the start was phenomenally successful. The three owners received generous salaries, and as subsequent dividend income strengthened their individual financial positions, they dropped out of the active management one by one and employed a salaried president in 1935 to manage the enterprise. The owners moved to Southern California and Florida and took no active interest in their corporation's affairs except to continue their dividend-financed standard of living.

The president, who had maintained the sales and profit growth trend, in 1959 indicated that he wanted to take a position in a Midwest university. It was at this time that the three owners assembled to reappraise the organization's position and discovered that there was no one within the organization believed to be qualified to assume the top management position. Also, no younger member of the three families wanted to move to Cleveland, preferring the milder climates of California and Florida. The owners considered employing an outsider to succeed the president but concluded that the risk was greater than the possible dividend rewards, whereupon negotiations were started to sell the company. In this case the absence of a management successor was described as a desire to set the family estate problems in order, a not unlikely explanation in view of the owners' ages.

One-Man Management

Related to the problem of management succession as a reason for selling is the recognition by the principal owner and one-man manager that the organization is getting too big for him and that because of his personal administrative shortcomings he is unable to multiply his effectiveness by delegating to others authority to build and strengthen the organization. We found many extraordinarily competent entrepreneurs who were able to organize small profitable companies but who were unable or unwilling to manage them as they grew larger. Here again, the reasons for the decision to sell were described in negotiations without revealing the owner's true reasons.

To illustrate, the Tap Electronics Company was organized in 1952 by an engineer, a civil service employee of one of the Armed Services. In his governmental position he had been responsible for the award of many contracts for the development of specialized electronics equipment. He recognized the growth anticipated for electronics, resigned his government job, and with very limited personal financial resources augmented by bank borrowings, established the Tap Electronics Company in the Midwest. With many contacts in the agency from which he had resigned, together with a risk-taking point of view, he built up an engineering group to work on military development projects. The owner was talented in securing government contracts, and when the organization carried these out successfully, additional and larger contracts for the development of more sophisticated electronics equipment were awarded to Tap. As the organization grew to meet the steadily increasing backlog of government business, it became apparent to the owner that he could not physically perform the increasing number of tasks required as chief operating executive. From the first day of business, this had been a one-man management and it had continued to be one even when employment reached 250 people. The owner's frustrations with his inability to handle all the problems led to a nervous breakdown, and when he returned to work several weeks later, he decided to realize a capital gains through selling the company as a going concern. During the negotiations he indicated clearly his desire to withdraw from management responsibilities because of his health, a befitting reason with the known history of his nervous problems. The actual reason for sale, however, was that he realized the increased management requirements exceeded his capacities.

A similar circumstance was found in the Ray Company, another in the electronics industry. Here the president organized a components company in 1950. The Korean War greatly increased the military requirements for electronic systems and the Ray Company was able to become profitable almost immediately. During the following years, the electronics industry continued its rapid growth and the demand for components was so great that product specifications were frequently waived in order to get delivery of needed items. By the middle 1950's, however, many new companies had been organized to fill the supply vacuum, prime contractors were exercising stricter quality control standards to comply with specifications, and loose cost control practices which were tolerable during a period of large margins became impossible with the increased competitive structure.

Mr. Ray, who performed all the management jobs, found himself overwhelmed by the greatly increased demands in the new situation; customers rejected deliveries; bank loans had to be renewed and increased; new sales had to be made. And yet, Mr. Ray found it impossible to delegate to others in the organization, partly because of his own administrative weaknesses and partly because the people occupying key positions were not competent to assume responsible decision-making roles. The organization chart included all the customary titles: vice presidents for engineering, customer relations, manufacturing, and finance; but the chart did not indicate that all decisions were made by one man: Mr. Ray.

As problem added to problem, Mr. Ray decided that his only answer was to sell the company. During the next few months he negotiated with three companies, introducing his "key executives" and representing the top five as a hard-working team of dedicated people. A sale was completed, and the same management personnel were retained by the purchaser. Shortly thereafter sales and profits declined, and the buyers decided that maintenance of even current levels of production could not be accomplished as long as Mr. Ray continued as president. The inevitable solution occurred: Mr. Ray was terminated and he departed with a handsome capital gain over his original investment. Then it was discovered that the hard-working team of dedicated executives had served largely as ministerial clerks for the president. A vice president of the acquiring company who moved in to manage the Ray Company stated: "Not only were the key executives not competent, they were incompetent which is even worse!"

Industry and Technological Change

Earlier the Craven Company was described to exemplify the many reasons, intertwined, which can lead to a decision to sell. In that case, one of the many significant factors was the necessity to raise more capital to finance the automation of the factory in order to reduce costs and thus remain competitive. Industry changes, and technological changes such as in Craven, are constants in the business environment and managements must continuously study their industries if the businesses are to survive.

In the Ace Company, an adhesives manufacturer in the West, the president stated that the uses of adhesives for industrial products were growing at a tremendous rate. Rubber-based adhesives had been used for years in the manufacture of shoes, but new applications were found in construction materials as well as substitutes for rivets and screws on industrial products. The new opportunities required high technical know-how and an applications staff to find new uses and to test laboratory compounds for these uses. Ace had a good name in what was developing into a smaller and smaller part of the total adhesives business. The two leaders in the industry were Minnesota Mining and Manufacturing Company and Armstrong Cork. Each had extensive technical and market development programs and the Ace management felt the encroachment of this competition as a threat to their existing business. They concluded that substantial money would be required to add to their present limited technical staff and that new and better laboratories would be needed in order to maintain a place in the adhesives industry. Ace was owned largely by a trust created several years earlier when the principal owner died. The trustee relied on the judgment of the five top executives of Ace and left the decision to sell or provide additional funds for the company's expansion to the group.

After evaluating the problems of raising the necessary capital to finance the essential product development, of recruiting additional experienced technical personnel, and of expanding their largely regional operations to cover other markets, the top executives concluded the more attractive alternative would be to recommend offering the company for sale to a buyer which had the capacity to fulfill these requirements. After a few prospective buyers from New York were rejected because the Ace management believed them to be "fast operators after the quick dollar," a sale was completed to a company with most of the desired characteristics. Again, for the Ace management this was a choice of alternatives and they chose the assistance of a much larger acquirer in order to meet the changing conditions in the industry.

Change in the structure of an industry was instrumental in the decision to sell by dozens of paper box manufacturers, as was mentioned earlier in Chapter II under reasons for buying. Mills seeking to integrate more fully commenced buying the independent box manufacturers in 1950; and by 1961 less than 20% of boxes were being made by independents as compared with 70% in 1939. One of these independents, an Ohio company founded in 1938, was owned by Mr. Smith, Mr. Jones, and the widow of the third founder of the company. Mr. Smith, the president, recognized early that the very large mills were buying box manufacturers throughout the country and saw the inevitable and untenable position of the independents. He and the other owners decided that the acquisiton trend of the industry could not be denied and they sold to a large eastern company.

In 1953 the owners of a company manufacturing special systems for reciprocating engine aircraft sold their business which was currently earning about $500,000 a year. It was clear to the sellers, but not to the buyers, that the demand was falling rapidly for reciprocating engine aircraft which was being supplanted by jet aircraft. This case raises important questions about the problem of evaluation, discussed later, but it should be noted here that a technological change was taking place in the aircraft business — a change which the sellers recognized and which motivated them to sell.

Many other situations were found where the basic reason for selling was a fundamental change in the technology or in the strucure of the industry. Some owners and managers found selling the most attractive solution; others stayed in the business and found ways to survive on their own.

Management Dissension

Dissension among the top management members in small and medium-sized companies is also a major reason for selling the enterprise. This was found to be so both in organizations where the top managers were owners and in companies where they were not. In the latter case, corporate owners, not caring to face these difficult problems of reconciliation or termination, chose the course of washing their hands of the problem by selling the company. In some cases the acquiring management was aware of the dissension and in others this motivation for sale was missed during the evaluation and negotiations.

The classic pattern of dissension can be illustrated by the Trace Company. In 1946 three ex-GI's joined with a 45-year-old inventor with what appeared to be a new and better way of manufacturing rotary lawn mowers. A corporation was organized with the limited capital of the four men and with bank loans. The mowers were designed and a prototype was made which was introduced at a trade show in St. Louis. Representatives of a large auto supply chain saw the mower and gave the Trace Company an order for 1,000 units. With the contract in hand, the four owners returned to their office in the East, arranged further bank loans to finance the production contract, and commenced operations. During the early history of the company the four owners dedicated their working lives to making the company a success: seven-day weeks, no vacations for anyone, careful budgeting and control of expenses, and all the usual struggle and crises of a new enterprise. The objective of the four was unified: to create a profitable company. These four were united, lean and hungry, and faced all company problems as a team determined to succeed and grow. The president stated that their objectives at first were very simple and all decisions were made on the basis of (1) can we afford it; and (2) if so, will it make money?

Ten years later, however, having established a position in the industry as a profitable leader, the four owners' motivations became more complex and divergent. One believed that more profits could be made in companies outside the lawn mower business; the second wanted higher sales and cared less about whether the increased sales were profitable; the third became interested in the city's chamber of commerce, accepted the presidency, and devoted a great deal of time and attention to noncompany affairs.   The inventor, now 55 years old, became concerned that if he should die his widow and children would have no capital except what was locked up in the Trace Company.   He wanted cash or listed securities and more time to travel.   In addition, he became bored with lawn mower designs and wanted to work on other equipment.   One of the four, largely responsible for the successful marketing of the mower, began to think of himself as an administrator — or executive — and his great ability as a doer became lost in layers of organization.[5]   The four owners found areas of disagreement in the amounts of money which should be borrowed from banks, possible new products which might be added to the line, the amounts of time each was expected to spend at the company, and their changed motivations carried over into the innumerable small problems involved in the day-to-day operations of a business.

What started as a unified objective with all efforts aimed at achieving success deteriorated to petty differences and unpleasantness.   This, together with a decline in annual profits and an offer to buy the complete company at an attractive price, resulted in its sale shortly thereafter.   The four owners received their individual shares and embarked on four new and satisfying business careers.   Motivations which held the group together during the trying days of establishing the enterprise failed to achieve the same goal when the company became financially successful.

Another situation that illustrates dissension as a reason for

[5] Several situations were found where men with great technical skills organized new small companies and later began to think of themselves as executives.   They left the laboratory bench, assumed the role of what they believed to be an executive, and shortly discovered that the executive world gained nothing and the technical world lost fine, competent scientists.

selling a company was that of the Sun Company, a machinery manufacturing organization in New England. The three top officers of the Sun Company were Mr. Harris, aged 64, chairman of the board of directors; Mr. Spade, aged 54, president; and Mr. George, aged 40, vice president and general manager. These executives each owned roughly one-third of the common stock; they received salaries of $60,000 per year in addition to dividends and the benefit of country club dues and company cars. In 1959 sales totaled about $10,000,000 and a satisfactory profit rate was realized.

During recent years considerable friction and tension had developed among the three top men. Both Mr. Harris and Mr. Spade regarded the general manager, Mr. George, as "their boy" and constantly overwhelmed Mr. George with conflicting statements for action. There was noticeable envy between the chairman and the president which was manifested in petty and ungenerous comments in the small town where the company had its headquarters. The wrangling and discord had reached a climax at the time the Sun Company owners were approached by a Taylor Company vice president, and the three owners-managers concluded a sale. The purchase by the Taylor Company was complicated by the longstanding feud. This was resolved by Taylor's establishing Mr. George as the chief operating executive, hiring Mr. Spade for a staff position at a salary of $25,000 a year in the Taylor headquarters in Chicago, and letting Mr. Harris retire gracefully, but completely, from the company as chairman, thereby enabling Mr. George to manage the enterprise unimpeded by the former harassing tactics of the other owners. Here again, the interests, motivations, and objectives of the owners changed over the years and a sale to the Taylor Company solved the dissension and permitted a successful organization to continue with new top management.

There is another type of management dissension which

seemed to be most prevalent among relatively new and growing companies. In the 1950's many able entrepreneurs, sometimes technically trained and sometimes not, organized small
research, development, and manufacturing firms and reserved
to themselves, or to at most one or two others, options for the
purchase of capital stock not needed for public issue or financing purposes. Many of these enterprises became unbe-
lievably successful, as to both sales and profits, and as to the
price of their securities on the market. During the years of
successful growth, the very limited number of owners became
wealthy while key research and development engineers, sales,
factory, and finance personnel continued on salaries consistent with the scale in the region where operations were conducted. The tremendous capital values accumulated by the
few owners were not unknown to other key people and they
expressed strongly their interest in being included in some
sort of stock option arrangement. The nonoption employees were aware that other companies spread options down
through the organization and many such employees had offers
to join enterprises where options were available to key executives.

We found several instances where the few owners decided
to sell the company and to realize a substantial capital gain
rather than include others in the plan. The owners' motivation may have been greed as well as a recognition that unless
the subordinates were given additional compensation, they
would resign to join other companies where stock options
were available. If the key people did resign, there would be
a sharp impact on the company's ability to produce a profit;
and as one president said, "I'd better get out while the getting
is good!" It is noteworthy that during the negotiations to sell
the enterprise in anticipation of a mass departure of key people, the owners would describe the great strengths of the key
people and urge the buyer to "be sure to include them in the
acquiring company's stock option plan." The dissension of

key subordinates resulting from the disparate sharing of the benefits of corporate success has motivated many owners to sell their companies.

Unbalanced Product Line

Discussions with owners of several companies disclosed that their primary reason for selling was to avoid the risks and high costs of a seasonal product line. The seasonal aspect may not seem to be a problem when the company first enters the market, partly because the high cost of starting a company conceals the real costs of idle plant capacity. Another explanation is that when a company moves into a seasonal specialty with a novel approach, gross margins in the beginning are likely to be considerably higher than later when competitors bring out similar products. Some companies with a seasonal line such as lawn mowers and other powered garden tools have sought counter-balancing seasonal acquisitions to smooth out the manufacturing load. Others, however, after searching briefly and unsuccessfully for balancing products, have sold their companies.

In the Magna Engineering Company situation, for example, one of the reasons for selling the company to Yuba Industries was that Shopsmith, Magna's principal product, was highly seasonal. Sales of the Shopsmith, a combination home workshop lathe, saw, and drill press, were made almost entirely in October, November, and December, inventory for which had to be built up during the months of May to October. In addition to the problem of nonproductive factory space during the idle months, another critical problem was estimating in the spring and early summer of each year what the fall requirements would be. If the estimate of fall sales was substantially in error, the obvious resulting problems of financing the inventory, plus space for storage, had to be confronted. These uncertainties for a company with sales of about $8,000,000 a year, a net worth consisting completely of plowed back earnings, and a corporate value representing the total personal capital of the three organizers, caused the owner-managers to consider alternatives and to conclude that selling the company was the best recourse. Prior to sale the owners had negotiated for the acquisition of a garden power tool manufacturer in the Midwest, but price had become an obstacle in the discussions and no acquisition was accomplished. If the seasonal manufacture and sale of home workshops could have been balanced by the winter manufacture and spring sale of lawn mowers, both products using essentially the same kind of space and factory equipment, there would have been an economical use of space as well as a broader product line to spread the risks.

In the course of our study we encountered several companies whose market was largely if not exclusively the federal government. In recent years, the government's military budget has grown steadily and engineers and others have organized hundreds of new companies hoping to share in this military market. It is interesting to note that within the five-year period after World War II several very large American companies decided to return to civilian business on the assumption that military requirements would not continue. The Korean War and subsequent events, however, changed this decision quickly, and today many of our largest corporations have significant divisions devoted completely to doing business with the government. This same market attracted hundreds of entrepreneurs who left going concerns or governmental employment. Electronic companies in particular sprouted up by the hundreds, inspired in part by the ready availability of outside capital, and also by the opportunity for profit. But after having established a position in the military market, many owners-managers recognized the risk of dependence on a single type of customer.

Some sought diversification, a spreading of the risk, by seeking buyers whose product line was closely complementary.

The management of one electronics company, manufacturing military products, for example, with sales of about $7,000,000 a year, realized that most of these sales came from one large government contract which could be canceled. They searched, negotiated with, and sold their concern to an electrical goods company. In this case the president stated that not only was the broader market coverage important, but also the new association provided opportunities for all key people to move up in the combined organization.

The management of another military products company in the Midwest persuaded the other nonmanagement owners that a sale to an old-line commercial company would be in the best interests of both organizations. The top managers of the Crone Company, having completed several years of work in one of the government's many World War II laboratories, had organized this enterprise in 1946 to do advanced research and development work primarily in the communications field. Small development contracts were received which led to more and larger contracts. By 1958 the company's sales were over $12,000,000 a year, all to federal government agencies. From the company's inception the managers believed that some day the military business would cease and their plans included the objective of developing an industrial or commercial business equal to about 50% of their total sales.

In 1956 and 1957, the Crone management tried to enter the industrial field by seeking commercial opportunities for some of the technical developments arising out of their military business. They hired an experienced executive familiar with large-scale ranches and the citrus-growing businesses, and he assured the Crone management that his contacts in the industry would result in tremendous sales for communications equipment. Two years and $100,000 later, the Crone management concluded that developing, introducing, and selling products for the commercial market were quite different from military marketing and that the best solution would be to sell out to an established, reputable company with the necessary organization and know-how.

Financial Considerations

One of the most common and frequent explanations given for selling a company is to gain access to cash for growth which, it was believed by the sellers, could not be raised any other way. One president said: "Our desire for a merger was created by our own success. We had borrowed up to reasonable limits and we simply had to have cash to maintain the jet speed rate of our expansion."

The need for cash or the lack of available money for growth was never found, however, to be the primary reason for sale. During our entire field study we did not encounter a single company that was required to sell because of the lack of money. There were always alternatives, such as a public stock issue. But this possibility was tempered with "but see how it dilutes the equity," or "this is a family-owned enterprise and we don't want outside money," or "a public issue for a company our size will result in our getting only 75% of the market price for the stock because the underwriting charges are sure to equal 25%." Our conclusion, therefore, is that the need for cash may be proffered as the reason for selling, but it must be regarded as the last possible solution after having considered and rejected the several different methods which might be employed to solve the financial needs of the company.

In the Smith Company, for example, the president, who had limited stock holdings, and the members of the board of directors, who were largely from one family and held most of the stock in their names, concluded that more capital would be required. Discussions were opened with an investment banking firm that offered to underwrite 60,000 shares of stock at a market price of $50 per share, an arrangement which would net the Smith Company something over

$2,500,000 after the selling fees. The president presented the proposal to the board and illustrated the delayed improvement in earnings per share while the additional plant space was being built with the rather sharp reduction in earnings per share in the meantime. The board members, who had watched the value of their shares rise from $8 to $48, recognized the possible impact on what they regarded as "their values in stock" and promptly rejected the proposal. Expansion could not be delayed, however, so the president, with the board's approval, negotiated a sale of the entire company to another able to provide cash. Money was made available promptly and the organization's strong growth trend continued. The owners were unwilling to accept a dilution of their equity, but they were willing to divest themselves of all Smith equity in exchange for the stock of a larger company. Reasons other than the need for cash must explain such management decisions.

The most important single reason for selling closely held family corporations, particularly when one or two of the leading members reach 60 or more years of age is a strong motivation to convert company stock for which there is no market into the listed stock of another company. There are two purposes:

1. To be able to establish a value on the holdings of each of the stockholders; and

2. To achieve some liquidity for estate tax purposes. Many family-owned companies in which provision has not been made for these two contingencies have been sold after the death of the principal owner at a fraction of the potential value as a going concern. There are many ways of providing for valuation and liquidity for estate taxes, but sale to another company is one useful and common solution.

Three other interesting financial motivations for selling were found in companies included in our study. In the first the owner-manager of the company, aged 45, concluded that with reasonable luck he could sell his company for a high enough price to net him a little more than $1,000,000 after the necessary taxes had been paid. His personal goal was to become a millionaire and while in fact he was one already in terms of the value of his wholly owned company, his wealth was not real to him. And besides, a few bad years could cause the value of his enterprise to deteriorate sharply. He had made his million, he had achieved his personal goal, and he did not want to risk the million to try to make another and another and another. He said, "I can't believe I'm wealthy and I'm scared to death it will evaporate." Accordingly, he negotiated a sale of his company, fingered the stock certificates with covetous care, and retired to become the unpaid mayor of his community.

Others in this situation have sold out in order to realize their personal financial goals but have stayed on as a management employee of the acquiring company. The Birch Manufacturing Company in the Midwest, for example, was owned by two mechanical engineers, aged 43 and 44. The younger was president and was described as serious and highly competent. The older man was vice president for engineering and had made substantial technical design contributions which added greatly to the Birch company's sales and profits. When it became clear to the two principal owners that their personal financial objectives in effect had been achieved through the capitalized value of their holdings, they decided to "cash in their chips but stay on in the game to see what happens." In this way they would provide security for their families and in the negotiations leading to the sale they could arrange for their continued employment and generous, but not exorbitant, salaries.

A vice president of a large East Coast company learned of the two owners' interests and immediately started discussions which eventually led to purchase of the Birch company.

The president, now financially secure, assured of the same salary and eager to qualify for promotion to a higher position in the acquiring company, worked harder than ever. He was cooperative during the difficult integration period and as the acquiring company vice president said, "has turned out beautifully." The technical vice president of Birch, however, behaved quite differently. During the negotiations he made strong representations as to his interest in staying on in the key engineering position. Shortly after the purchase of Birch was closed, his wife became aware of their new tangible fortune and encouraged her husband to follow leisure class office hours of 10:30 A.M. to 2:30 P.M. This was followed by unannounced and lengthy vacations to a recently acquired summer home in Maine, more easily reached by their new amphibian airplane. In the case of the Birch company owners, the motivation to sell to reduce their security to tangible, touchable, and salable stock resulted in two quite different performances after the sale was completed.

Finally, in some situations where a company is owned by one man, he is able to adopt very conservative accounting practices — expensing everything possible and thereby keeping the reported earnings very low. While net income may be understated for accounting statement purposes, appropriate adjustments can be made by the seller when negotiations are under way. When the company is sold at a price which takes into account its real and larger earning capacity, the owner realizes a substantial capital gain. And the gain is especially attractive if the seller is able to negotiate a deferred payment plan based upon his company's earnings, say, over the next five-year period. The decision to sell in such a case is based essentially on an offer which is "just too good to turn down."

In this chapter we have discussed some of the principal reasons for selling one company to another. Usually the reasons were interrelated but the one single factor found in almost all the situations studied was fear by the owners and managers as to the competitive future of their enterprises. These fears were rarely expressed explicitly; rather they were disguised with self-serving statements.

CHAPTER IV

Planning for Growth Through Acquisition

THE basic responsibility for charting corporate growth is an inseparable part of the chief operating executive's job. It is he who must set short- and long-term goals and outline plans for attaining them. He may draw upon the advice and counsel of the company's line and staff officers, but the ultimate responsibility is his. The board of directors, typically, does not initiate corporate plans, even though corporation law usually charges the board with the management of the corporate entity. The board clearly controls the achievement of corporate plans for growth through acquisition by its necessary vote and approval, but it usually does not create the operating plans themselves.

Once defined and outlined, a corporate plan for growth should be submitted to the board of directors for their concurrence. The requirement for this step is more a matter of sound management procedure than it is of complying with the legal requisites. Since the board of directors must vote on any proposal for acquisition, its participation in approving the plan ahead of time expedites the implementation of a corporate program. In the Sykes Company, for example, the president proposed the acquisition of a small company in an unrelated field. The board members, whose average age was over 60 and whose main board preoccupation was following the company's slowly but steadily increasing earnings and dividends growth, turned down the president's proposal. The discussion of the subject disclosed that the board was happy with the company's present lines of business. The president, on the other hand, realized that, while currently profitable, the company's operations during the next five years might not continue to be so, and it was important to move into other fields. Rebuffed by the board, the president prepared an analysis of the company's current position and made forecasts of sales and profits for the following five years. At the next board meeting he presented his findings and raised two fundamental questions:

1. Is substantial growth our objective and, if so, are we willing to spend the money, take the risks, and devote the energy necessary to accomplish the desired result? And
2. Is our growth effort to be confined to our present fields or do we wish to diversify into other types of enterprises?

This was followed by a specific management recommendation to continue present operations, to seek opportunities for the use of $10,000,000 in other ventures considered to have superior growth potentials or high return on investment, and to maintain an open mind with respect to investment of additional amounts in other fields depending on performance of initial activities, future prospects, and opportunities, and related requirements for funds. The board concurred and two subsequent specific recommendations for acquisitions by the president were approved. During the past two years the company has moved into two new areas and studies are under way not only to strengthen these by further acquisitions, but also to embark on ventures in one other major product area.

In those situations where the president has not included the planning function as an important element of his personal concepts of his job, board members have both the opportunity and the responsibility to stimulate planning by asking discerning questions as to where the company is going.[1] In one such situation it became clear to one outside board member that it was important for the company to de-

[1] M. T. Copeland and Andrew R. Towl, *The Board of Directors and Business Management*. Boston, Harvard Business School, Division of Research, 1947.

velop foreign markets, particularly the European common market. At a board meeting in late 1959, he asked what plans the company had to expand abroad and the president's answer showed clearly that insufficient time and thought had been given to this facet of operations. The president stated in December 1960, that he realized the value of the board member's query, but that as of late 1961 the company still had not decided upon a clearly defined program to grow through acquisitions abroad. We found during the course of our study that unfortunately too few board members apply the standards of performance, including the asking of discerning questions, outlined by Professor Copeland and Mr. Towl. This is especially true in established organizations where current sales and profits seem reasonable for the industry.

One way of considering planning for growth through acquisition is to divide the function into three phases:

1. Establishing objectives;
2. Defining criteria to meet those objectives; and
3. Organizing to fulfill the objectives.

ESTABLISHING OBJECTIVES

During our study we found several situations where top management executives had failed to think through their corporate objectives for growth and, caught up in what seems to be a fad for acquisitions, had spent considerable amounts of money and tremendous amounts of time in a fruitless search for what they thought would be growth opportunities. In one situation the president stated that with a goal of "adding complementary product lines with good profits," he had looked intensively at 50 widely divergent companies and had acquired none. It was clear that he had not defined his own company's strengths and weaknesses. In another case the president had employed a consultant to aid in finding "companies for diversification." The consultant with no further guidelines brought 20 companies to the attention of the president and each situation was dismissed with, "We are not interested in that kind of company."

Unless the chief operating executive is willing to take the time and energy to define carefully what the company's objectives are, it is wasteful to employ consultants or to spend time considering candidates for acquisition. The absence of objectives can only result in haphazard search and it is a fortuitous circumstance indeed if any sensible acquisitions are made.

The real danger is that without objectives defined, a management may be induced to buy what seems to be a worthwhile and profitable venture. A basic resin company, for example, bought a plastic boat manufacturer because this seemed to present a controlled market for a portion of the resin it produced. It soon found that the boat business was considerably different from the manufacture and sale of basic chemicals. After a short but unpleasant experience in manufacturing and trying to market what was essentially a consumer's item, the management concluded that its experience and abilities lay essentially in industrial rather than consumer-type products.

Definition of objectives requires careful analysis of what strengths and weaknesses the company has in personnel, product line, manufacturing and distributing facilities, finance, and research and development. Working with this background of experience, and with forecasts of the future market for present product lines, the president then has a basis for evaluating what if anything needs to be done to strengthen the company's position.

We did find, however, many case situations where impressive jobs were performed by the mangements in adapting their goals to changes in their industries and in creating a new set of objectives. In the Brunswick Corporation, for example, the top management in 1952 did a "deep soul searching of the Brunswick corporate image." Sales that year were

about $26,000,000 and net income after taxes was under
$1,000,000. With its history in bowling and billiard equip-
ment manufacture, the management studied the possibilities
of capitalizing on its past strengths by moving into related
markets. Staff studies indicated that leisure time, health, and
education were important areas of opportunity for the future.

More paid vacations, less hours worked, more leisure for
the new developing families. In addition, the booming
population was certainly going to place particular emphasis
on the growth in schools and hospitals. Old age insurance
and the future studies of geriatrics and longevity indicated
that the health field would be something that would fit into
our patterns as long as we did not become too technical and
attempt to compete with the pharmaceutical companies.
So, recognizing what we were, what we had to offer, and
what would fit into our talents, tastes, and preferences led
Brunswick to establish this diversification program. Thus,
our slogan of recreation, education, health, and defense was
born. . . .

Our basic objective in setting up this business development or diversification program was to expand and diversify
into newer dynamic growth fields in the recreation, education, and health areas, while at the same time maintaining
and strengthening the existing product structure of Brunswick by acquiring new products, additional channels of distribution, and research and development activities having
future profit possibilities. This was an attempt to fulfill
two interrelated objectives. Basically we were committed to
continue building Brunswick through a sound acquisition
program. We, therefore, were going to look for companies
or products that represented a true growth picture and met
our financial requirements. Also, we were looking for the
leaders of specific products in their respective fields. At all
times we hoped to avoid companies that had difficult seasonal problems.[2]

2 "Brunswick: A Study in Planned Diversification," by L. T. Peifer, Director of Business Development, Brunswick Corporation. *Proceedings of the*

With these newly constructed corporate objectives, the Brunswick management designed a set of criteria and organized a program of growth through acquisition to achieve these objectives. During the eight years 1952–1960, Brunswick acquired 10 companies in recreation, education, health, and defense segments of industry, and in 1960 sales had increased to $370,000,000 and profits after taxes to over $38,000,000. In 1955 Brunswick earned $.21 per share; in 1960 $2.28 per share.

An interesting aspect of the Brunswick soul searching creation of new objectives and their implementation through acquisition is that many other companies, similarly situated in 1952 when the program started, could have made essentially the same analyses and come to the same conclusions as to areas of opportunity in the future. During our field studies several executives said, "Hasn't Brunswick done a good job — we certainly missed the boat. Why didn't we recognize these needs and do something about them earlier? Now it is probably too late."

But there will be opportunities in future markets that can be recognized today, and in some companies five years from now executives will say, "How did we miss the signs so clearly visible in 1962?" Doing something today about the opportunities of tomorrow, five years away, depends upon the willingness, and particularly the ability, of each company's chief operating executive.

The managements of two relatively young electronics companies also did impressive jobs of stating and following through a set of thought-out objectives: Litton Industries and the Itek Corporation.

In early 1954 when Litton was organized, its three key executives, Charles B. Thornton, Roy L. Ash, and H. W. Jameson, studied the total electronics industry and decided upon a program to establish leadership in several parts of that industry. This plan was to be accomplished through acquisitions as well as through internal research and development. The major initial areas selected were electron tubes, military equipment and systems, communications, business machines, and certain components. There was nothing fortuitous about Litton's growth; the acquisitions and internal growth were planned in detail. Each year the top executives review the five-year plan, extend it where appropriate, and embark on a continuous effort to create a large, profitable, and successful company.

The management of Itek Corporation also prepared a set of goals in the fall of 1957 when the company was organized. Mr. Richard Leghorn outlined a plan to establish a strong position in office equipment, publishing, manufacturing of highly technical products, communication, education, and reconnaissance (space and military). Mr. Leghorn and other top executives of Itek started by creating a strong research capability and then acquired companies with the capacity to manufacture the hardware. In 1959 Itek purchased the Photostat Corporation, thereby acquiring a commercial product sales capacity. This strength, plus the products of research and development will, it is planned, result in total sales of over $100,000,000 in a few years. Here again, we found an example of thoughtful management charting a course and then taking the steps to assure its achievement.

In some companies the phrase "a philosophy of growth" was used instead of the word objectives. For many years prior to January 1955, the Pfaudler Company of Rochester, New York, was one of two industry leaders in manufacturing glass-lined steel tanks for chemical, pharmaceutical, drug, and brewery companies. For some processes, the glass-lined tank was currently the only vehicle which could be used, for example, for many of the wonder drugs and substantially all of certain kinds of plastics. The company sales and profits were tied rather closely to the trends in the capital goods business and there was the ever-present risk of technical obsolescence if a better substitute could be found for glass-lined tanks. In 1954 a representative of a large American company approached Pfaudler management and proposed that Pfaudler sell out and operate as a division of the larger company. The proposal was reviewed by the Pfaudler board of directors and it was agreed that the acquiring company could make no contribution to Pfaudler and that Pfaudler could not gain by "being a small part of an investment trust."

Stimulated by the interest of another in acquiring them, the Pfaudler executives evaluated their position and decided to generate an internal and acquisition program for growth. In March 1955 Mr. Donald A. Gaudion, the president, wrote a memorandum entitled "A Philosophy for Bigness" which outlined the advantages to be gained by Pfaudler through the acquisition of other companies. It was not proposing an objective of bigness for bigness' sake, but rather a goal of larger size which would provide greater profits by economies in administration and operations. The philosophy document became the charter for an aggressive program to create a stronger enterprise than it was before.

In those cases where programs for growth were initiated by defining corporate objectives, it was noted that there were no set patterns, either as to the procedure by which the objectives were arrived at or as to the formality with which the objectives were reduced to written documents. In some companies a planning staff or a planning committee of line executives prepared the background material for discussion, and in others the president and one or two others concentrated on setting up the program. The only common factor found in those companies where effective goals were established was that the president or chief operating executive took a leading role in seeing that the job was accomplished. In those companies where the president did not take this interest, the objectives derived through staff studies became documents and memoranda more remembered for their waste of time than for their usefulness as tools for top management decision and action.

And whether the objectives were reduced to writing in brief one-page simplicity or elaborated into many-paged booklets was relatively unimportant. The document was not the desired end. The important purpose performed through its preparation was requiring the top executives to think through their ideas as to where the company should go. It was the process, not the document, which gave value and meaning to the plan. Many executives stated that this phase of planning is the most difficult — it involves projections and forecasts, laborious at best. But once the direction of a company's growth is defined, creating criteria and implementing the program are relatively easy. Perhaps it is because constructing objectives and thinking about the future involve dealing with intangibles that some managements shy away from the task. We believe that no corporate growth program can be successful without a clear definition of objectives. It is dangerous and risky to embark on an acquisition project without this first step. The purchase of other companies without clear objectives as to the reasons for their acquisition can lead to loss of profits except under the most accidental circumstances.

The failure to define objectives seems to result in a sense of top management dissatisfaction, a feeling that something needs to be done. Under these circumstances top executives may become overanxious to buy something that looks good to them without defining what is good, and too often they embark on purchase programs later to be regretted. They think of defining objectives as an academic exercise without realizing its elemental importance. But as one vice president stated, "The need and desire for acquisition stem from top flight plans, not poor plans — nor from in between."

The demands of their day-to-day jobs make it very easy and conscience-comforting for some executives to neglect considering the market, looking ahead to opportunities of 1963, 1964 and 1965. In such companies, managements often satisfied with current sales and profits will say in 1967, "We should have done something about this five years ago." Many managements are evaluating their current situations and creating objectives related to their potentials. And if the pattern of the past is any clue to the future, the thoughtful top executives of today will be the successful top executives of tomorrow.

DEFINING CRITERIA

Once a corporation's broad objectives have been thought through and accepted, the second step in planning growth by acquisitions is to construct a set of criteria which describes more narrowly what kinds of companies should be considered for purchase.

Reasons for Criteria

There are at least three reasons for establishing useful criteria:

1. As definitive guidelines for line and staff personnel involved in acquisitions: We found several situations in which the chief operating executives evidenced dissatisfaction with their companies' current growth rates and notified all key executives that "favorable consideration will be given to suggestions for desirable acquisitions." In one case the president employed a staff vice president for plans, and with no further guidelines except "favorable consideration will be given" waited for results. Mr. Young, the newly employed vice president, spent several months becoming acquainted with the company: background, strengths, weaknesses, internal developments, and executive interests. He was unable to get the

top executives to be more explicit than "expand through acquisition," and therefore he developed his own criteria as to
what he thought would be appropriate areas and potential
acquisitions. Having selected the most promising, he made
detailed studies of the company, its industry growth trends,
and all the other time-consuming aspects of corporate evaluation. With these data and a personal recommendation that
a purchase be negotiated, he presented the proposal to the
president whose response was, "at best, lukewarm." The
president took the possibility to the board which summarily
rejected the suggestion. During the following three years,
Mr. Young repeated this procedure several times and in each
case was rebuffed.

Mr. Young, reviewing his experience, stated:

> It was much more difficult than I supposed it would be to
> get agreement as to what the corporate objectives and cri-
> teria really are, and to get some sort of preliminary answer
> as to whether a specific case was or was not sufficiently in-
> teresting to justify (1) taking time to investigate (which is
> not only money but time diverted from other cases), and
> (2) wasting other people's time which is bad even for the
> lowest reason, namely, that people will stop discussing ac-
> quisitions with you because you acquire a reputation for in-
> decision and aimlessness.
>
> Had I spotted these problems or really given them full
> weight, I would never have taken the job. I find most peo-
> ple who have had this type of assignment find these points
> more difficult and frustrating, but I guess it is more or less
> inherent when a company starts from scratch.
>
> It beats me how anybody can think you look in the same
> place for rapid growth and a stable, mature industry. Beats
> me how people can think you look in the same area for
> $100,000 and $50,000,000 acquisitions. Beats me how any-
> body can decide which type to look for if he doesn't know
> how much his total program in a certain time span is. And
> how do you know how much money you have if you can't

decide (a) how big should your cash or equivalent reserves be; (b) your earnings and retained earnings after dividend policy; (c) what you can and should borrow; and (d) in what types of situations stock will be used for acquisitions. While all this sounds basic and, you might say, academic it seems as inescapably practical as deciding what type of plane, what amount of gas, what kind of navigation equipment, and what altitudes to fly if one is to reach an intended destination.

2. For screening possible acquisitions: Once an acquisition program as a method of growth is embarked upon, candidates for acquisition can be identified both by internal staff studies and by outside agencies. Unless carefully drawn criteria have been established to screen large numbers of potential companies quickly, enormous amounts of time will be spent and largely wasted on abortive evaluation attempts. There is no point in considering a company which deals in consumer products if the acquirer is interested only in industrial product lines. Too, even relatively small companies take considerable evaluation time if the desired thoughtful job is to be done. Many managements, recognizing that small and medium-sized companies require essentially the same amount of time and energy, disqualify for consideration any company with less than $1,000,000 in sales.

What has been described as "quick and dirty" appraisals frequently disclose critical factors which result in immediate decisions not to spend any time on intensive evaluation. One acquiring company, for example, will not consider any enterprise with a closed shop, because it fears that if a closed shop company is added to its operations, closed shop contracts will be negotiated in existing divisions where the clause is not now in effect. Another company disqualifies any industry or company with gross margins below a stated level on the grounds that the potential acquisition does not have the earning capacity to include headquarters overhead allocations as a cost of doing business. It was found that the creation of such criteria does assist in eliminating quickly dozens of what might appear to be appealing additions to a company's area of activity.

3. For use by bankers, brokers, and board members: There are many sources of leads as to the possible availability of companies interested in selling, which will be discussed in a later section. But if these sources do not have a fairly clearly described set of criteria, their proposals will waste the time of corporate evaluators on nonuseful and diversionary studies. In some cases acquiring company management representatives have made personal calls on potential sources of suggestions and have described their interests orally in great detail. It was found, however, that something gets lost in the spoken communication and what might be a useful source of leads turns out to be, if not unproductive, at least unrelated to the kind of industry and company desired. There is merit in personal discussions of an acquiring company's areas of interest, but the results of such discussions are likely to be more productive if the potential purchaser gives a written memo of the specific criteria he has set up. Plough, Incorporated, for example, prepared a two-page "acquisition program" brochure which included not only pertinent information about Plough's business and financial history, but also described their areas of interests and criteria for future acquisitions.

Typical Statements of Criteria

Statements of criteria ranged from: "interested in the whole spectrum of industry; idea must make business sense and be available at an attractive price in relation to earnings and assets; price would vary depending on the method of payment; method of payment might enable paying considerably higher than asset value over a period of years"; to a 20-page document which outlined in great detail what the specific elements of the company's criteria were. The latter, incidentally, was written by the management of a company after it had acquired three companies, all of which turned out to be mistakes.

In one company a carefully prepared document was written and then used as a topic for discussion with the top 50 key people. Distribution of the printed material was not believed to be enough and the president concluded that a series of management meetings would result in a clearer understanding of the company's program.

The document first stated the broad corporate objectives to be:

1. To achieve leadership and growth in related fields by serving efficiently the needs and wants of present and future customers;

2. To produce earnings sufficient to pay shareholders an adequate return and to provide for long-term growth and stability;

3. To provide opportunity and incentive for employees;

4. To conduct our relationship with suppliers honestly and fairly and expect from them maximum value in goals and services; and

5. To take our place as good citizens in the community and to earn and keep the goodwill of the public.

For each of these broad objectives, detailed elaborations spelled out further the full meanings of the company's philosophy. In the section on earnings, the company's growth plans were detailed in part as follows:

> Growth is to be achieved internally through increased sales of present products and through new products from research and development; externally it is to be achieved by carefully selected acquisitions. Businesses which do not complement our existing operations and which do not show long-term growth possibilities will not be considered for acquisition or increased investment irrespective of their profit

outlook. Similarly any growth or acquisition move must satisfy the criteria of our ability to manage successfully and to service technically.

. . . . .

Acquisitions should be based on long-range plans and needs which are the result of accurate determination of our major growth possibilities. We should then decide if it is better to build such facility or business or if it can be acquired more advantageously.

. . . . .

Criteria for Judging New Ventures

To qualify for acceptance, a new product or acquisition shall be judged by the following criteria:
1. Offer a substantial growth potential;
2. Be in an industry which is at the early stage of its growth cycle;
3. Offer a return on investment of at least 20% before taxes;
4. Provide a relatively quick payment period. Such periods will vary according to the type of industry. However, in no case should the payment period exceed five years;
5. Be an industry in which we are qualified by know-how, capital, and experience to offer equal or better service, performance, and economy than competitors. This does not preclude entry into new industries but it does mean that we must have some reason — other than the opportunity — for entering the business.
6. Serve industrial markets.

In another company, the following criteria were established and distributed internally and externally to possible sources of leads:

1. Size and growth potential:

Sales volume should not exceed $50,000,000, and unless very closely allied to our present fields, should exceed $5,000,000. The investment should not exceed $30,000,000.

There should be an anticipated growth over the next five to ten years of over 5% per year and preferably over 10%.

2. *Profitability and basis of acquisition:*

In the case of cash purchases, it is desired that the return on investment should be at least 25% before taxes, if not immediately at least in the foreseeable future. In those cases where the sales price of the company is in excess of approximately $5,000,000 the acquisition would probably be based on exchange of stock or a combination of stock and cash. In those cases present earnings per share should not be appreciably diluted initially and the prospects should be that earnings per share will be increased. Any exchange of stock should not result in an unduly high concentration of our stock ownership in the hands of one or a few persons.

3. *Type of business:*

The business should be a manufacturing business in, or closely related to, the chemical or chemical processing industries. The products should have a high technical sales and service requirement rather than being in the category of basic chemical commodities. Sales should be to industry rather than to the ultimate consumer. The business should not be competitive with our major customers nor should sales to our present competitors be a major element. The business should not require widely different management concepts from ours, i.e., it should not require high advertising budgets, high capital investment-sales ratio, or highly speculative raw material purchasing problems. On the other hand the business should require a sizable research and development investment.

The company should have a good reputation and be an important factor in its field. The business should not be dependent on one or a very few large customers.

4. *Management:*

The company acquired should have competent management willing to continue operating their business as a division.

It should be noted that statements of criteria must be constructed to give detailed meaning to the individual company objectives and to reflect realistically what is practicable in view of the acquirer's condition. The criteria for a company in a nongrowth industry, subject to wide cyclical changes, with a low price-earnings ratio and unlisted stock, will be quite different from the criteria for a company in a growth industry with listed securities and high price-earnings ratios. To serve the purposes indicated earlier, statements of criteria must be tailored to each company's objectives and situation.

Based on the evidence obtained in our study we believe that establishing company objectives and criteria are important steps in a successful acquisition program. One executive, however, pointed out that he preferred to omit these two steps in that, in his experience, a list of objectives and criteria can become "sacred cows": rather than serving as guides, the goals begin to control the acquirers. He added that criteria served no useful function as a source of leads. The company's board and the public recognition of their interest in acquisitions produced more leads than could be handled administratively. Finally, the industry technology was changing so rapidly that criteria current and useful today would be obsolete tomorrow. This executive's observations of the values of objectives and criteria expressed a minority view held by managements in the situations we studied.

ORGANIZING FOR ACQUISITION

With the creation of corporate objectives and criteria, the next and extremely important step is to organize for the job. That the unique nature of "the job" was not fully understood was evident from peculiar kinds of organization offices set up in some companies. Apparently in these situations the chief operating executives assumed that setting up an organization for acquisition was much like establishing a marketing or a financial function, and since no one in this area with experience was available, anyone could be assigned to the job. The results were odd on two counts: (1) The office, whether called corporate development, or plans, or acquisition, had no clear definition of authority and responsibility in the corporation; and (2) the people assigned typically were castoffs who had proved incapable in carrying out their duties in other segments of the company.

Often, a chief operating executive, having given intellectual lip service to doing something about an acquisition program, belied his real interest by returning to the demands of his day-to-day operating tasks. In one case the president instituted a staff group for acquisitions and assigned to it some former key executives who had been found incompetent in operations. The office was regarded as a respectable dumping ground for people who had failed or who were on the аownside of their curves of interest and energy. These executives were assigned the functions relating to acquisition with fervent hopes that something good might happen. As one president said, "and besides, they can't do much harm in that area. Who knows, maybe they will come up with something worthwhile." This same president, not content with one staff group concerned with acquisitions, set up two others in competing roles. With no top management direction, the groups' compounded efforts resulted in frustration and no action. Even today it is not generally recognized within the company that this approach is costly, wasteful, and nonproductive.

In another company the president organized an acquisition committee which included six vice presidents and the manager of research and development. Weekly meetings were held and minutes maintained on the flow of discussion. A review of these minutes indicates the wandering and nondirected use of busy executives' time, again with no results.

The size of the group and the absence of conviction of the usefulness of the activities soon led to the inevitable conclusion to disband the committee and start on another tack.

Personal Involvement of the President

We found that in every company in which there was a successful acquisition program, the chief operating executive was personally involved. There were no exceptions. In some companies the president worked closely with another key executive, such as a vice president and general manager of a division or a vice president for plans, a staff officer for acquisitions, or in one case, vice president and general counsel, an extraordinarily capable top management executive, where the skills, capacities, and working relationships between the two enabled the joint consummation of six acquisitions in two years. This is not to say that staff groups especially organized or other functional line and staff specialists do not have significant contributions to make. They do, but the leadership and drive must come from the chief operating man or his representative with his support. We believe that the personal involvement of the president is crucial and its absence explains the many unsuccessful acquisitions programs extant today.

There are many reasons why the chief operating executive's involvement is critical in acquisitions. Some of the more important are described below.

1. He has the responsibility to plot the growth of the enterprise. If, in addition to internal growth methods, he decides to augment this growth through acquisitions, he has a powerful motivation to be sure that the program succeeds. One president stated, "Having announced and embarked upon the acquisition route, I am determined to make it go." Another said that the "successful acquirer is the president or subordinate who wants more than anything else in the world

to acquire. He has an active driving desire to achieve this objective and the job cannot be performed by one accustomed to advising, persuading, and suggesting, and not being responsible for results."

2. The chief operating executive, subject as noted to the board of directors, has the authority to represent the corporation in relations with others. In a sense, he speaks as the company and carries a powerful mantle of prestige and position in all negotiations.

3. Today's high interest in acquisition as an approach to company growth has resulted in what many describe as a sellers' market. Sellers' representatives, usually the president or in some cases members of the board, like to be approached by the chief operating executive of a potential acquirer. The subtle but meaningful equivalence of position has important influences on the degree of acceptance by sellers.

4. The chief operating executive usually has had line experience in the industry or has someone with him who has had line experience and therefore either or both can talk the language of the business with executives of companies to be acquired. It was observed that sellers are more likely to trust someone with business backgrounds similar to their own. But if the representative of the prospective buyer has not had experience in that industry, sellers, involved in the process for the first time in their lives and "scared to death they will be taken into camp by some fast talking slickers," become "frightened, clam up, and negotiations might as well end right there to save everyone's time."

The acquiring chief operating executive can talk shop with his counterpart. This has two purposes: (1) to create a rapport between knowledgeable executives; and (2) to enable the acquiring executive to calibrate the responses to industry questions. In one situation, for example, the acquiring president, with many years' experience in the camera business opened a discussion by noting the effect Japanese competition was having on American products and wondered how the potential company to be acquired had handled this threat to the market. This query was followed by such questions as the following: Just how do you sell your products? Do you use distributors? Are they effective? What problems have you had with manufacturers' agents? Have you considered selling direct through salaried salesmen? How has your profit margin held up? What product development are you doing? And so on. Such a conversation can better be handled by line executives chatting with line executives in the company under consideration for acquisition.

Because of his long acquaintance and experience with the important elements in his field of business, the chief operating executive generally has developed a sensitive ear and a penetrating eye. The former makes it possible to listen for discords among the executives approached, to ferret out whether the organization is filled with dissension and distrust. The penetrating eye permits the accumulation of evidence that the company being considered has poor production control, uses old, obsolete, and inefficient machinery, or has superb special-purpose machine design as manifested by the products manufactured.

5. The president with long experience in an industry becomes acquainted with his competitors and customers in the business. These friendships, built up through trade and professional associations, result in rather intimate knowledge of who is doing what in the industry and which companies might be amenable to being acquired. The president of an eastern mechanical instrument company, for example, reported that with the company's broad line of equipment he knew practically every customer and competitor in the United States. In this case, two somewhat related instruments companies were identified and acquired.

6. He must convince the board of directors of the desirability of growth through acquisition. During our study there

seemed to be four broad categories of boards of directors. In the first, the president owns all or control of the voting stock, the board consists typically of the president, his wife, the company attorney, perhaps one or two employees, and, in rare situations, a few outsiders. In this situation the president makes all major decisions and the board exists to give the necessary legal approvals. Here the president makes the decision to acquire or not to acquire and the board complies with the legal requirements. Relationship with the board is no problem for the president in these situations.[3]

The second category is the medium-sized or large publicly held company in which the president ostensibly is elected by the board of directors each year but, in fact, the election is a formality and the president largely controls the election of members of the board. In this type of corporation, the board may include a few outside directors who ask discerning questions but most presidents we observed during our study were sufficiently able to answer the questions satisfactorily and essentially decide whether an acquisition should be made. The president's role in category two is more difficult than when the president owns the company, but not much. There were a few cases of problems with the board, but these were a very small percentage of the total.

In publicly held companies where the board consisted of both insiders and outsiders, it cannot be reasonably expected that a vice president insider, for example, would raise any objections in a board meeting to a presidential endorsed proposal to acquire another company. In one company such a vice president asked the president before the meeting if he should express his doubts at the meeting and he was advised succinctly and clearly that his question or opposition would be inappropriate. Needless to report, the vice president remained silent.

[3] Myles L. Mace, *The Board of Directors in Small Corporations.* Boston, Harvard Business School, Division of Research, 1948.

The third category is the medium-sized or large publicly held company where the board membership includes some sharp, perceptive, outside directors who do recognize their responsiblities to the stockholders, the employees, and the public. Aware of these duties, they conscientiously fulfill their roles with the highest sense of corporate management trust. They do their homework and come to meetings prepared to exercise their best judgments. With such mentors, the president, although he enjoys the greatest confidence of the board, has a more difficult job with regard to acquisitions than is the case in categories one and two. In category three situations, the president must be prepared to make the acquisition proposal and to answer the penetrating questions which always can and seem to be asked. Answers to such questions by a subordinate in the company do not carry the weight of those given by the president.

The fourth category, and the most difficult one to deal with from the president's point of view, is the company where the board consists of members who are substantial stockholders and the president, owning little or no stock, is basically a hired, salaried manager. In such a situation, the president has real problems. This was found to be especially true in three companies we studied where the average age of the board members was over 70 years and whose general philosophy was, "We have done all right in our industry for 50 years and we just don't like some of these newfangled ideas to grow through acquisition."

The four categories of boards of directors are raised here to indicate the importance and influence of each company's chief operating executive. As the manager of the corporation, and with firsthand knowledge of the merits and shortcomings of a proposed acquisition, he is in an extremely important position, in category three and four situations, to affect the ultimate decision. If the president is personally involved in the acquisition process, he is able to present his recommendations with the necessary conviction and persuasion. But if the president is not involved himself but instead relies upon a subordinate to evaluate and negotiate a deal, he will find himself as a relatively uninformed filter between the subordinate who makes the proposal and the board. In such situations, the boards seem to take a much more careful look at the proposals made and our studies showed that they frequently turn down opportunities.

In one case the head of a planning department located, evaluated, and substantially alone negotiated a possible acquisition, subject to board approval. The key factors were reviewed by the president who concluded it was a good proposition and asked the planning department head to make the presentation to the board. The board was a category four board — substantial stockholders. The presentation was made and several board members raised penetrating questions of the sort that can be asked about *any* acquisition. The answers by the planning department head were accurate but unpersuasive. The president, also a salaried employee, was unable to change their conclusion — a disappointing result after months of careful work by the planning department.

Working Through a Subordinate

For the reasons outlined above we believe that the personal involvement of the president is crucial to the success of a company's acquisition program. We found several instances, however, where success was achieved by a senior executive who worked closely with the president. The relationship between the two top executives was characterized by complete rapport, confidence, and unity of thought and concept. When this relationship existed it was possible to increase the number of active evaluations and negotiations being carried on. But in all cases the president was fully aware of what was being done by his senior executive and participated to the extent necessary to accept or to reject the opportunity for acquisition, whichever the indicated course of action was.

Examples of effective working relationships between the president and senior executives were found in Litton Industries, among others. Mr. Charles B. Thornton, chairman of the board and chief executive officer, has a very close and intimate working affiliation with Mr. Roy L. Ash, president, and Mr. Glen McDaniel, senior vice president. Mr. Ash and Mr. McDaniel both represented Litton Industries during a number of negotiations, kept Mr. Thornton completely advised, and consummated several acquisitions for Litton. Also, in the Thompson Ramo Wooldridge Company, Mr. Warren Hayes, vice president and general manager of the components division, represented his company effectively, but at all times he was in communication with Mr. Dean Wooldridge, president of Thompson Ramo Wooldridge. Here again, we observed the unity of purpose and business accord between these two executives.

SPECIAL PROBLEMS IN DECENTRALIZED COMPANIES

For companies with a relatively small headquarters organization consisting of the chief operating executives plus specialized staff or service groups, and with operations decentralized into several divisions and departments, particular care must be taken to define meticulously what the acquisition activities and responsibilities are for these headquarters and for the operating divisions and departments. The decentralized divisions are created typically to establish autonomous profit-and-loss measurable entities and to bring the decision-making process as close as possible to customers and suppliers. In effect, the division and department managers are to administer their organizations as separate medium-sized businesses, subject only to the limited control of headquarters and to use of the staff groups at headquarters which, theoretically at least, can perform the staff functions better and more economically than could be done at each of the divisions and departments.

Each division and department manager is responsible for the complete operation of his organization, including planning its growth in sales and profits. These managers, closer to the competitive conditions in their segment of business than anyone else in the company, constantly get ideas for improving their respective product lines either through internal developments or through the acquisition of other companies in related businesses. This is an important part of their general management function. But unless their authority to investigate, evaluate, and negotiate for the acquisition of a promising company is circumscribed thoughtfully, unforeseen and undesirable company liabilities can be created quite innocently.

In the Bares Corporation, for example, a division vice president and general manager was aware of his responsibilities and the need for growth planning. In addition to expending house research and development money on internal development projects, he initiated a search for possible companies to acquire which met stated criteria. During the search he learned of a potential candidate for acquisition, and without coordination with his headquarters started discussions and negotiations with the principal owner. Later, the division manager reported to the president with some pride what he had accomplished. At this stage experienced headquarters executives took over the negotiations and completed the acquisition. But the problems of negotiation were compounded by the general manager's inexperience and a liability for a $50,000 brokers' fee was incurred, a fee which, in the judgment of headquarters executives, was not justified or appropriate.

Division and department general managers typically do not have the background of skills and experience which is critical in the successful conduct of acquisition proceedings. They have important roles to perform in identifying desirable product areas and perhaps in identifying prospective companies to be acquired. But beyond these steps in the acquisition cycle, authority and responsibility should be vested in and carried out by headquarters executives. The division and department general managers and subordinates may in some situations have had pertinent industry experience which can be most helpful in evaluating a possible acquisition and this experience should be called upon in evaluating proposals. The main responsibility for leading the acquisition process, however, should be assigned to a headquarters executive.

In one company, organized on a decentralized basis, a policy statement on the acquisition of other enterprises was issued which, after listing criteria, stated in part:

1. The headquarters' executive vice president has the primary responsibility for evaluating potential acquisitions and for conducting negotiations for acquisitions.

2. Operating division general managers have the primary responsibility to plan the growth of their respective divisions. This will include, among other approaches, recommendations as to potential companies to be acquired. Division general managers shall study their requirements, prepare proposals for achieving division growth plans, and submit these proposals to the headquarters' executive vice president. Under no condition is the division general manager to open negotiations with the owners and management of a potential acquisition without the express approval of the headquarters' executive vice president, nor are conversations to be carried on with business brokers or other sources of leads.

3. The headquarters' executive vice president shall see that all division proposals for acquisition are analyzed and evaluated. After concurrence by the company's executive committee, the executive vice president will be responsi-

ble for all negotiations leading to acquisition. He may call on any executives in the company, including the division general managers concerned, in order to carry out this role most expeditiously.

ROLE OF STAFF GROUPS

In many corporations presidents have organized new and separate staff groups to be concerned with acquisitions. Typically their functions are described as:

1. Advise and counsel corporate and divisional management concerning the effect of significant outside financial, social, and economic factors on the company's plans and objectives;

2. Perform economic and financial analyses on which to base short- and long-term plans; and

3. Identify, evaluate, and prepare recommendations on opportunities for growth in new areas, either by acquisition or by internal development.

We found that most staff groups of this type performed very valuable analyses and recommendations. Their principal functions were to locate promising fields for growth, internally and by acquisition, and the members of these groups developed a professional skill in doing this job. The size of the group ranged from a one-man specialist in a small West Coast company to a 12-man organization in a very large East Coast company. In the latter situation the group included market analysts, lawyers, technical specialists, and financial analysts. Over the years a considerable library of information had been accumulated and was available to top line executives responsible for managing the growth of the enterprise.

The assignment of functional specialists to a staff group for planning acquisitions has many advantages. The processes of acquisition are markedly different from the processes of administering a going business.   Acquisition involves financial and personnel evaluations quite divergent from the usual operating problems found in a company.   Various concepts such as pooling of interest, tax-free exchanges, new bases for depreciation, and the integration of substantial plant and people resources are everyday facts for those involved in acquisitions, but not for those whose experience has been entirely in the customary corporate operations. Many staff executives, however, who have gone through the process once, have become immeasurable aids in subsequent negotiations and agreements to acquire.   They perform the dual function of specialists on both operating and acquisition problems.

Other staff officers, unaccustomed to the new intricacies involved, served largely as dampeners and critical fault-finders. Their attitude and behavior seemed to indicate that their principal function in evaluation of a company, for example, was to find every conceivable thing wrong with it.   One president, confronted with such a staff performance, said, "My staff executives, asked to participate in an evaluation, were determined to outline why it wouldn't work.   They just will not help me find what can be done to make the acquisition worthwhile.   They are great on our regular operations, but on possible acquisitions, they appear dedicated to protecting themselves so that if we do acquire a business they can say, 'Of course, the problems resulting were pointed out by me in a memorandum to the president, dated December 7, 1961.' "

To provide the professional and specialized services needed to carry through one or more acquisitions, some company managements have employed consultants.   The president of a West Coast company, for example, wanted to explore the feasibility of growth in the electronics and chemical industries.   He retained on a one-year basis two outstanding and nationally renowned professors from California universities to work on the problem and sought the advice of others on the appraisal of technical and personal competence. The president stated that he was able to get the thinking and judgment of knowledgeable professionals and avoid the continuing cost of salaried specialists working as staff members in an acquisition group.

During our study we found that some consulting firms had done eminent and impressive jobs in helping managements construct a philosophy of growth through acquisition, had elaborated detailed criteria for the objectives, had assisted in constructing an effective organization to achieve the goals, and had performed the other important functions essential to a sensible acquisition program. But, as is the case when employing consultants for any management assistance, it is important for company executives to evaluate carefully the experience and qualifications of the individual consultants who will work on the assigned project as well as the recommendations which result from their studies.

Effective planning for growth through acquisition, then, consists essentially of establishing the company objectives, defining meaningful criteria, and assuring the personal involvement of the president. Many instances were found where neglect of these three relatively simple, basic concepts resulted in wasteful, time-consuming, and unproductive acquisition efforts.

CHAPTER V

Locating Companies to be Acquired

With carefully defined objectives and criteria, top management is then prepared to search for promising leads for acquisition. We found a wide array of approaches ranging from the extensive dissemination of written statements of a company's history and its criteria for the kind of companies it sought to acquire, to the selection and study of one company in an industry to which an approach was made. One management, for instance, mailed several hundred letters which stated substantially:

> Gentlemen:
>   We are a listed company and one interested in acquiring other companies as divisions for diversification and growth. We are in a position to pay cash or stock or a combination of both. If you are interested in the sale of your company, would suggest that you send in full details.
>
>   Yours truly,

This approach was described during our interviews as "casting literary bread upon the waters of trade with hopes of a return." Unfortunately, however, this method of searching for promising companies for acquisition was not found to be useful. Responses were forthcoming but the sender of the letters was swamped with offers to sell from restaurants, gas service stations, bowling alleys, and manufacturing companies quite unrelated to his existing business. Responses were received, also, from dozens of business brokers into whose hands the letter had drifted. One president who initiated his search this way said: "With no expressed limits to our interests in our letter, our haul included haddock, cod, sea bass, whales, and even a few sharks."

On the other hand, Drake, Inc., mailed a four-page brochure to investment bankers, commercial bankers, brokers, and finders. But here the areas of interest were carefully outlined. The criteria were explicit and the reader could get a clear idea of what kinds of companies might be of interest to the top management of Drake. It was reported that many worthwhile opportunities were located through the brochure mailing which was accompanied by a personal letter from the president or a vice president.

Studies by Staff Groups

In those companies where a program of growth through acquisition is accompanied by the participation of a staff group, the approach, although more complicated, is relatively straightforward. With areas of interest clarified, the staff members can study various segments of business and decide whether these segments include candidates for acquisition. In a large chemical company in the Midwest, for example, search was limited to firms making industrial type products and compounds. A member of the commercial evaluation department and an assistant studied the adhesives field and their memorandum stated in part:

Industrial adhesives have a great deal in common with our present operations:
1. We are now manufacturing some adhesives, although in relatively small quantities.
2. The role of adhesives is "our kind of business," a chemical compound, and requires much the same approach as our other products.
3. Our entrance into this business would not raise any difficulties for our salesmen or conflict with our present products.
4. Some of our important customers are large users of adhesives.

5. Few users of adhesives are staffed to develop their own adhesives, yet they have expressed dissatisfaction with the service and technical ability of most suppliers.

6. There are unsolved technical problems that require fundamental development work.

7. The use of adhesives is growing rapidly in all outlets, owing to technical advances and to increases in labor costs.

We believe there is a fine opportunity for a supplier with our background. By selecting those types of adhesives that involve more development and technical service, and by giving greater attention to the needs of the field, there is a profitable market with a modest investment.

The term "adhesives" covers a wide range of materials used to bond two surfaces. Several years ago, adhesives would probably have been classified into three groups of glues, pastes, and other. Glues included hide, bone, and fish glue; pastes included viscous cooked starches; and other was chiefly some of the natural gums, rubber cement, and silicate of soda. These materials are still used but they have been modified and others have been developed to give a long list of compounded adhesives suited to the greater variety of materials and surfaces and to the demands of high speed fabrication. The adhesive business now is a complex one.

The study then set forth in more detail the various classifications of adhesives, the principal industries using the several kinds of adhesives, the ways in which the materials are used, and the nature of selling to the users. A brief description of three companies recommended for acquisitions followed; these companies had been selected from a list of 66 companies on which some information had been obtained. The information for the study was collected through interviews with the acquiring company's employees, the executive secretaries of the Adhesives Manufacturers Association of America and the Tapioca Institute of America, box manufacturers, large users of adhesives, packaging engineers of large users of packaging materials, tire companies, fabric and steel manufacturers, aircraft companies, auto companies, printers of catalogues and books, and chemical customers of the company who were buying their adhesives from others. The study required eight months to complete and demanded the full time of the two employees of the commercial evaluation department. But based on these findings the president initiated discussions with the owners of one of the three companies recommended for acquisition and shortly thereafter an agreement was reached.

We found hundreds of staff studies such as this. Many, of course, suggested that no acquisition be made after the facts about conditions in the industry were disclosed. But the systematic and orderly collection of information on segments of an industry does provide an abundance of facts about the industry and a listing of companies active in it. The process is slow and costly but, we believe, it is effective if a program for acquisition is to be accomplished sensibly.

Staff groups organized for acquisition purposes have a large number of sources of information. Industry trade associations, United States Department of Commerce statistics and industry studies, reports by Poor's, Moody's, and Dun and Bradstreet, and the company's marketing and purchasing organizations all combine to enable the seeker to learn a great deal about an industry and its inhabitants. We found that a company's own employees frequently provided data of great value, but we found also that this source of information was frequently overlooked by members of industry study groups. There is much to be learned from company employees. But getting a flow of information upward through succeeding echelons of management requires active work by those at the top. Somehow the process of upward movement of ideas does not happen automatically.

In addition to acting on suggestions from lower echelon employees, acquisition staff groups make studies as requested by the chief operating executive and operating vice presidents within the company. The president obtains ideas and recommendations from a wide circle of contacts, including his board of directors. In one case, the acquisition staff head lamented that the president had been asked by a board member to consider the acquisition of a small manufacturing company in an area completely foreign to existing operations. Without asking for a staff study in the small company and its industry, the president recommended that the company be acquired and the action was approved by the board of directors. Two years and several hundreds of thousands of dollars later, the president concluded that his "whim" was not attractive and had turned out badly and the abortive venture was sold to a company in the same industry. It should be noted, however, that this same president has accomplished an incredible list of successful acquisitions during the last 15 years and as was stated by one of the company executives, "he is entitled to a few boo-boos."

Another common complaint of acquisition staff groups was that they were requested by the president to devote inordinate amounts of time to evaluating random companies which came to his attention. Numerous times the companies suggested were well outside the orbit of clearly written criteria, but detailed studies were asked for nevertheless. Two observations: Many top executives are aggressive, imaginative, and constantly searching for new, better, and more profitable areas to exploit. They accept the values of established criteria, but do not permit a limitation on what they envisage as other worthwhile ventures. These chief operating executives are willing to explore what to them is virgin territory and as one planning department head said, "Our president can afford to take the kind of risk which the planning department cannot." Second, sometimes members of a planning department or acquisition group implicitly resist suggestions as to new areas for development which do not derive from their own studies. The feeling is related to the not-invented-here concept mentioned earlier. Acquisition staff departments, many of which are doing outstanding work in the field, must include as a built-in ingredient of their function carrying on some studies apparently outside the confines of existing criteria.

Suggestions from Boards of Directors

We cannot generalize on the merit of suggestions for acquisitions by members of boards of directors. In some companies board members understand the operating objectives and are alert for opportunities that will increase the company's growth through acquisition. With a clear understanding of the industry in which the company operates they recognize new areas and bring them to the attention of the chief operating executive. In other companies, however, board members have never come up with suggestions for areas or companies to be considered for acquisition, nor are they likely to do so. The willingness of board members to serve useful roles in finding new sources of potential acquisitions is a function of their interest in the company as well as the leadership provided by the president.

Working with Investment Bankers

Investment bankers have proved helpful in locating prospective companies for acquisition. Their staffs typically include experienced partners with wide acquaintances in business — industry specialists who know intimately the status of companies in their respective industries and sometimes one or more staff members whose functions are specialized in the acquisition area.

Some companies have investment bankers on their boards of directors and thus naturally have available if desired the facilities and services of the banking firm in locating potential acquisitions. It is not always true, however, that the particular banking firm represented on the board can be helpful to the company seeking search assistance. The quality of the help depends on the qualifications of the members and staff of the banking firm as well as the personal time and interest taken by the banker on the board.

In those companies where the board of directors does not include an investment banker or where the company has not established a relationship with an investment banker, the decision must be made as to whether to approach one or several investment bankers for help in locating prospective acquisitions. One banker stated that if the management of a company talked with several different banking firms, there was bound to be duplication of effort. Also, if a banking firm knows that other bankers are working on the same problem, it will have less incentive to make an intensive search. We believe that the most satisfactory solution is to work with one banking firm on an exclusive basis for a limited period of time. If the results are not productive, the company management can then make arrangements with another banking firm.

When approaching an investment banking firm for help, it is important for the management interested in acquisitions to have already defined the specifics on the product area, the size of company desired, and the kind of management the acquirer is looking for. As one banker said, "My first question when a client comes in and wants help in locating a seller is, 'Do you really want to acquire and what criteria have you defined to give real meaning to this desire?'" He added, "I have found that if a potential acquirer comes in with his goals thought out, I know he is not frivolous about the affair."

In one case the president of a very large company asked a well-known New York investment banker for help with only sketchy verbalized ideas as to the area desired. A young partner in the bank made a trip to the company headquarters, talked to all the top executives and divison managers, and wrote up a memorandum stating what appeared to him to be what the company was looking for. The memorandum represented a top management consensus which was discussed further and after some changes became the guidelines for the banker's search. In this situation the partner noted that the management did define the goals carefully and that these were basic to an intelligent search for acquisitions.

There are many varied fee arrangements which can be made with investment bankers. In some cases the bank will work on a retainer fee basis; in others the fee will vary according to the results and to the amount of work put into the task; and in still other circumstances, a fee will be negotiated after an acquisition is achieved. In all cases, however, we believe that managements seeking help in locating companies should have a clear understanding in advance of the fees and costs involved.

Use of Commercial Banks

Commercial banks, too, represent a fertile source for leads to companies which might be acquired. Sometimes a borrower from the bank may be losing money and the bank officers will actively seek a potential buyer. Bank officers, in their particular geographical areas, usually are well informed about the kinds of industries and the individual situations of companies there. They know of companies where the management is getting old and seeking retirement, where capital for growth is limited by a company's borrowing capacity, where company management members are anxious to devote full time to first loves such as research, development, or product development, and so on. Bringing these situations to the attention of prospective acquirers serves the interest of both the buyer and the seller, and in our field studies we found no commercial banks which charged fees to either party of an acquisiton for any of the work performed. Commercal bank officers can provide leads, but typically do not make financial analyses of corporate values, thus avoiding any conflict of interest. The bank's incentive of course is to serve as the depository for the combined company or to be the lending source for the two companies when they are joined.

We found many situations in which commercial bank officers were helpful in providing leads to company managements interested in buying and introductions to owners interested in selling. In one, the vice president of an East Coast company asked a loan officer of a Chicago bank about two manufacturing companies in that area. During the conversation the bank officer learned about the type of companies desired and suggested that consideration be given to another company not on the potential buyer's list. Six months later the East Coast company acquired the company the bank officer had proposed.

Use of Consultants

Another source of leads for acquisition is the consultant. There are many professionally qualified and helpful consultants, some of whom specialize in work on acquisitions and others who include assistance in acquisitions as part of a general management consulting practice. Several examples were found where consultants came into an organization when the only progress that had been made toward an acquisition program was a conviction by the president that his company should diversify. The experienced consultants discussed and studied the company's history, evaluated its manufacturing, marketing, and financial strengths and weaknesses, and gained insight into the organization structure and financial capabilities. With this background they worked with the chief operating executive in outlining corporate objectives, establishing criteria, searching for desired companies to acquire, evaluating and screening candidates against the prescribed requirements, and, in some cases, participating in the negotiations for purchase. Working as professional consultants on a fixed fee basis, they represent only the client's management and thus avoid any possible conflict of interest. Consultants, also, have served effectively in situations where the managements have defined their own objectives and criteria, by conducting intensive industry searches to identify companies which meet them. In fact, competent consultants can come in at any phase of the acquisition cycle and perform useful roles.

Some managements, interested in only one or at most a few acquisitions, have relied upon consultants rather than establishing an acquisition or commercial development staff group as a more or less permanent part of the organization. The cost of the consultant's fee was believed to be lower than the expense, short- and long-term, of creating a staff department. Other managements, however, contend that even for a limited acquisition effort it is better to establish a company's own section to do the work in that the accumulated background and findings inure to the benefit of the company rather than to the consultants. All managements with whom the role of consultants was discussed in our study agreed that before consultants are retained it is imperative that the scope of work be defined and fees agreed upon. Reputable consultants appreciate the importance of this clear understanding and typically will propose a phased program of work at the end of each part of which the client can decide to continue or terminate the relationship.

PROBLEMS OF DEALING WITH BUSINESS BROKERS

Business brokers constitute another fruitful source of leads for managements seeking companies to acquire. There are competent, professionally qualified brokers who have been in-volved in acquisition arrangements for many years. But the recent sharp increase in acquisitions as a method of growth has attracted innumerable others who, as one president stated, "have turned the role into a racket." It is of the utmost impor-tance that a management seeking acquisition through brokers determine at the start whether arrangements are being made with a reputable or with a less than reputable broker. To il-lustrate a broker's lack of authority to represent a selling man-agement: The vice president of X Company, active in acquisi-tions during the last 15 years, reported that when the Federal Trade Commission ruled that the Y Company must divest it-self of an earlier acquired subsidiary, the X Company vice president received 35 telephone calls in two days from brokers suggesting that the divested subsidiary should be purchased by the X Company.

There are, however, a number of brokers who observe the highest levels of integrity and professional ethics. One of these, aware of the increasing unfortunate connotations of "broker," described his function as that of an "intermediary." He reported that his firm serves almost exclusively as an agent for the selling company. The two partners of the broker's firm are a lawyer and an engineer with aeronautical and me-chanical engineering degrees. They do not provide tax or technical evaluation advice, but suggest that appropriate specialists be employed to provide those services. They stated that ideally the broker's function is to know a segment of business sufficiently well so that when retained by a seller's management, it is possible to bring together the most worth-while buying company and the seller. To fulfill this task, the two partners travel extensively, attend trade shows and asso-ciation meetings, and visit companies which might be pos-sible purchasers in the future. They try to assure that before approaching a prospective buyer, the acquisition would make business sense from the point of view of both the buyer and the seller. Fees to the seller for these services are 5% of the first $2,000,000 of cash or stock value involved; and for the larger deals 3½% on the first $3,000,000 and 1½% thereafter.

Reputable brokers such as this do perform a useful function and appropriate fees are inevitably part of the agreement. While the brokers' arrangements are typically with the seller, whether or not the amount of the fees is included in the total purchase price, it is always a part of the negotiated price for the acquisition.

Some brokers upon learning that the owners of a company might be interested in selling their enterprise or even upon suspecting that they might be interested in selling, write and send hundreds of letters to possible prospects worded essentially:

> Does your growth program include the possible acquisition of a West Coast company which manufactures and sells construction materials? This field is growing and may be of interest to you. The company we have in mind has operated for 15 years, has sales in the high seven figures, and profits after taxes of approximately 7% after adjustments for executive salaries and bonuses. Please let us know if you would like to pursue this fine opportunity.

Another broker called the head of a corporate planning department to report that he knew of a company which might be of interest and while he did not represent the prospective seller, he wondered whether he could make a financial fee arrangment if the company's name were disclosed. A similar call was received by a vice president of a refrigerator manufacturing company on the East Coast in which the caller said, "Did you know that the X Company can be purchased? It has a large backlog and would give you a midwest base of operations." The availability of the company was already known to the vice president and later, after he had acquired it, the caller filed a lawsuit to collect his commission. In another situation, one of many we encountered during our study, the president of a company was approached by a broker who suggested a possible acquisition and stated that he would be compensated by the seller. When the deal was completed, the broker submitted a bill for services in the amount of $300,000. The president of the acquiring company paid the broker $45,000 to avoid litigation and told him to sue for the balance if he did not regard this amount as fair.

Another broker when queried about fees wrote, "Remuneration would be due us only if an acquisition is accomplished, would be payable by the selling company (to be reflected in the price paid by you for the company), and you would have no additional liability to our firm."

Companies with experience in acquisitions have established careful safeguards to avoid unanticipated liabilities for brokers' fees. In one company the following memorandum was circulated among all key personnel who might be the recipients of telephone calls or letters having to do with acquisitions:

Subject: Liability to a Business Broker or Finder for Compensation:

In any transaction in which the Curt Company acquires a business or the assets of a "going concern" there is likely to arise a question of whether some third party is entitled to a fee or commission for his part in arranging the transaction or bringing the parties to the transaction together. The problem becomes more acute as the Curt Company steps up its activities in this area, because there is apt to be an increased flow of unsolicited opportunities presented to the Curt Company.

The problem can arise regardless of the form of the transaction, i.e., whether it is a purchase for cash or notes or stock, whether it is a merger or tax-free reorganization or some other form. It can arise regardless of the type of property subject to the transaction, i.e., stock, tangible or intangible assets, etc.

The third party may be anyone including a broker, whose sole business is to arrange such deals or a person who has never acted in such a capacity before.

The amount of work performed by such a third party may seem appallingly small, yet he may, unless proper precautions are taken, become entitled to a substantial "fee." The problem is not always to avoid paying for the services of such a third party, but to avoid paying a fee that the Curt Company did not knowingly intend to become liable for or to limit the fee, if any, to an amount agreeable to the Curt Company.

All compensation of the type referred to is payable only pursuant to a contract. The contract may be expressed or implied. The latter, of course, is the type which gives the greatest trouble, and should be avoided.

The only sound way to avoid making an unintended implied contract is to have a written understanding that no compensation is to be paid by the Curt Company or, if compensation is to be paid, the exact amount or a formula for determining the exact amount, and a clear statement of when and under what circumstances the fee is payable.

However, the preceding statement is the conclusion and there are pitfalls to be avoided even if one has the problem clearly in mind and contemplates ultimately having a written understanding. These pitfalls can be avoided by observing the following:

1. Whenever the Curt Company is approached by anyone who wishes to propose a business opportunity, find out whether such a person is a "finder" or "business broker." Perhaps the best way is to find out whether the person is a principal. If he is not a principal, his position is one where he may later claim a fee, and it should be determined whether he expects to receive any pay from the Curt Company before he makes any disclosures to us.

In this connection, note

(a) the mere fact that the person is acting for the sellers and is to be paid a finder's fee by them does not preclude him from also collecting a finder's fee from us.

(b) the mere fact that such a person expects to benefit indirectly from the proposed transaction may not preclude him from also claiming a finder's fee (e.g., a broker who might expect to make a broker's commission on the transfer of stock), and

(c) disputes over such fees are a common source of litigation and have on occasion involved representatives of very reputable firms, so do not be misled into thinking the third party is "not the kind of person" who would claim a finder's fee.

2. If such a person denies that he wants us to pay him, it is highly desirable to have a statement to that effect in writing signed by the individual. (A sample form of such a statement is attached as Form A.) * It may not always be feasible to ask for such a written statement. In that event, we should write a letter to the individual stating our understanding on the question and asking for an immediate written reply if the other party disagrees. (A sample of such a letter is attached as Form B.) Any disagreement with the latter statement should be cleared up before any further disclosures or negotiations take place.

3. If the first approach to the Curt Company is by letter, no disclosure made in such a letter can be the basis for claiming compensation, but any reply to such a letter should contain statements of our position with respect to a fee. (A sample of such a statement for incorporation in a reply is attached as Form C.)

4. If, in any of these situations, the third party indicates that he does expect to receive a fee from us, *then before any disclosures are made* we must decide whether we want to

---

* The attached forms are illustrative. Wherever possible, the Legal Department should be asked to prepare or review any letters or other statements on these subjects.

pay, and if we are willing to pay, then to work out the amount and terms of payment. Such an agreement must be reduced to writing and signed. No form of such an agreement is attached as the terms and provisions would be too varied. Such an agreement should be prepared by or reviewed by the Legal Department before it is signed. Do not accept any information from the third party until the fee agreement is signed.

5. The foregoing and the suggested forms were written to apply to situations where a proposal is brought to the Curt Company. The problem of liability for a finder's fee can arise just as well where we ask a business broker to find possible transactions for it. In such situations, we should determine whether such "finders" expect to be paid by us. If they do, then it is essential before such a "finder" expends time and effort, and, in any event, before any proposal is disclosed, to agree on the amount or a formula for determining the amount of such compensation and the terms and conditions on which the fee becomes payable. Such an understanding should be written by or cleared with the Legal Department. It should, of course, be signed by the "broker" and by an officer of the company.

Any correspondence bearing on the matter of such fees or commissions is important evidence which should be carefully preserved. It is suggested that it be sent to me for filing in the Legal Department.

Form A

—————, 19———

The Curt Company
St. Louis
Missouri

This letter confirms my oral statements to you. I represent Mr. John Jones, the owner of all of the capital stock of XYZ Corporation. Mr. Jones is interested in entering into a transaction with you for the acquisition by you of his interest in said Corporation. In the event that you enter into any such transaction with Mr. Jones or any transaction with the XYZ Corporation for acquisition of its business and assets, I expect to receive compensation from Mr. Jones or the XYZ Corporation for my services in helping to arrange the transaction. The Curt Company is not, under any circumstances, to be liable to me or my firm for any services in connection with such a transaction.

Yours very truly,

Form B

Dear Mr. _____:

It is our understanding, based on Mr. _____'s conversation with you on _____ 19_____, that you are acting solely for the owners of XYZ Corporation and expect to receive compensation from them in the event that the Curt Company enters into a transaction with them or with the XYZ Corporation, but under no circumstances is the Curt Company to be liable to you or your firm for any services in arranging such a transaction. If you do not agree with our understanding on this matter, please let us know by return mail.

Very truly yours,
THE CURT COMPANY

Form C

Dear Mr. _____:

We acknowledge your letter of _____ regarding _____. We are interested in considering this matter further and suggest you call us to arrange a suitable time to discuss it.

However, before receiving any further information, we must have a clear understanding with you regarding your position in this matter. (Since you state that you are acting for _____, we assume that if we enter into any sort of transaction with _____ you will be compensated by them. Under no circumstances is the Curt Company to be liable to you or your firm for any services in arranging such a transaction. Kindly confirm whether or not you

agree with us in this regard.) *   (We must know whether
you expect to receive any compensation from Curt Company if we enter into a transaction with _____.) *

Very truly yours,

THE CURT COMPANY

---

* These provisions in parentheses are to be used as alternatives.

The president of an East Coast company received a letter
from a broker stating, "A manufacturer of electrical goods,
our client, is for sale. Your purchase of the company would
provide a highly competent scientific staff, a technical product
line, a large backlog, and a substantial tax loss to carry over.
Please advise us with regard to your interest."

The president wrote the broker, "Before exploring this
matter further, we would like to receive, from the company
referred to, a letter signed by one of its principal officers au-
thorizing your representation of it. You and your principals
may rest assured that we will treat this matter with a high
degree of confidence."

The broker's response was that he was insulted by such a
letter and that he would not reveal whom he was representing.

The precautions which should be taken in dealing with
brokers have been discussed at some length because of the
unfortunate experiences many companies have had. It
should be pointed out again, however, that there are numerous brokers serving useful roles who can supply constructive
sources of leads to potential acquisitions.

THE SEARCH FOR LEADS

Locating companies which might be attractive and desirable acquisitions is a long, tedious, and man-hour consuming
process. There are many sources of leads which can be helpful, but the top executives of the acquiring organization must

spend the time and energy to search out and identify promising candidates. In a few situations, presidents announced their interest in acquiring other companies and then sat back waiting for applications to come in. They did not and it is not likely that they will.

The task is particularly difficult for the company embarking on its first attempts to acquire another. As one president said, "There just is no substitute for wearing out shoe leather pounding the pavements." But after one or two companies have been acquired and publicized, the interests of the acquirer become clearer to others who can be helpful in the search for leads and the experience gained in a few acquisitions contributes greatly to the skills of the acquirer.

CHAPTER VI

Strategy of Approach

WHEN a company has been selected as a possibility for acquisition, executives of the interested acquirer can learn a great deal about the company from published sources before approaching the management and owners. For companies listed on financial exchanges, it is possible to get considerable data; for unlisted, closely held, and family companies, much less information is publicly available. But even for the latter type, a substantial number of facts can be obtained and a search for relevant information should be made before any approach to the management is attempted.

In some companies with development or planning staffs, a continuous search is carried on and all the information obtained is sorted and compiled in files organized by industry and company. Local newspapers, the *Wall Street Journal* and trade magazines are read carefully. News items relating to the industry or companies which might be of interest are clipped and filed for reference in the future. The collection of bits of evidence over a period of months can result in the disclosure of a pattern of information, of inestimable value in making an evaluation of a company's competitive situation.

PRELIMINARY STUDIES

After a possible acquisition has been chosen for investigation, the typical procedure is to secure a Dun and Bradstreet report, and to review Thomas' *Register of American Manufacturers,* Poor's and Moody's for pertinent data. If the company has had a public offering, the prospectus is a most useful document. If the company is listed, the 10K Form is filed with the stock exchange and with the Securities and Exchange Commission, and this too is public information. In addition, annual reports, trade literature such as catalogues and brochures, advertisements in trade journals, special reports by the many investment services, and newspaper and magazine stories provide considerable information about the company. The collection of these data enables a summary of facts to be made which gives top managers some understanding of:

1. Financial status, balance sheets, profit-and-loss statements, earnings per share; price-earnings ratios, etc.;
2. Identity, ages, and compensation of officers and directors;
3. Ownership of the company's stock;
4. Product line;
5. Company markets;
6. Number and location of plants and offices; and
7. Research and development areas and sometimes the amounts spent on R & D.

The results of a preliminary search permit a quick screening against the criteria previously set up by the interested acquirer and a decision can be made whether more time should be spent on investigating the company. Summary reports vary in length from a few to 20 pages, require a few to 30 days or more to prepare, and constitute a reasonably low-cost, but essential, step in the total acquisition process.

A typical report prepared by the National Chemical Company from published information about the Zarka Company, Inc., is reproduced below.

Zarka Company, Inc.

1. *Brief Description of Operations*
   Company produces and sells textile chemicals for processing cotton, wool, and synthetic fibers, molded rubber parts used in the assembly of various products, and metal treating chemicals.

2. *Financial Data*

| | 1960 | 1959 | Millions of Dollars Year ended December 31 | | | 1955 | 1954 |
			1958	1957	1956		
Sales	30.4	27.6	25.2	28.6	29.4	30.0	30.0
Net	1.8	1.9	1.2	1.9	1.9	2.0	1.6
Marketable Securities	2.3	2.2	1.5	1.7			
Net Worth	19.4	19.0	18.4	18.4	17.9	17.9	N.A.
Return on Net Worth	9%	10%	7%	10%	11%	11%	N.A.
Return on Sales	6%	7%	5%	7%	6%	7%	5%
Shares Outstanding	901,022	899,651	896,305	896,305	896,405	N.A.	N.A.
Dividends	1.50	1.50	1.35	1.50	1.50	1.60	1.60
Earnings per Share	2.00	2.11	1.33	2.12	2.08	2.14	1.74
Price-year end	26	25					
Price/Earnings Ratio	13.0	11.8					

3. *Location*

Plants:

Wyandotte, Michigan — main offices, laboratories, and principal manufacturing

Middletown, Connecticut

Los Angeles, California

Birmingham, Alabama

Hamilton, Canada

Branches:

Waterbury, Connecticut

Birmingham, Alabama

Los Angeles, California

Cincinnati, Ohio

Detroit, Michigan

4. *Foreign Associates:*

London

Rome

Dusseldorf

Manila

Caracas

5. *Personnel*

Name	Age	Position	Remuneration					Company Paid Benefits at Retirement	First Became Director	Shares Held
			1956	1957	1958	1959	1960			
Alfred L. Deringer	57	President	$57,700	$59,200	$61,750	$63,500	$63,500	$9,000	1945	5,105
Fred R. Moffitt	51	Exec. V.P.	24,000	26,800	28,000	29,300	29,300	8,000	1949	1,500
John L. Grainger	61	Senior V.P.	18,000	20,100	22,175	25,000	25,000	8,500	1930	4,010
Howard P. Fanning*	71	Director	7,500	7,500	6,950	6,000	N.A.	2,300	1928	7,000
Philip R. Molner		Director	950	900	500	900	N.A.		1950	860
Charles T. Henley		Director	850	750	400	850	N.A.		1946	9,137
Walter J. Mann		Director	850	750	400	850	N.A.		1948	300
Arnold G. Harrington		Director			500	800	N.A.		1959	800
Michael J. Duffy	64	Secretary								
Arthur J. Linskey	58	Treasurer								
Andrew R. Foley	53	Controller								
Francis S. Gilson		Asst. to Pres.								
William T. Keane		V.P. and Sales Mgr.								
Martin F. Ridley		Assistant Secretary								
Carl J. Reynolds		Technical Director								

* Formerly an officer.

6. *Biographical Notes*

Alfred L. Deringer, born 1904, married; attorney with subject corporation since 1934, and an officer of and director since 1945, elected president in 1958.

Fred R. Moffitt, born 1910, married; chemist by profession, has been associated with this business throughout entire adult life.

John L. Grainger, born 1900, married; accountant by profession. Associated in that capacity with Fenwick & Royd Co., Nashville, Tenn., employed by subject corporation since 1927.

Howard P. Fanning, born 1890, married; came to this country in 1923 from England, lawyer by profession. U. S. citizen.

Philip R. Molnar, a director since 1950. Vice president of Jackson Investment Co., Detroit, Mich.

Charles T. Henley, a director since 1946, chemical engineer by profession.

Walter J. Mann, married; a patent attorney by profession, associated with the ABC Co., Detroit, Mich.

Arnold G. Harrington, married; made director in 1959, Vice president and director of Key Corp., Detroit, Mich.

Michael J. Duffy, born 1897, a lawyer, associated with Finch & Reane, Detroit, for 14 years before joining subject company in 1936.

Arthur J. Linskey, born 1903, married; an accountant by profession, joined company in 1936.

Andrew R. Foley, born 1908, married; an accountant, formerly associated with family business, joined company in 1951.

Francis S. Gilson, a chemical engineer by profession, joined company in 1948, formerly employed by Ace Chemical Corp.

William T. Keane, a sales engineer, joined company in 1946.

Martin F. Ridley, married; has been associated with subject corporation entire adult life.

Carl J. Reynolds, married; has been associated with subject corporation for the past ten years, formerly associated with Chemical Research Co. Inc.

7. *Significant Excerpts from Annual Reports*

1956:

We look for good business in 1957. In anticipation we have just about completed a $500,000 expansion in our customer service section. We have also installed a large new molding machine, new testing facilities, and many other new development devices which will greatly expand our service facilities to solve customer problems.

1957:

A new pilot plant has now been completed at our Detroit location. The plant will be ready for operation in April 1958. This unit with its enlarged and modern facilities will assist us in increasing the efficiency of our present manufacturing operations and the development of new processes and products.

A new unit for the manufacture of wax sizes for the paper industry has been installed in our Middletown, Conn. plant.

1958:

Part of the decline in operating revenues was due to the disappointing business this year in the appliance industry. We had expected greatly increased orders from the appliance industry this year with our new Zarka pretreatment process which is designed to give the appliance manufacturer considerable savings in enamel frit. However, with their business down from the previous year this industry was not disposed to invest in equipment for a new process. The result was, of course, less business from appliances than we had the previous year. Also, a segment of the automobile industry was down over the previous year. Our textile chemicals sales continued strong.

1959:

Our aim for this coming year is to continue our policy of doing new things for industry on an ever-increasing scale. In our fiscal 1958 we saved our customers hundreds of thousands of dollars with new Zarka processes. As recognition of our efforts we were given a citation by General Electric Company as "Supplier of the Month" for saving them considerable money in their Commercial Laundry Division with this process that also contributed greatly to employee comfort and safety. We were selected from among thousands of suppliers for this award.

Our steel treatments are gaining wide recognition as the most efficient available, and as uses for this metal increase in the building field and others, we see an ever-expanding use of these processes. 1960 should show great expansion here. Our rubber products division is developing new applications every day throughout the country and the coming year should show great progress in industrial uses.

Nearing completion, but not yet ready to announce, is an arrangement concerning the purchase of stock and merger of a smaller company whose sales and service would supplement Zarka's in fields not now served by Zarka. It is believed that the benefits of the acquisition, if consummated, while they would be more long range than immediate, would be a step in the direction of diversification.

1960:

During the last few months we have perfected and introduced to the automobile industry several new products. One of the Big Three seems about to adopt one of these as an aid in their campaign to improve the corrosion resistance of their finishing system and probably others will gradually do so. This should help our sales and earnings picture. Other inventions discovered in the last few months for other fields will, we believe, catch on, and should gradually build up sales.

8. *Comment*

With two listed companies having widely traded securities, any merger would probably be made on the basis of an exchange of securities bearing approximately equal market values. Where the larger company is the one actively seeking the merger — as in this case — this might be modified to the extent that an exchange slightly more favorable than market price would be required to induce the smaller company to give up its independent corporate existence, assuming of course that it was interested in merging at all.

In the case of Zarka and National Chemical, there is an additional reason, it seems to me, why National Chemical would probably have to give to the Zarka shareholders slightly more than the current market value of their shares. Zarka is now selling at about $26. It earns about $2 and pays a dividend of $1.50. It has no debt or preferred outstanding and has ample cash resources. Zarka has maintained a rather steady dividend over the years. It has paid no less than $1.50 since 1953, with the exception of the recession year 1958, when the dividend dropped to $1.35. Zarka has always had a high payout of earnings, averaging 75% over the past decade. At its current price and current dividend, the stock is yielding 5.8%. As such, the stock is a typical "high income" stock, one that undoubtedly appeals to investors who are more interested in current income than in growth.

On a common-for-common exchange at relative market values, the Zarka shareholder would get 26/40th of a National Chemical share for each Zarka share held (figuring NC at $40). At the current dividend of $1.40 per National Chemical share, this would give the Zarka shareholder a dividend of 91¢ per old Zarka share, a drastic reduction from his former dividend of $1.50. True, this new holding would have better dividend coverage, greater growth potential and less dependence on the progress of one or two industries. Nevertheless, it would be a long time before this 91¢ dividend got back up to $1.50, and for many Zarka shareholders, a switch to some other high income security would be necessary to meet the objectives of their particular investment programs. Such a switch would involve both time and expense: time to investigate a good substitute stock and the expense of broker's fees in making the switch. On this basis alone, National Chemical might have to offer securities carrying market values of at least $1 to $2 over Zarka's $26 per share to obtain sufficient support among Zarka directors and stockholders for such a merger.

No combination of National Chemical common and preferred would provide the Zarka shareholder with a continuation of the $1.50 dividend because even our preferred stock carries a lower yield than the Zarka common:

	Dividend	Approximate Market Price	Yield
Zarka Common	$1.50	$26	5.8%
National Chemical Preferred	4.00	80	5.0
National Chemical Common	1.40	40	3.5

The highest dividend we could offer and still be on a relative market value basis would be an exchange involving preferred only. This would involve 26/80th of a preferred share for each

Zarka share held, providing a dividend of $1.30 per old Zarka share.

If a new *convertible* preferred issue were offered, it presumably would sell for a price yielding something under 5.0%, since it would have the safety of our present preferred, plus the opportunity for a possible attractive conversion. Thus, its current dividend would be something under $1.30 per old Zarka share if the exchange were made on relative market values. (Some theoretical market value would have to be computed for a convertible preferred, since it would have no actual market until issued.)

Assuming that a stock exchange would require National Chemical securities having a value of at least $28 per outstanding Zarka share, the central question for National Chemical is whether the company is worth the price.

Once this is decided, the additional question arises as to the combination of common, preferred, or convertible preferred that would be best from National Chemical's point of view and would make the exchange most "salable" to the Zarka shareholders. Because National Chemical now has a balanced capital structure with both common and preferred outstanding, I believe that, from National Chemical's point of view, a merger that is not attractive based on a common-for-common exchange would probably be equally unattractive if equivalent market value of preferred or convertible preferred were substituted for the National Chemical common, in whole or in part.

From the standpoint of the Zarka shareholder, it would appear that something other than a straight common-for-common exchange would be best. Either a convertible preferred or perhaps a choice of two types of preferred with different dividends and conversion privileges might be most attractive to the Zarka shareholders.

In looking at the central question of whether Zarka is worth $28 per share to National Chemical, it might be helpful to divide this analysis into two parts:

1. Worth of Zarka as a separate, going business, ignoring any increases in worth stemming from a merger with National Chemical.

2. Increase in the value of Zarka, or of National Chemical, over the simple sum of the two businesses that would be expected to arise from a merger.

Looking at 1, it might appear at first glance that a value of $26 per share should be put on Zarka. This is the price investors have put on the stock. By definition, it takes into account earnings, dividends, safety, growth prospects and many other factors that go into valuing a security.

Should some adjustment be made in this market figure in valuing the stock to National Chemical? There are at least two factors that come to mind which have probably affected the market price of the Zarka stock but whose effect on National Chemical's valuation of the stock would be quite different.

One of these, probably the most important, is Zarka's dividend payout. Zarka's payout of 75% of earnings presumably has resulted in a higher market price for the stock than would a more "normal" payout of around 50%. Operated as a subsidiary, with all its earnings subject to National Chemical control, Zarka's high current dividend would be of no particular value to National Chemical. In appraising the worth of Zarka to National Chemical, it would seem appropriate to estimate the market price that Zarka's shares would command if they followed a dividend policy more in line with National Chemical's.

The other point is that the stock price probably suffers from moderate instability in earnings more as a separate company than would be warranted in appraising the unit as part of a larger company. (Zarka's relatively stable earnings of about $2 per share for years was broken in 1958 when earnings dropped to $1.33.)

We have now suggested that in thinking about the worth of Zarka to National Chemical, we first look at the current market value of Zarka's shares, and then attempt to adjust by estimated differences in value that would be warranted if the company were part of National Chemical. Admittedly, setting down factors that would seem to have an impact on this valuation is easier than making a quantitative evaluation. This is a matter of judg-ment on which no two experienced security analysts would probably agree exactly. I shall give a rough idea of what the numbers look like to me, with the suggestion that persons expert in this field be called upon to render a judgment at an appropriate time in the course of this investigation.

Some analysts believe that a dollar in dividends is worth four times as much as a dollar in earnings in valuing a stock. (Such guidelines do not apply to companies with high growth rates and/or very low dividend payout.) Using this formula, the market price of Zarka would decline by 25% if Zarka were to adopt a policy of 50% payout of earnings:

	Current 75% *Payout*	50% *Payout*
Earnings	$2.00 \times 1 = 2.00$	$2.00 \times 1 = 2.00$
Dividends	$1.50 \times 4 = 6.00$	$1.00 \times 4 = 4.00$
	5/8.00	5/6.00
Composite factor	1.60	1.20
		$1.20 = 75\%$, or a decline of 25%

This would mean a price decrease from $26 to $19.50 per share. I suspect this overstates the case slightly. If a lower payout had been in effect for awhile, the earnings would have been slightly higher because of the investment of excess funds in interest-bearing securities. Using a 3–1 dividend-earnings ratio instead of 4–1 assumption, the decline would be 23.1% and the resulting price just $20 per share. I would guess that this is about where the stock would be if Zarka was paying a dividend of $1 per share.

A figure of $20 is ten times last year's earnings. This does not seem unreasonable for a company whose sales and earnings have been approximately level for the past ten years (except 1958) and whose earnings showed a moderate degree of instability under the impact of the 1958 recession.

The second factor, mentioned for consideration, was an adjustment for the probable greater weight put on the company's large dependence on one or two major markets compared to the weight this consideration would warrant if Zarka were part of National Chemical. This factor is far more nebulous to appraise. The business conditions within which Zarka operates would not change after a merger with National Chemical. Theoretically, an investor could presently own both Zarka and National Chemical shares, and for this particular investor this risk factor would be no different after the merger than before the merger. For this reason, we probably should not give this factor too much weight. Perhaps investors would upgrade their appraisal from 10 times Zarka's earnings to 10½ or 11 times if these earnings were part of the earnings of a larger more diversified corporation. This would boost the "worth" of Zarka to National Chemical to $21 or $22 per share.

Clearly, while there is much room for difference on the specific figures, this first phase of the analysis seems to point to a conclusion that Zarka would *not* be worth $28 per share to National Chemical considering only its underlying value as a separate, independent subsidiary.

Based on the figures developed so far (which are subject to further study and evaluation) the second phase of this study would be to evaluate the potential advantages of the merger, to ascertain whether they are sufficient to upgrade Zarka's worth to National Chemical from $21 to $22 per share to something over $28.

Such an upgrading of the value of Zarka could come from three main sources:

A. Acceleration of the growth of Zarka and/or National Chemical. If a merger with National Chemical would result in a pattern of *growth* for Zarka in the future, a proper evaluation of Zarka's current earnings could increase from the 10½–11 assumed above to perhaps 14 times. This alone would upgrade Zarka's worth enough to justify the $28 per share assumed above as the minimum acceptable. This would mean a growth rate close to National Chemical's. Careful study would have to be made to determine whether such accelerations of growth would be likely as a result of National Chemical contributions in the areas of management, customer contact, research and development, etc. Any contribution Zarka could make to help speed growth in National Chemical's present lines would also have to be considered. Such a possibility might exist in the areas of customer contact and research and development for National Chemical's Automotive Supplies Division.

B. Direct dollar savings resulting from the merger. We suspect there might be some savings from elimination of some duplicating functions, from possible joint use of some facilities, and perhaps from some joint research programs. As an offset, there will probably be increased expenses due to the adding of lines of communication and the aligning of personnel benefits. At this stage, we do not foresee sizable net savings.

C. Corporate image and size. The market assessment of the combined company might be somewhat more favorable than would be expected just from the practical business reasons given above. This could be true because of an enhancing of National Chemical's corporate image of increasing aggressiveness. Some slight benefit might be gained because of the greater number of shares that would be available to trading, particularly in making purchases by large institutional buyers more likely. Although sales are only $30.4 million, Zarka is better than $1/4$th our size in earnings and market value; the merger would be a "major" merger. On the other side, there is a possibility of a temporary dip in the market, assuming some National Chemical common shares are offered, as some Zarka shareholders switch to other "high income" stocks.

While not at all sure at the present time that Zarka is worth over $28 per share to National Chemical, we feel that there is enough chance that this is the case that we consider exploratory talks with Zarka warranted.

Besides the advantage of screening out clearly unsuitable companies, the preliminary study has other merits. A review of the study can result in the definition of key areas about which there are questions and for which considerably more information is needed. When an approach is made to a company being considered for acquisition, not only will the representative of the acquiring company have some facts about the company in itself impressive to the management members he approaches; he will also have in mind during the early discussions an awareness of the areas for which he needs additional facts. Sometimes the early discussions disclose other problem areas which lead immediately to a termination of further negotiations. Here again, time and money can be saved if it is discovered early in the investigation that there are clear indications of undesired characteristics in the company under consideration.

In one company an analysis was made of a summary report on a potential acquisition and the following key areas were defined as requiring further information, not available from published sources.

1. With substantial foreign operations, what percentage of the company's total sales and profits come from foreign markets?

2. What is the future of the industry, sales, earnings, and return on investment?

3. How do our other product lines complement each other?

4. To what extent would our research contribute to their needs?

5. The president is 73 years old. What is the quality and depth of the next level of management?

6. What percentage of their sales are in capital goods? This is a field with which we are quite unfamiliar.

7. Are they dependent upon a few large customers?

8. What possibilities are there for realizing economies through consolidation of staff functions?

9. What business will be lost if these two companies consolidate?

Clearly these and many other questions would need to be answered before a decision could be made about an acquisition, but the preliminary study does help to identify early a few of the critical areas.

PLANNING THE APPROACH

Once a company has been identified as a possible candidate for acquisition, the management of the interested acquirer should make no approach until careful thought is given to the strategy. Even with the relatively limited information provided by a preliminary study, it is possible to define some of the critical areas to be discussed and to determine how to deal with them once negotiations have started. We found many situations in which acquiring managements neglected to take the time and care to plan their strategy, and in most of these cases what might have developed into constructive discussions terminated quickly because of inappropriate approaches. It was surprising to find some managements skilled in planning marketing strategy for their own companies failing to apply the same concepts to their approaches to potential acquisitions.

In two large companies we encountered a point of view among top management people which weakened and mitigated against effective strategy. Both companies were internationally known, were listed on the New York Stock Exchange, and were leaders in their respective fields. But the two or three top executives of each company were obsessed with the idea that they were successful, an idea which was manifested in the attitude: "Our name should be good enough to any potential seller to persuade him to accept our idea of acquisition."

Another implicit facet of this attitude was a management preoccupation with the question, "What can the company to be acquired do for us?" and omission of the question, "What can we do for the acquired company and why should its management sell out to us?" Discussions with owners of companies who had been approached by representatives of these two large companies indicated clearly that the basic attitude of the potential acquirers had precluded effective negotiations shortly after the initial approach. One prospective seller of a company said, "Sure, I have heard of the president, but when he gave me the impression that I was being given, in effect, a private audience in his 60-foot office, that I was a peasant type owner-manager, and that I would be blessed by exchanging my unlisted stock for his company's listed securities, I decided the deal was not for me."

One of the significant kinds of information to be derived from a preliminary study is a characterization of the principal owners and executives of the company to be considered for acquisition. Published data about companies include the names, ages, business experience, salaries, bonus arrangements, and stock ownership of the principal officers, directors, and owners. From this information an appropriate method of approach can be planned in advance.

Several cases illustrate the importance of an awareness of the regional backgrounds of the owners. In the first company, published information indicated that the two principal owners were over 68 years of age, had lived and worked in New England during their entire business careers, and were generally known as crusty New England Yankees. The president of a larger company with headquarters in New York invited them for a two-day visit in New York to get acquainted with his key personnel. A Cadillac limousine met the two Yankees at the airport and they were transported to the Waldorf-Astoria Hotel where a two-bedroom suite had been reserved. Elaborate lunches, dinners, and entertainment were provided and the two owners returned to New England to consider whether to carry the discussions further. By the time they arrived at their more frugally equipped offices, their decision had been made and no further conversations took place with the New York company.

A few months later the management of a midwestern company decided to approach the two New England owners, but here there was an appreciation by the potential acquirer that some New Englanders are not impressed by fancy and lavish entertainment. The first meeting was arranged to take place at breakfast in a small hotel convenient for the owners, and the approach of the potential acquirer's representatives took into account the owners' backgrounds.

In another case, the president of a West Coast company,

upon learning that the president and some substantial stock-holders of a Boston company in which he was interested planned to attend a trade convention in San Francisco, tele-phoned Boston and invited the president and his associates to visit the company's offices on the West Coast. His invitation was accepted, and the reception was planned to be in good but not flamboyant taste. In this case, a most favorable im-pression was made on the prospective sellers and negotiations were started which resulted in an acquisition.   .

In another situation, Mr. Jones, the chief operating execu-tive of an active acquirer, contrasted his experiences in Bos-ton and in Dallas, Texas. He reported that he went to Bos-ton to talk with two brothers who owned a company in the suburbs. They met after breakfast in a Boston club and sat down to have some coffee. During coffee the two brothers called in two of their associates. Mr. Jones found himself do-ing all the talking. Coffee extended into lunch, Mr. Jones was still doing all the talking, and by dinnertime he had learned nothing about the New England company. The next day conversations were resumed, the partners began to talk, and Mr. Jones was able then to learn something about the af-fairs of the company. In Dallas, Mr. Jones stated, he spent three hours with two owners and when they put him on the train, they were kissing cousins and had decided on the essen-tials of an agreement.

The important point here is not to characterize all New Englanders as thrifty, provident, and taciturn people but to emphasize that a plan of strategy should be developed based on the characteristics of the personalities involved. Each company is a unique combination of owners and executives, and a unique approach should be established for each situa-tion. And it is much better to amend and adjust a plan of strategy to unanticipated conditions as they arise than it is to make an initial approach with no plan at all.

Facts about the professional education and training of

owners and executives of companies are also available from published sources. In the Cann Company, for example, the three top executives held Ph.D. degrees in Science. During the history of the company, which was organized immediately after World War II, sales and profits grew steadily and with this growth the three scientists became less occupied with re-search and development and moved into general management positions. Initial financing was provided by a venture capi-tal group which resulted in two financially oriented mem-bers on the company's board of directors.

Throughout the company's growth, there were many con-flicts between the engineer-trained top management and the financial specialists board members. In the five-year period, 1955–1960, the Cann Company management was approached, according to the president, at least once a week by companies interested in acquiring Cann, and in each case the overtures were turned down because the management of the interested company was not "our kind of people." Early in 1960 a vice president of a machinery company, and an engineer by train-ing, talked to the principal executives of Cann and there was an immediate rapport. The Cann executives, with technical educations and with a background of misunderstanding by the financial specialists on their board, found in the machin-ery company management a satisfying intellectual accord. Our kind of people!

This phrase, "our kind of people," was encountered in al-most every acquisition situation included in our study. Own-ers and managers of companies amenable to acquisition re-ported that many of the potential acquirers' representatives were not their kind of people. In the Cann Company, the phrase meant that an approach and a possible association with people other than technically trained engineers would not be acceptable. In a midwestern plastics company owned by the two founders, an approach by the head of a commercial devel-opment department with a Ph.D. in Chemistry was resisted because he did not understand dialectric materials, one of the principal uses for the company's resin products. The two founders stated that if the acquiring company's representative did not have a sufficient understanding of the research, production, and marketing costs of developing new materials for new markets, how could they possibly expect to have a reasonable working relationship with him after being acquired? In another situation the president of a manufacturing company was approached by a vice president of research, a vice president of sales, and a consultant. Here again, the three representatives of the interested acquirer were not "our kind of people" who could establish a feeling of common interests. The research vice president became too involved in technicalities, the sales vice president talked in "global generalities," and the consultant was ineffective in trying to represent the acquiring company. The strategic plan of approach should take into account the background, training, experience, and age of the key personnel of a company desired for acquisition.

Many examples of thoughtful planning for a strategy of approach based on available information were found during our study. The management of a large western manufacturing company learned, for example, that an eastern company needed several million dollars in order to exploit new product ideas and for plant expansion, preferred not to dilute its equity by a public issue, and was managed by an executive who had been employed several years before in a key position by one of the largest heavy equipment manufacturers. With this background information the president of the acquiring company manifested in his initial conversation that his company had substantial cash resources, that the management was accustomed to considering investment of millions of dollars, and that the big business background of the principal executives of both companies would contribute to an effective and profitable relationship.

In a second situation, a large family company was owned by

six heirs, one of whom had been removed as chief operating executive by the other five. Relations between the former president and the five were strained, although all six continued on the company's board of directors. The former president resented his removal from his position as chief executive, and he attended all meetings of the board in what was described as a "stony silence." Facts about the relationships among the six owners were well-known in the industry. Before the acquiring company's management made their initial approach, a plan was developed which assigned individual executives to each of the six owners and provided that the former president and the five other owners should never be parts of the same acquisition discussion meeting. The plan was carried out and at the first meeting the former president said to the man who was assigned to talk with him, "If the infamous five do not want to sell to you, then I will vote for the acquisition by you!" Careful attention was given to each of the other owners involved and the conduct of the negotiations enabled the former president to recapture some of his lost prestige. Within three months of the first approach, agreement was reached by the six owners to sell their company.

In each of these situations, the top management of the acquirer took the time to collect all the information publicly available, to evaluate the facts, and to develop a plan of strategy prior to making any approach.

ANTICIPATORY QUESTIONS

Thoughtful planning includes also (1) anticipation of possible questions which might be raised, particularly in the first discussions, and (2) answers to these questions which will not result in a premature termination of negotiations. In almost every acquisition case studied, one question came up early in the conversations and was high among the concerns of the company to be acquired: "If we sell to you, where will our company fit in your organization? Will we be absorbed into one of your divisions or can we continue to operate as an autonomous, profit-and-loss measurable, independent operation?"

For example, three executives of a New York company, with relatively little experience in acquisition and with no plan of approach, met with the owners of an organization at breakfast. Pleasant conversation was carried on until the dishes were cleared and then the president of the company to be acquired asked, "Where will we fit?" With no previous thought as to an answer, the three executives tried to improvise and suggested three different solutions, none of which was satisfactory to the owners. This is an excellent example of how not to approach prospective sellers of companies. The discussions continued during the rest of the morning, but it was clear that the potential sellers had concluded earlier that no sale would be made to the unprepared New York executives. The question, "Where will we fit?" seems to be basic in the minds of all prospective sellers, and before any approach is made by potential acquirers, an answer should be thought through.

A second question frequently raised by sellers which should be anticipated when the two companies' product lines are closely related is, "How would you organize the joint product line resulting from a merger?" To illustrate:

A large eastern manufacturer selected a St. Louis company as a desirable acquisition because it had a strong national marketing organization. The eastern company, with regional distribution and excellent products that had been developed in its research laboratories, needed a national sales organization in order to get the products distributed quickly. The president of the possible acquirer telephoned the owner of the St. Louis company and arranged a meeting at a St. Louis motel two days later. The president then asked his vice president of research and vice president of finance to meet him in St. Louis. The three eastern company representatives arrived separately at the motel where the St. Louis company owner, the president, the executive vice president, and two vice presidents of the company were awaiting them.

An early question raised by the owner was, "How would you organize the joint product line that would result if our operations were merged with yours?" This issue had not been considered by the acquisition team prior to the meeting and the vice president of research quickly responded: "We would split the country into two geographical areas. We would take the East and you could have the West." This brought an immediate chill to the tone of the conversation, and the St. Louis owner and key executives made motions to leave, saying they had other business engagements to attend to. An attempt was made to save the situation by the vice president of finance, but the case had been closed. Shortly thereafter the St. Louis company was acquired by another purchaser.

It is not possible to anticipate all the critical questions which may come up in the initial approach, but in this case the post-acquisition marketing structure should have been thought about by the acquiring company group before any conversations took place.

A third question by sellers which should be anticipated is, "What plans do you have for our key people?" It was found that in most cases owners and managers have a very strong feeling of responsibility toward their employees; and few owners are willing to divest themselves of title without assurances by the buyer that the employees of the acquired company will have opportunities for continued employment and promotion after the sale. A related question is, "Will you keep the plant and offices in the present location or do you plan to move our operations into your facilities?" And a question associated with what can happen to the acquired company employees is, "Will I, the principal owner, be

elected to the board of directors of the acquiring company?"
These questions relating to people involved are usually raised
in early discussions and, again, prospective acquirers should
be ready with answers thought out in advance of the approach.

Also, owners and executives of companies which might be
acquired generally ask, "If we sell to you, what can you contribute to our operations?" Here again, we found that unprepared acquiring management representatives stumbled,
floundered, and improvised in an attempt to disguise the fact
that the question had never been thought about deeply. The
president of a midwestern company, for example, said that he
had been approached by over 25 companies and his first question was "What benefits will accrue to my company if we sell
to you?" He stated that the typical response was that the
two organizations had overlapping sales, manufacturing, and
research functions, and that a merger could eliminate people,
reduce costs, and increase profits. The president then asked
for a specific and complete outline as to just how costs could
be cut, and the potential acquirers had all been unable to satisfy him that they really knew what the savings might be.

The arguments stressing the alleged economies that will result from merged operations often oversimplify the problems
involved in their achievement; and reasonably sophisticated
sellers will not be persuaded by general and usually unwar-
ranted arguments that these great economies will materialize.
In one situation the president of a Connecticut company was
approached by a vice president of a large New York company
who "came roaring in not knowing anything about us, and
never did get specific as to what his company could do for us.
Based on what he said, the sale did not make any sense and
we decided not to sell to people who had not thought out
what mutual benefits might be achieved."

A contrasting situation, however, was found in the approach of a Chicago chemical company to the management of

a Boston industrial paint company. Here the Chicago company president realized the rapid technological changes that were going on in the paint industry and in his plan of strategy included the participation of his vice president of research as a key member of early discussions. As had been anticipated, the potential sellers asked, "What can you do for us?" The vice president of research reviewed the many projects which had been worked on in his laboratories that were related to the Boston company's line of products, suggested that the results of this advanced research would be available, proposed that more intensive projects would be initiated with the guidance of the industrial paint company's technical director, and suggested that the key people doing research and development on paint in Boston visit the Chicago laboratories at an early date to learn more about the company's technical achievements. The owners of the paint company reported that it was clear that the vice president of research appreciated the technical character of their problems and that the potential acquirer did, in fact, have substantial contributions to make.

Another intellectually disarming question which some prospective sellers asked was, "Why do you want to buy us?" The representative of a prospective buyer who was unprepared to answer such a question usually rambled on and the essence of his response was heard by the seller to be "because we would like to have your profits," a reason which rarely contributed to an atmosphere of further useful discussion. In other cases this question had been anticipated; indeed, the basic reasons for their desire to purchase had been thought through and their replies tended to be persuasive.

The executive vice president of another company commented on the importance of a plan of strategy and stated that sometimes an important unanticipated question arises in the first discussion and his technique is to say, "We have thought about the problem a great deal and admit that we do not have very good answers. Before doing anything, we would want to work out with you what the most effective solution might be. What thoughts do you have now as to how this problem might be handled?"

An executive with considerable experience in acquisitions noted that some of the owners and managers of companies he had approached for acquisition were relatively naive and did not raise the kinds of questions with which this section is concerned. We found, however, that most of the managements who had been approached by potential acquirers did, in one form or another, ask such questions and that they appraised the potential acquirer in terms of the validity of the responses. The owners of several companies, for example, having decided to consider selling, not only listed the critical questions they would ask, but also prepared a list of criteria to describe the characteristics of the best possible company to which a sale might be made. In one New England corporation the owners described their ideal acquirer as meeting the following criteria:

1. Sales over $100,000,000;
2. Profits over 6% after taxes;
3. Listed on the New York Stock Exchange;
4. Strong financial position;
5. Management composed of our kind of people;
6. Strong technical position with competent research laboratories; and
7. Company is not a polyglot of a wide variety of unrelated businesses.

Approach by Whom?

After an evaluation has been made of the available data about a potential acquisition from all possible sources except from the company itself, the acquiring company's president or some other key executive should decide who should make the initial approach to whom. It must be decided whether the particular management and owners under consideration should be approached by the potential acquirer's president alone or whether he should be accompanied by others with special qualifications to answer any unique questions that might be raised. Every effort should be made to match the experience, training, and personal idiosyncrasies of the acquiring members with those in the management of the company to be acquired.

The executive vice president of one company, for example, outlined his method of approach as this: He studied carefully everything he could learn about the owners and management of the company to be acquired and then asked key executives from headquarters to go with him when he felt that they could make a contribution. One of the vice presidents had been deer hunting in Minnesota with the owner of a prospective acquisition, and although the vice president was described "as an Ivy League lush-well," he assisted in consummating the purchase. In another situation the executive vice president learned that the owner of a company to be acquired always drank two martinis at lunch. An executive of the acquiring company of about the same age and with the same inclination toward luncheon martinis was asked to participate in the initial approach. The luncheon discussion went superbly, the two executives had their martinis, and the executive vice president stated that this was the easiest acquisition he had ever made.

Frequently we found that a president asked a distinguished member of his board of directors to accompany him on a first visit. In a Cleveland company, for example, one of the board members was nationally known as an eminent business executive who had been president of a large company and who had occupied a high position in the United States Government during World War II. His presence added something to the image of the acquiring company and in several cases it contributed substantially to the acquisition process.

Need for Secrecy

Secrecy of approach is very important in most situations. Rumors about the interest of Company A in Company B travel through trade circles with unbelievable speed and many acquisition possibilities have been lost by public knowledge that discussions are taking place. We found many case examples where rumors reported in newspapers brought an abrupt end to negotiations. Too, when the employees of a company learn that consideration is being given to a possible sale, the organization's morale suffers and much employee time is devoted to projecting what is likely to happen to them: Will I be moved to the acquiring company headquarters? What about their salary, bonus, option and retirement benefits? Will I be competing for advancement with a lot of people from the parent company who have the inside track? These and similar questions inevitably arise, and in several instances we found that the concern about their future became so great that many key employees resigned and took positions with other organizations rather than run the risks involved in being acquired.

Relations with customers suffer as well. When a possible acquisition is rumored, competitors are quick to bring this to the attention of their customers: "Did you know Company A has given up and will sell out to Company B?" Certainly during the early exploratory approach and discussions, secrecy should be paramount. One president reported that he learned the importance of secrecy while he sat in the waiting room of a possible acquisition. A salesman of a competitor of his came in and said, "Is this your next acquisition, Bill?" The next day he read in a New York paper that there was a well-founded rumor that the acquisition was about to take place. Thereafter, the president said, all conversations with owners of companies to be acquired were held in hotel rooms or at the company's offices after regular office hours.

In some situations we found that the president used an outsider to make the preliminary approaches. The purpose was to avoid identifying the acquiring company. It was believed that if the large and successful acquiring company were identified, (1) competitors would learn of its interest and attempt to make the same purchase, and (2) the purchase price, especially if the company to be acquired had its securities listed, would increase as people learned of the large company's interest.

But, as noted earlier, the critical element found in most successful strategies of approach is the personal involvement of the chief operating executive or the competent subordinate with whom the chief operating executive has an effective working relationship. Others in the organization may be asked to participate when analysis indicates the value of their presence; but the leadership of the chief operating executive is a crucial requirement.

And an approach by the executives of an interested acquirer is the beginning of another important phase of the acquisition cycle — the negotiation of terms.

PROBLEMS OF NEGOTIATION

Skill in the art of negotiating is critical to the success of any acquisition agreement. The long hours and hard work of corporate planners, operating executives, analysts and outside parties who are involved in the process can be in vain because of mistakes made during negotiations. And what is said or implied by either party to the agreement eases or complicates the subsequent task of integrating the two operations.

Resourcefulness on both sides is required in order to effectuate a mutually acceptable agreement. Experienced negotiators stated that early determination of the basic needs and desires of the buyer and the seller is important to useful discussion, and when the basic requirements have been clarified, the foundation is provided for tailoring the contract of purchase. The financial vice president of one company active in acquisitions said that he looked upon the variety of terms available as a "bag full of goodies" and that any goody or combination of goodies could be used to meet the objectives and needs of the two parties. The distinguishing characteristic of successful negotiation is the willingness of representatives of the buyer and the seller to discuss all the elements of a possible contract until it becomes clear to either side of the transaction that there are no "unlivable with" conditions.

One active negotiator stated that early discussion should focus on the economic benefits to be derived from a combination, and that discussion of the means to accomplish these goals should come only after the participants accept, at least intellectually, the validity of the anticipated benefits and agree on the merits of further detailed consideration. If prolonged discussion of these benefits to result from the combination reveals that what seemed initially to be good reasons are not so significant as was believed, then further negotiations are likely to be a waste of time. Emphasis placed first on the economic factors seems to stimulate both parties to think about a potential agreement in a constructive manner.

The techniques and approaches used by various negotiators tended to vary greatly, but one concept employed in many situations seemed to be effective — avoidance of a take-it-or-leave-it ultimatum. Two food processing companies, for example, were located in the same midwestern city. Owners of the two companies had considered merging several times because of the economic advantages that could come about primarily from combining their distribution facilities. The companies had similar and complementary product lines; one was about 20% larger than the other in terms of dollar volume of sales. The larger company's management was highly regarded and its members' average age was a few years younger than the other's. Both companies' stocks were widely held and had performed about equally well. Many outsiders had recognized what seemed to be a logical merger of the two companies, and their managements had been bombarded with merger proposals from brokers and investment bankers.

In 1955 the managements of the two companies talked over the possibility of a merger and decided to let each of their investment bankers study the other company and recommend terms for an exchange of stock. The two recommendations resulting from the bankers' studies were based primarily on relative market values and differed by about 5%. Despite the near-agreement, the managers and owners of a substantial percentage of the stock in the smaller company thought that their shareowners should be paid a 15% premium over market price. Negotiations were broken off when the other company (whose management would take over the top executive positions) offered only a 5% premium over market value.

One year later merger talks were begun again. This time each company was represented by its president and an outside director. The business advantages were still self-evident and there were no disputes about top management positions. But again, negotiations were stalled when the smaller company representatives again insisted on a 15% premium over market value.

Both sides agreed to hold one more negotiating session. With offered and asked prices 10% apart, the outside director of the larger company sought a way to avoid making a take-it-or-leave-it proposal. At the final meeting, he began to talk away from the price question, outlining again all the advantages of the proposed merger, and maintaining that the stockholders of both companies would benefit in the long run. He pointed out that the difference in the exchange ratios acceptable to each side was minor in relation to the long-run advantages. Finally he suggested that both sides caucus independently, consider solutions to the impasse, and meet later in the day.

As soon as the representatives came back to the negotiating room, he asked the smaller company's representatives to state their proposal for breaking the impasse. They suggested an exchange ratio that split the difference and the merger was agreed upon. The price value of the combined company's stock almost doubled in the year after the merger took place.

The management representatives of acquirers interested in purchasing a company typically will not permit a negotiating meeting to end without agreement on a date and place for the next meeting. A discussion which ends with, "We will think the problems over and let you know later," frequently jeopardizes the possibility of agreement. Misgivings and doubts enter the minds of the executives of both the buyer and the seller and silence is interpreted as a signal of noninterest.

The importance of another meeting may be illustrated by the experience of two vice presidents of the Flor Company in negotiating with Mr. Edar for the purchase of his privately owned enterprise in which he was the only stockholder. Mr. Edar insisted upon secret meetings to avoid the disruption that would occur in his organization of about 300 people, and the two vice presidents, the president, Mr. Flor, and his attorney met in a hotel room in a city near Mr. Edar's company headquarters. At the end of the first day, Mr. Edar stated that he was not satisfied with the progress of the discussion and suggested that subsequent meetings be postponed. One of the vice presidents then said, "If you want to meet with us again, we will be having breakfast in our room here tomorrow at 8 A.M. Think over the problems tonight and join us in the morning." The next morning Mr. Edar and his attorney arrived for breakfast and the discussion was continued. But for five consecutive days the same exchange took place at the end of each day-long meeting, and each time Mr. Edar and his attorney returned for breakfast. Late on the fifth day an agreement was reached, papers were prepared and signed, and the acquisition contract was completed.

The most successful executives in negotiating acquisitions are those who are patient and listen carefully for clues as to the real wishes of the other party. These desires are frequently covered up by misleading statements, but the astute listener is able to penetrate the verbal camouflage and guide the discussion so that the interests of both sides of the negotiation will be clarified. And in some circumstances the agent of the buying company will create an atmosphere of mutual confidence and acceptance by bringing out points which are to the advantage of the owners of the selling organization.

Specific Negotiating Problems

Problems of Price and Payment

Disagreement over the purchase price offered is given most frequently as the reason for the termination of acquisition discussions. And in some cases failure to agree on a mutually acceptable price is the real reason. In today's sellers' markets, many owners and managers, particularly of small and medium-sized unlisted companies, have inflated ideas as to what they can extract from eager buyers. The executive vice president of one large western company reported that the price requirements of many small companies are so high that he prefers to talk with the owners on the "third or fourth bounce — after they have discovered how fallaciously high their demands are, and after they have been 'humilified' by rejections from prospective buyers." And as will be noted in Chapter VIII, the problems of determining the value of an unlisted company are complicated by the absence of a stock market appraisal. Owners and managers of these companies naturally seek to establish bases for valuing their companies which will bring them the maximum price.

A small company in the office equipment industry, for example, had sales of about $5,000,000, a net worth of $800,000, and net profits after taxes of $150,000. The cash position was poor, accounts receivable and inventory were pledged as security for a $600,000 bank loan, and an additional $200,000 was owed on equipment purchases and debentures. Credit reports indicated that the company was slow in paying its bills. Some upward adjustments in the figures shown on the balance sheets and profit-and-loss statements were appropriate because of management efforts to expense as many costs as possible, but these adjustments were nominal.

The president of the Leonard Company arranged a meeting with the five owners, and after a joint review of the financial statements, it became clear that the owners of the office equipment company expected that in setting a price for their stock, a price-earnings ratio equal to others in the industry would be used. Other companies, much larger and more stable, had experienced a recent rapid rise in their listed stock prices — one competitor's stock sold for 65 times earnings and another sold for 58 times earnings. Therefore, said the five owners, "some earnings multiplier in that range of 58 to 65 would be expected to enable you to get into this growing and dynamic industry." The president of the Leonard Company concluded quickly that a $9,000,000 price for the business was exorbitant and negotiations were terminated. The five owners, however, remain adamant in their conviction that the high price earnings ratio of a few companies in the industry should be applied to their profits to arrive at a price. In November 1961 the company was still being offered to prospective buyers, and it is likely that "several bounces" will have to take place before a realistic price will be asked by the owners. In the meantime the company with its precarious financial position is becoming known throughout business circles as "corporate junk — maybe it will have some salvage value but not much more."

Price represented a negotiation problem in the acquisition of the Bridget Company by the Logan Manufacturing Company. The Bridget Company was owned by the two top executives who wanted to convert all or part of their entire personal estates into cash or the securities of a listed company. They discussed the possibilities of a public issue with some investment bankers who suggested that a portion of the stock could be sold at 20 to 25 times earnings. Shortly thereafter an executive of the Logan Manufacturing Company approached the two owners about a possible sale and price became the major issue. The Logan stock was selling on the New York Stock Exchange at about 45 times earnings and the owners of the Bridget Company expressed the view that the earnings of their company should be capitalized at the same rate. The president of Logan countered with an offer of 14 times the earnings of Bridget stock and this was rejected promptly. The two owners of the Bridget Company stated their belief that the company's earnings would increase sharply over the next five years and that this factor should be weighted heavily in determining an exchange rate for the two companies' stock. If the convictions of the two owners were true, the value of the Bridget Company to the Logan Company was something more than 14, 20, or 25 times the past year's earnings.

Recognizing that the representations of the owners of the Bridget Company might have some validity, the president of the Logan Company offered to make a down payment of Logan common stock equal to 15 times the Bridget Company's average earnings for the last three years. In addition he offered at the end of five years to pay the Bridget Company's owners in Logan stock twice the total amount of earnings in excess of an annual increase of $10,000, the amount forecast by the Bridget Company's owners. The Bridget Company's average earnings for the previous three years had been $80,000 after taxes and the current year's earnings were $100,000. Earnings for the next five years were forecast by the Bridget owners as $110,000, $120,000, $130,000, $140,000 and $150,-

000; or a total for the period of $650,000. If the total earnings for the five-year period were $1,250,000, for example, the Logan Company agreed to pay the Bridget Company's owners twice the difference between $1,250,000 and $650,000, or $1,200,000 in Logan stock at the end of five years, the exchange rate to be based on the market price of the Logan stock five years hence.

The proposed solution of deferred payment was satisfactory both to the Logan Company management and to the two owners of the Bridget Company. The Logan Company was able to reduce the financial risk of paying more than seemed reasonable according to previous years' earnings, its earnings per share outstanding were increased sharply by the acquisition, and an important incentive was provided the two owners to dedicate their management efforts to increasing the yearly profit increase to more than $10,000 per year. The two owners of Bridget received immediately the listed securities of the Logan Company and received, also, the opportunity to double the dollar value received as a down payment by doubling what was regarded as a normal rate of increase in annual profits after taxes.

From the point of view of the acquiring company, a deferred payment proposal has many advantages. Almost all sellers of corporate enterprises state during negotiation meetings that they are "on the threshold of new and higher earnings rates." A responding statement by the representative of the prospective buyer that he hopes this is true and that he will agree to share on some basis the greatly increased profits forecast by the sellers, tends, as one executive stated, "to flush out the confidence factor the sellers have in their own forecasts of profits. An offer that ties future payments to the seller's performance in accordance with its owners' own forecasts gives great meaning to what otherwise is loose management talk about future sales and profits."

Another major advantage to the acquiring company of a

deferred payment plan is that the former owner-managers are given an incentive to make the operation succeed as they have said it would.   When former owners stay on as managers of the acquired company, they have a personal stake in the results over a three- to five-year period.   Incentives of executives change, of course, and this was found to be especially true of owner-executives who found themselves suddenly with tangible indications of wealth — cash or the listed securities of the acquiring company.   But if only part of the total amount to be paid is available immediately and the balance is to be based on results after, say, five years, the selling managers have a strong incentive to realize the greatest possible return.

The executives of some acquiring companies, however, do not wish to become involved in deferred payment plans. They point out that it is impossible to anticipate every contingency and to provide for these in a contract.   Also actions taken by the buying company can have drastic effects upon the profits of the acquired entity: the amount of cash which is made available for growth, decisions as to plant use or disposition, pricing policies, and a myriad of decision areas about which there can be considerable disagreement between the seller-managers and the new owners.   One executive said that an agreement which attempted to spell out what action would be taken on all conceivable future problem areas "would be almost infinitely long and would still miss many problems which could lead to controversy."   He added that the effectiveness of a deferred payment plan depends in large part upon the faith and integrity of the two parties to the agreement.

There are other shortcomings to deferred payment plans. If the former owners of the acquired company turn out to be less effective than was believed by the acquiring management, there is virtually nothing which can be done until the deferred payment period has expired.   A need for a change in management of the acquired acquisition may be indicated clearly within a relatively short time, but the operating managers have what is in effect a five-year employment contract. Efforts to change management in less than the term of the deferred payment plan are complicated by extensive negotiations and ill will. The purchasing company's executives can attempt to persuade, counsel and advise, but they are essentially precluded from taking action which could be interpreted as prejudicial to profit reporting for deferred payments.

Another disadvantage was cited by the president of a western manufacturing company and illustrated by a recent experience. The acquiring company had embarked on a growth program through the purchase of going concerns and its first purchase was of a small company in Chicago under a five-year deferred payment plan. Two years later, another company in the same industry was acquired in the Chicago area for cash. Logically and economically the two operations should have been combined; they made essentially the same products which were sold to the same customers. But this action was prevented by the deferred payment plan which required the autonomy of the first company for three more years. The president of the acquiring company added that an additional disadvantage of the deferred payment plan is that the long-term welfare of an enterprise can be jeopardized by decisions made at the acquired company level in order to assure greater short-term profits and hence a higher price.

But when the acquired company can be operated as an autonomous unit for the period agreed upon for deferred payment, when the additional payments are related to the selling company management's forecast of earnings, and when an atmosphere of faith and integrity can be established and maintained between the managements of the buyer and the seller, a deferred payment plan can be a most effective method of solving the price conflicts of acquisition negotiation.

When negotiations are terminated between prospective buyers and sellers, the reason proffered by both parties usually is disagreement on price or related financial terms. A failure to agree on corporate values is plausible and reasonable, and allows both parties to the potential acquisition to achieve a corporate and industry face-saving. But while disagreement on price may be suggested as the cause of the lack of agreement, frequently other and important *real* reasons have led to the termination of discussions.

Top Management Perquisites

The president and majority owner of a small or medium-sized company typically has control over his board of directors whom he has himself selected and elected. In some few cases these directors perform useful and constructive functions. But rarely do small and medium-sized board members ask discerning questions which will cause embarrassment to the president; they are content to go along with his performance and recommendations with a "don't rock the boat philosophy." These same characteristics are also to be found in some large companies with securities listed on national exchanges in which the president occupies a position of great influence.

In addition, the owner of a small company derives satisfaction from the title as "President." Also provision of a company automobile is not unusual, the controller never questions the president's expense account, combination business and pleasure trips are taken at company expense, and the president's decision to buy new equipment or to sell excess facilities is accepted without question by the board and by company subordinates.

Consideration of a decision to sell his company, to continue on as vice president and general manager of the company as an operating division of the acquirer, and to accept a drastically different corporate relationship role frequently results in his decision to maintain an independent status and even to decline acquisition offers which overvalue his company.

Skilled negotiators of acquiring company managements recognize these perquisites, tangible and intangible, of the company president and are prepared to discuss and suggest solutions which will permit the president to continue at least some of the trappings of his job. In some cases he is elected to the acquirer's board of directors; in others he is named a vice president of the acquiring corporation. The company automobile is continued because "it is important to have transportation available for visiting customers." And other adjustments are negotiated which permit the president to find satisfactions in a new, for him, corporate relationship.

Some negotiators, upon discerning the president's fringe benefits, err in stating abruptly and finally, "Of course, we can't go along with these extras. We have a policy manual on expense account allowances, company cars, and entertainment expenses, and we couldn't live with a situation where you would enjoy benefits which even our own president doesn't have." Too often such a statement is the beginning of a cessation of discussion which culminates in "negotiations were terminated because of differences as to price." It is not price, but the possibility of a change in corporate life which terminates the acquistion negotiations.

The perquisites of owner-managers of small- and medium-sized closely held companies frequently constitute difficult problems of negotiation. The management of a large corporate acquirer with carefully drawn policies on salaries, bonuses and company cars may hesitate to add an acquired organization as another operating division when other equivalent division executives enjoy considerably lower benefits. If the seller insists on the continuation of what are considered to be out-of-line salaries and bonuses, for example, the management of the buyer may be compelled to forego the acquisition. But here again, resourcefulness by the buyers in negotiations can, in some cases, provide alternatives which are acceptable to both sides.

The president of the Paul Company, for example, learned that what was believed to be a desirable company to acquire had a cash bonus plan for its three top management owners based on sales. Each of the three executives received a base salary of $33,000 per year and a bonus at year-end of 6% of all company sales in excess of $700,000. In 1960 the total compensation for each of the owners exceeded $90,000. The Paul Company conducted operations through eight profit-and-loss measurable operating departments which were headed by departmental general managers. Their total annual compensation was a base salary of $30,000 plus a small bonus based on department profits of from $1,000 to $5,000 per year. It was clear to the president of the Paul Company that it would not be feasible to add a new operating department with three executives each of whom earned more than twice the amount paid to existing department managers. Negotiation between representatives of the buyer and the sellers resulted in an agreement to reduce the salaries of the three owner-managers to that of the other department heads and to provide deferred retirement pay of $12,000 annually for ten years after retirement.

Many other examples of success in negotiating adjustments of what seemed to the acquirers to be excessive compensation plans were found but the significant element in the negotiations was the willingness of both parties to seek out, discuss, and agree upon different methods of compensation which were acceptable to both parties.

Negotiating Critical Problems

There is another aspect of the Paul Company situation which should be noted. The issue of the compensation of the three owners arose very early in the cycle of negotiation.

Inability to resolve the problem satisfactorily would have prevented the acquisition. Some negotiators, faced with such problems, prefer to defer the "sticky problems," come to an understanding on other phases of the agreement, and then return several days or weeks later to the major obstacle areas. An important shortcoming of this deferred approach is that if agreement cannot be reached on the difficult problems, enormous amounts of time and energy have been wasted. Generally we believe that if a major obstacle to a contract arises, the problem should be faced immediately. If acceptable solutions cannot be found, discussions can be terminated without the unnecessary and wasteful expenditure of time on a contract never to be signed.

Another illustration of this sort of negotiation problem was found in the Andrews Company, the president of which wanted two provisions included in the contract for the purchase of the Townsend Company which provided that:

1. Each foreign license agreement of the Townsend Company will be canceled or renegotiated to a form satisfactory to the Andrews Company; and

2. The rate of earnings for the 12 months' period after the end of the Townsend Company's fiscal year shall be equal to that shown on the profit-and-loss statement for the previous fiscal year.

The principal owner of the Townsend Company stated in a letter:

> There is no intention on our part to guarantee that we could obtain revision or cancellation of any one or all of our foreign license agreements any more than it is our intention to guarantee that sales and profits will continue at the rate established for our last fiscal year. The writer would use his best efforts to obtain the desired revisions or cancellations, but it would be unrealistic to approach any of these people at a time when they would know that the sale of the

business depends upon an ability to get them to revise or cancel the contracts. In that situation we would be at their mercy. And where would we be if we obtained the acceptance of new contracts by less than all of the licensees and the sale of our business failed by reason of this or other deficiencies. . . .

As to sales and profits we cannot make the sale contingent upon the rate of earnings shown on our last profit-and-loss statement. . . . As you know, our major seasonal sales occur in the second half year and while we are confident that sales and profits will equal or exceed those of last year, we cannot guarantee that these results will occur. We are not good enough forecasters to make this a condition of the sale.

Recognition by representatives of the buyer and the seller that agreement could not be reached on what both parties believed to be critical conditions led to an early termination of further negotiations.

Numerous other problems of negotiation were found in the situations we studied, but those we have cited seemed to be common to many. Resourcefulness by representatives of both the buyer and the seller is required in order to reconcile the needs and desires of the two sides of an agreement.

Again, it should be noted that the acquisition of one company by another does not proceed in mechanical step-like phases. We have separated the various elements arbitrarily into segments for purposes of presentation, recognizing that evaluation and negotiation go on concomitantly. Whether the consideration of negotiation problems should precede or follow the consideration of evaluation problems is less important than separating these problems for purposes of discussion.

CHAPTER VII

Nonfinancial Evaluation Problems

AFTER negotiations have been initiated between the representatives of the prospective buyer and seller, each becomes involved in the complicated task of evaluating the other. Determining whether two organizations should join is, typically, a complex and time-consuming process. But a thoroughgoing size-up and analysis of the present condition and future potential of both parties is critical to a mutually worthwhile acquisition.

The purchase of the Anderson Electronics Company by the Wood Company illustrates some of the pitfalls and problems resulting from inadequate evaluation. The Wood Company was organized in the early 1920's to manufacture and sell small parts and assemblies to the automobile industry. The enterprise prospered under the leadership of H. B. Wood, Sr., the founder, and became the largest employer of labor in the small midwest city where the company's only plant was located. The Wood family included two sons and two daughters, who, upon the completion of their formal educations had married and returned to their home city. The two sons and two sons-in-law were employed by the Wood Company, and when H. B. Wood, Sr., died in 1949, the four family members constituted the top management echelons of the company. During the following ten years the company continued its steady growth of sales and profits; by 1959 it had incurred losses in only three years, and had a net worth of slightly more than $1,500,000.

The company's dependency on one industry, automobiles, became of great concern to the owner-managers, and in early 1959 they decided to look actively for companies to acquire which would provide them with product diversification. Also, with the larger size they would achieve through acquisitions, the management planned to have a public issue of the company's stock which was owned entirely by the two sons and two daughters.

One of the Wood Company's salesmen suggested that consideration be given to the acquisition of the Anderson Electronics Company, located in the same state but in another small community some 85 miles away. This company had been organized in 1947 by Charles Anderson as a proprietorship (later incorporated) to develop, manufacture, and sell electronic components for radio, television, and military uses. This relatively new and rapidly growing industry appealed to the Wood management; a venture in this field through Anderson seemed to meet the defined objectives of acquisition.

Discussions were initiated by H. B. Wood, Jr., president, who pointed out to Mr. Anderson the reasons why he thought the merger would be a natural one for both organizations. They were as follows: The Wood Company, with a long history of success, had cash resources which could be used to finance Anderson's growth into new markets, the Wood family management needed and wanted new blood and new ideas, and both the Wood and Anderson families would achieve stock liquidity when, subsequent to the acquisition, a public issue of the stock could be arranged. These points appealed to Mr. Anderson who at 55 years of age realized that his total savings were represented by his ownership of the company and that he needed help in marketing problems. During the following weeks, visits were made to each other's facilities, and each party to the negotiations engaged in the evaluation process of the other.

The Wood management was impressed by Anderson's 1958 earnings of $150,000 after taxes, Mr. Anderson's capacities as a successful entrepreneur in creating a profitable enterprise, and the prospects for new and larger markets described with great enthusiasm by Mr. Anderson. At the same time, Mr. Anderson learned that the Wood family members were prominent in their community; they were active in town and church affairs, Mr. Wood was president of Rotary, chairman of the community fund drive, and a trustee of a local college; and all the key executives seemed to be the kind of people with whom he would like to be associated and identified. Mr. Anderson did observe when visiting the Wood plant that nothing was being done about new product development, but Mr. H. B. Wood stated that drawings were provided by the auto companies for most of the existing volume and that new product development was an area where Mr. Anderson could be especially helpful — another reason for bringing the two companies together.

The Wood family members and Mr. Anderson negotiated the financial terms which were agreed upon after brief discussion, and the Wood Company agreed to provide cash for new buildings and equipment at the Anderson Company facility. Mr. Anderson was elected to the board of directors of the Wood Company. A few days after the agreement was signed, the Wood Company sent Mr. Anderson a check for $125,000 to start the plant expansion immediately.

During the following 14 months the management of the Wood Company learned that: (1) Anderson's 1958 earnings of $150,000 after taxes was attributable to one large, exceedingly profitable contract. When it expired and a new contract was negotiated, profit margins were reduced by 80%. (2) Anderson's 1959 operations resulted in a loss of $40,000. (3) Mr. Anderson had developed several new electronic components, tooled for their production, and then discovered that equivalent competitive products sold for 30% less than he could make them. (4) Mr. Anderson asked too many questions at the monthly board meetings; and (5) more and more friction was developing between the executives of the two organizations.

Mr. Anderson, in this same period, discovered that: (1) No management help on marketing and distribution was provided by the Wood executives, and a management committee organized to help Mr. Anderson met seldom and then only to criticize the lack of profits at the Anderson Company. (2) Board meetings were held with no agenda, without current financial statements, and without minutes of the meetings. (3) Wood executives purchased two small companies without Mr. Anderson's participation or approval. (4) The Wood management members were narrow, provincial, and not sources of broad, enlightened, constructive help. (5) A significant portion of the Wood Company's inventory consisted of obsolete parts which had been on the shelves for over 20 years.

The Wood-Anderson situation, greatly abbreviated, illustrates dramatically the disenchantment and disillusionment which can result from inadequate evaluations, both by the acquirer and by the acquired. Neither the Wood family management nor Mr. Anderson was happy. When last reported, a way had been found to disentangle the unfortunate alliance but only after months of expensive negotiation and the loss of three years consumed in "spinning our wheels." The case is not unique, however. We found several others with similar unpleasant results. The specific problems involved varied, of course, but in many cases both the buyers and the sellers stated, some time after the acquisition, "How in the world did we ever miss so many important problems in the other company?"

"This is easy," said one acquiring president, "when you first embark on a program of acquisitions, the enthusiasm to do something blinds you to the realities. Everything seems to be as you would like it to be and with rose-tinted filters on the evaluator's eyes, you begin to say to yourself, 'How long have I been missing these junior grade Fort Knoxes?'"

There is an interesting combination of attitudes required in the acquiring company executives. Having decided on the basis of public information that Company X would be an ideal acquisition, the acquirer's representative, aware also that the acquisition market is essentially a sellers' market, approaches the prospective selling management and owners with a salesman's point of view. The acquiring representative is trying to persuade another management group that their mutual best interests will be served by getting together. The efforts to manifest to the sellers that the buyers are "your kind of people" must be combined with an objective, tough-minded, evaluating point of view. Many major shortcomings of companies are not discernible from published information, and the purpose of evaluation is to ferret out strengths and weaknesses so that a prudent judgment can be exercised on a decision to buy or not to buy.

TIME SPENT IN EVALUATIONS

We found many examples of managements who made fast and superficial evaluations of companies which were acquired. A West Coast company, for instance, wanted an established East Coast manufacturing base of operations. Trade information and published data indicated that the Palm Company, owned substantially by Mr. Mann, the president, might be acquired. The president of the acquirer asked two vice presidents to approach the owner of the Palm Company, to negotiate its purchase quickly, and "don't make any mistakes." The two vice presidents arranged an appointment with Mr. Mann at a hotel in a nearby city and negotiations started. Mr. Mann stated that no visit to the plant could be arranged because any suspicion of sale would affect the morale of his employees. "Perhaps we cannot come to any agreement and if we can't, I certainly don't want my employees to know that I am even considering a sale. Tell me whatever you want to know and I can arrange to get the information for you without arousing any suspicion." The two acquiring company vice presidents made a list of desired data which were provided during the next two days. Negotiations continued, and on the sixth day an agreement was signed to purchase the Palm Company. The legal requirements were completed later and the West Coast acquirer had its eastern base of operations.

It was discovered shortly, however, that the Palm Company key employees were not competent, the backlog included a number of loss contracts, and the inventory was loaded with materials for which no short-time use was anticipated. Some of these problems were covered by warranties included in the sales agreement, but the protections were of little comfort when the acquired company turned out to be something other than what the two vice presidents believed they had purchased. This was a case of too fast action, and while it would have been possible to withdraw completely from the agreed purchase because of the many breaches of warranty, the acquiring management was reluctant to retract in view of the recent publicity announcing its newly acquired capacity to serve the eastern market. One of the acquiring company vice presidents observed several months later that much more information should have been requested — "There just is no substitute for looking long and hard."

On the other hand, it is possible to move too slowly. The Prout Company, to illustrate, learned through a broker in April 1960 that a medium-sized school equipment manufacturer could be acquired. The broker's letter was circulated among the headquarters' line and staff executives, and one month later a reply indicating interest was sent to the school equipment company. Visits between the two company managements took place in June, financial statements were exchanged, and the Acquisition Department of the Prout Company was given the figures to analyze and come up with a recommendation. There seemed to be no urgency until the broker called the Prout Company in late August 1960 to report that the school equipment company owners had sold the business to someone else. The indicated purchase price was well in excess of the amount the Prout Company management planned to offer when they got around to it.

We found that some chief operating executives or heads of acquisitions programs took enormous amounts of time to search out and evaluate every conceivable facet of a company's business operations. Sometimes the significant factors were not distinguished from the insignificant, and the hundreds of hours of work required led prospective sellers to withdraw from further negotiations. It might be concluded that concern for all the details is a good sign of thoughtful, penetrating, and analytical management in the acquiring company; but on the other hand, it could be concluded that endless staff studies and analyses result in overstudying the problems and procrastinating the taking of action. Certainly there is no clear bench mark as to what is the right amount of evaluation. Each situation is unique, but on balance we found more unfortunate experiences resulting from too little evaluation than from too much evaluation.

Deciding on Evaluation Criteria

A notable factor in the problems of evaluation derived from managements not knowing the kinds of things to evaluate, i.e., what to look for. The obvious and reasonably standard financial statements provided tangible documents which could be studied, and plants, equipment, inventories, products, and so on could be observed. But the intangible qualities of management, personnel, and organization which give value to physical assets were frequently neglected. Preoccupation with reasonably measurable quantitative factors resulted in overlooking equally important qualitative elements.

Again it should be noted that what to look for in the evaluation process is a function of the specific objectives of the acquirer. If the buyer is searching for companies to co tinue operating as going concerns, this goal will determin the factors to consider. If the objective is to increase borrow-ing capacity, another set of ingredients must be looked for. And if the buyer plans to acquire companies for the purpose of liquidating the physical assets at a profit, thereby increas-ing the earnings per share rate of the acquirer, still other ele-ments must be considered. With regard to the last objec-tive, it was surprising to find the number of companies which bought others with liquidation for a profit as the main objec-tive. Once embarked on this route, they found it necessary to engage in the same practice on a regular basis in order to maintain a continuing record of increased earnings per quarter. Most acquisitions we studied, however, were made with the conviction that the acquired organizations would continue as going concerns and for these it is important to evaluate more than just the touchable and seeable assets of an enterprise.

Some companies have established very specific criteria to be used in evaluating the qualitative and quantitative factors in companies that are being considered for acquisition. For in-stance, Mr. Warren Hayes, vice president of Thompson Ramo Wooldridge, in an address to the Security Analysts So-ciety of Denver, summarized briefly the qualities and strengths he hopes to find in electronic companies which are candidates for acquisition.

I. Personality, character, and attitude of management.

    A. *A Compulsive Drive to Succeed as a Business.* It is reas-suring to find a management which hates to lose, which will fight hard to win, and fight harder as the chances of winning seem to decrease, believes it can win until de-feat is a final fact, is exhilarated by victory, or depressed by defeat, but only until the next opportunity to do bat-tle.

B. *Courage.* In every business there are times when hard, difficult, decisions must be made, sometimes adversely affecting individuals, involving risk of failure, exposing weaknesses or failures to public view. Many managements stumble at making timely, resolute, necessary decisions. The ability to make such hard, sometimes seemingly ruthless decisions is an essential quality of management.

C. *Established Leadership.* It is difficult to develop confidence in an amorphous, leaderless management group, or in a group where there is unsettled competition for leadership.

D. *Profit & Loss Consciousness.* It doesn't take long to determine whether a company's management really translates its plans and actions into effects in P & L performance. Realistic profit consciousness is a vital quality in a successful company.

E. *People Skillfulness.* Healthy managements are usually able to engender and maintain healthy attitudes among themselves and the whole family of people who do the company's work. A depressed disinterested working group is usually a product of poor management, while an enthusiastic group is rarely an accident, but rather the result of management skill in dealing with people.

F. *A Selling Atmosphere.* It is reassuring to discover a selling orientation across the board, and correspondingly discouraging to discover a lack of market consciousness in parts of the company not directly involved in the selling process.

G. *Positive Internal Competition.* Internal competition is an ever-present process. However, in some companies it is an internal game of musical chairs where power is the prize; it is a pushing down process. In other companies, it is more nearly based on individual contribution to total company accomplishment. Usually company goals are subordinated in the first type of internal competition;

it is possible, and important, to channel competitive energies toward company achievements, and to develop an atmosphere of mutual respect.

II. Operational Program

A. *Understanding of the Industry.* There needs to be in an electronics company a well-developed knowledge of the industry from the business point of view, its structure, characteristics, markets, trends, and problems.

B. *Understanding of the Technical Issues.* Each electronics company is affected directly or indirectly by the process of technological change. A measurement of a company's ability is its understanding of the significant technical issues, and the character, extent of effect, and timing of technological changes.

C. *Comprehension of the Company's Fit in the Industry.* Each company has characteristics which should be taken into consideration in planning its program — size, skills, resources, deficiencies.

D. *Specific Company Program.* I am a believer in concept — that is, that a company which has a well-organized, well-analyzed, logically definitive concept of where it's going, and why, is more likely to succeed than a company which bounces around in an instinctive, opportunistic fashion. Especially in the difficult decade ahead, successful performance, perhaps even survival, will be greatly dependent upon the intelligence and discipline of forward planning.

III. Leverages

It is important in looking at any company to understand what are the leverages which will cause it to be successful. Mere presence in the electronics industry is certainly no assurance of long-term success. The kind of leverages one might look for would include: a front position in a dynamic technical art; a growing or changing market situation; an entrenched position in a good market; distribution strength; demonstrated management skills.

In this growth industry, I especially look for a favorable relationship between sales, gross profit, and net profit. In addition to paying its present costs of doing business, an electronics company must generate enough gross profit to support the technical work necessary to keep up the flow of new products, and have enough left over to provide the capital funds required to exploit such developments. A number of previously sound electronics companies have seen a price-cost squeeze on older products cut gross profit so much that, because of inadequate development of new products, their ability to sustain growth has been impaired. Once it has fallen behind, a company in this position has a real bootstrap problem on its hands.

IV. Specific Skills

    A. *Habit of Accomplishment.* Many electronics companies have existed for several years without really accomplishing much. They have drifted from project to project, never really becoming established, but somehow able to survive. It is reassuring to develop evidence showing a record of successful product development and engineering, effective transfer of the product into manufacturing, and the development of a firm market position.

    B. *Survival in Adversity.* Many electronics companies have not had to face adverse circumstances. Hard times, and the associated problems, are quite a shock to the uninitiated. One can breathe easier knowing that a company has experienced and survived periods of extreme difficulty.

    C. *Pyramidal Insight.* The top managers of a company sit on a pyramid of organization and people, large or small dependent upon size of the company. It is surprising how frequently top managers do not really know what is going on in their pyramid, usually because they are dependent on a straight-line communications channel, up through the organizational structure, involving filtering, adjusting and interpreting of the information as it is passed upward, and sometimes because they have filter-ears and filter-eyes, hearing and seeing only what they want to hear and see. Such a management can easily be in trouble without knowing it, until perhaps too late. The alert management develops techniques to maintain pyramidal insight, ouside of its straight-line organizational communication, and is well aware of the key operational problems existent, independently confirmed.

What I have given you is, perhaps, an idealized set of checkpoints. In most situations, information necessary to draw conclusions with respect to these various questions will be difficult, perhaps impossible to obtain. But I hope I have made clear my belief that the electronics company which proves to be a good investment in the decade ahead is the company which proves to be a well-run business, that the qualities which are essential to good management of an electronics company are not uniquely different from the qualities required to manage effectively almost any other type of company.[1]

Mr. Hayes outlined what he regarded as the critical elements for success in the electronics industry. It is noteworthy that many of the factors are concerned with management attributes: a compulsive drive to succeed, courage, established leadership, people skillfulness, positive internal competition, management programs, and others. The significance of research and development in the success of an electronics company is covered by his points, *Understanding of the Technical Issues* and *Habit of Accomplishment*. Marketing is included in Mr. Hayes' elements: *A Selling Atmosphere* and an *Understanding of the Industry*. And financial factors are part of the factors — *Profit & Loss Consciousness* and *Leverages*.

Other industries or segments of industries in which an organization operates have specific requirements a company

[1] Warren B. Hayes, "A Look at Electronics Investments," an address to the Security Analysts Society of Denver, February 9, 1960.

must meet if it is to succeed. For some it may be skill in consumer advertising, advanced research and development, careful cost control in manufacturing, effective sales coverage by technically trained salesmen, competent engineers who explore for oil and gas, or any one or more of the many functions of business. The evaluation process should include careful consideration of what is required for company success in its industry or its segment of industry.

Except for the financial considerations — and even here, as will be discussed later, there are difficult problems in determining the meanings of values and profits — most of the factors involve the characteristics of the management of an enterprise, and for these, as Mr. Hayes notes, "conclusions will be difficult, perhaps impossible to obtain." How does the interested acquirer, for example, evaluate the top management group of a company?

PSYCHOLOGICAL TESTING

The evaluation of management personnel remains today one of the unscientific functions of business. This conclusion will be disputed by some who rely greatly on psychological testing programs. But during our field case studies, we found no substantive evidence to change the judgment expressed by one of the authors in 1950:

> Perhaps the most important conclusion on tests is that no test or group of tests was found which could be used by every company to measure accurately executive traits. Some commercially minded psychologists, pseudo-psychologists, and others have made extravagant claims with regard to the universal applicability of their testing procedures, but no substantial evidence was found which supported the claims. It is unfortunate that a few have engaged in practices bordering on charlatanism, first, because some companies have wasted money and effort by accepting the glib representations, and secondly, because considerable damage has been

done to responsible and reputable psychologists whose scientific approaches hold real promise in this important field of study.[2]

Some progress has been made in the last ten years in constructing tests and in validating results, but we know of no professional psychological service which provides accurate measurements of executive skills and traits. Also still unanswered is the question, what are the skills and traits required in an executive for a particular position in a particular organizational situation?

In a few acquiring companies where psychological tests are required prior to the employment of any new personnel, attempts have been made to require tests for key executives of the company to be acquired. In one situation, the president of Pane, Inc., an East Coast company, started negotiations with a proprietary drug company in Chicago. The New York company management was most anxious to acquire the Chicago enterprise; it had a long history of increasing sales and profits, a fine reputation in the industry, and a young vice president of sales who was outstanding and largely responsible for his company's marketing effectiveness. When the sales vice president from Chicago visited the Pane Company headquarters, the vice president of research and engineering suggested to the president that the company psychologist spend two days testing the Chicago visitor. He said they could tell him that everyone in the company's employ who had become acquainted with the psychologist regarded him as a good friend and this ought to impress him as well as giving Pane the chance to "find out what makes him tick." The Pane Company vice president of personnel, upon hearing of the proposal and knowing the delicate qualities of negotiation required, protested immediately to the president and the suggested visit to the company psychologist was can-

[2] Myles L. Mace, *The Growth and Development of Executives.* Boston, Harvard Business School, Division of Research, 1950, p. 84.

celed. The personnel vice president observed later, "Nothing would have killed our chances quicker than asking a young old pro in the industry to have his square root extracted by a psychologist."

For some situations psychological tests are accepted as standard tools helping to evaluate key people, and in these cases there is little or no resentment to the use of tests as a tool that is only part of the total evaluation process. In many other cases, however, tests are thought of as the implements of head shrinkers and the suggestion that the key people of an organization which might be acquired be subjected to tests is likely to jeopardize rather than help the acquirer's chances of acquisition.

Evaluation by Interviews

We found that many company managements do a much more careful job of evaluating one man for possible employment than they do in evaluating five, ten, or fifteen people who would occupy key positions if the purchase was consummated. For the employment of one executive who is to occupy a high level position, many companies have extensive interview procedures in which several executives have opportunities to evaluate the prospective employee. Also, references are checked and efforts made to talk with former employees and associates. It is a time-consuming process, but the time and money required are regarded as a minimum price to assure competence at the executive level.

When the possible acquisition of an organization is being considered, however, the standard and extensive interview procedures seem to be forgotten. Even with all the shortcomings and infirmities of personal evaluations by interviews, it is extremely important to arrive at the best possible conclusions as to the abilities and skills of key people to be employed through the purchase of the acquired company.

When evaluations are being made of key executives of a possible acquisition, formal interviews in the employment sense typically are not carried on.   Rather, executives of the acquirer chat informally with executives of the organization to be acquired as an essential part of getting acquainted, learning about each other's operations, and evaluating the capacities and abilities of the people involved.   Unless executives have clearly in mind what they are looking for during these discussions, the conversation tends to drift off into casual, interesting, but nonrelevant subjects.   We found, for example, that some executives, after a two- or three-hour discussion with a key employee of a candidate for acquisition, learned that he liked to fish, play golf, and tend the home garden.

A structural concept of critical factors to look for in management personnel is a vital requisite.   Most executives think of themselves as skillful and penetrating interviewers.   With many years of business experience and participation in the employment of dozens or hundreds of people, they conclude that they can spot strengths and weaknesses, and forecast future performance on the job.   Some can, but many of those who pride themselves on their interview abilities have quite unimpressive records of employee selection and evaluation. Nevertheless those who can carry on a business conversation effectively and weave substantive questions into the discussions can learn a great deal about people's capacities and the company's operations.   We encountered several during our field study who were able to extract enormous amounts of information through informal discussions.   With years of experience in top management positions, they were able to lead pleasant conversation into useful and disclosing avenues, so essential in the evaluation of management personnel.

Some acquiring company executives limited their interviews to the president and the executive vice president level of the organization to be acquired.   In very small enterprises, this may be sufficient, but for medium and larger companies, it is clear that evaluations should be made of key people in the second and third levels of management. Frequently efforts to probe the additional levels will be resisted by the top executives for fear that weaknesses will be uncovered. We found that some presidents of companies to be sold will describe in glowing terms the "great team of capable and responsible executives" in the lower echelons and point with pride to the company's fine financial record as evidence that his team is competent. Occasionally such comments are disguises for weaknesses within the group. The president may be an extraordinarily capable executive who has run what is basically a one-man show. His departure after the acquisition or a change in his motives for continuing to work as hard as he did in the past can result in unanticipated management personnel changes. In most situations, we believe, investigation and evaluation of more than the top one or two executives are important.

While we emphasize the importance of interviewing as many people as possible, we recognize that the accomplishment of this significant step is most difficult. Insistence by the prospective buyer was interpreted by the seller, in some cases, to be a reflection on his integrity, on the validity of the representations he made as to the high quality of his team. It is hard to create the favorable atmosphere desired to demonstrate to sellers that the buyer's management is "your kind of people" and, at the same time, maintain the toughness of mind required for objective evaluation. But unless the acquiring management can be reasonably sure of the capabilities of the acquired key personnel, it is probably wiser not to run the risks of purchasing what can be a hollow organizational shell.

In addition to interviewing key people and evaluating their performance through financial records of the company, it is helpful for acquiring company representatives to check with former employers and former employees of the people being evaluated.   In one situation a former employee of the president of a company under consideration for acquisition reported that the president was a dictator and a tyrant, the company was not building for the future by research and development, the five vice presidents were weak and completely dominated by the president, and several competent men had left because of the internal mess in the company.   These significant conclusions about the management were confirmed by other discreet inquiries and it became clear that purchase of the enterprise would not be wise.

FORECASTING MOTIVATIONS OF KEY PEOPLE

The evaluation of executives' capabilities and potential is critically important but exceedingly difficult.   Even when every effort has been made to interview people in depth and to check on a firm's business associations, there can be surprises after the acquisition has been consummated.

We found many examples of apparently competent and highly motivated executives losing interest in their assignments after their companies were sold.   Part of the explanation for their lack of interest was the manner in which the integration process was administered and some of these problems of integration are presented in Chapter IX.   But in some situations where the acquiring organization seemed to follow useful and practical methods of integration, acquired chief operating executives deviated from their demonstrated record of achievement.

Several executives of acquiring companies reported that they knew of no infallible way to forecast the incentives of key people in the acquired group.   One president, for example, was 36 years old when he sold his company to a larger one in return for listed securities.   During the negotiations he stated repeatedly that his ambition was to continue administering the company as an operating division and to manage the division so as to make higher and higher sales and larger profits. Within six months after his company was acquired, the president found new interests in the local chamber of commerce, in part-time day study of languages at a nearby university, and in extensive travel in Europe. It soon became clear to the acquiring management that the president had decided not to work hard any more and it was necessary to find an early and unplanned-for successor for the position. This case was only one of many we learned about during our study, and it serves to emphasize again the importance of doing as much as possible to evaluate the people employed by the company to be acquired.

One acquiring company president stated, after many experiences in coping with acquired managements, that he would never consider for acquisition any company the management of which were owners and who, by selling out, would receive substantial amounts of cash or securities. The risks, he said, of changes in the basic motivations of people with new, tangible symbols of wealth are too great. They find security, lose the lean and hungry look, and become second-rate managers.

CHECKING ON BACKGROUNDS

Checking on the background of an individual or several members of an organization to be acquired is a very delicate and difficult job. But if these people are to occupy key positions after the purchase, their character, ability, and personal objectives should be investigated most carefully. Affirmative reports from knowledgeable and responsible sources constitute the most significant evidence about their corporate values and company potentials.

Members of acquired management groups, too, should explore the backgrounds of the management personnel in the organization to which their companies are to be sold. Disillusionment and disappointment were found among key executives whose organizations had been acquired. Here again, the evaluation methods of informal discussions and checks with outsiders are valuable. But in addition, confirmation of what their business lives are apt to be like in an acquired relationship can be gained by discussions with key people of companies acquired earlier by the same purchaser. Care must be exercised to assure reasonably unbiased comments by executives previously acquired, but this is usually possible through business or professional contacts. For example, the president of the Glenn Company, a substantial but not controlling stockholder, was approached by a New York company which had acquired two years earlier a company in the same community in which the Glenn Company was located. After negotiations began, the Glenn Company president checked with his friends who had experienced working with the New York organization and learned that many of the prepurchase representations had not been fulfilled. This bit of evidence was controlling in a decision not to sell to the New York enterprise, and a short time later a sale was completed to another company in the same industry.

Perhaps the single most important caveat for both acquiring and acquired key management executives is not to be time pressured into brief, superficial evaluations of the other, but to insist on the time necessary to provide maximum assurances that the key people are the kinds of people with whom continuing, satisfying, and profitable relations can be realized.

Check Lists for Evaluation of Company

During our study we found that many acquiring companies prepared check lists of factors to be taken into account and for which detailed information could be organized for analysis. The lists ranged from a few pages of rather broad headings to an extreme example of 36 pages of single-spaced typed questions regarded as fundamental for all possible acquisitions. Check lists are useful tools for executives engaged in the collection of data for evaluation purposes. Not only is complete information called for to provide some understanding of the operations, but also essential data are supplied which expedite the legal and accounting needs for the final closing of the deal.

In a few situations, representatives of the acquiring managements early in the negotiation stage mailed or handed long check lists to the organization to be acquired with requests that the information be collected and forwarded within a few weeks. The response by the receivers of such documents was usually negative and adverse to continued negotiations. With no conviction that a sale of their company would be attractive, the imposition of an encyclopedia-like questionnaire raised serious questions for the owners about the acquirer. Later in the negotiations when both the acquirer and the acquired have tentatively concluded that a useful relationship can be created, check lists do serve a purpose. But asking detailed questions prematurely through a check list was found to be untimely and ill-advised.

To illustrate the elements included in a typical check list, the following is an example of one used by an East Coast corporation, entitled "Desired Information for Evaluating a Company Acquisition Possibility."

Company Survey Check List
General

1. History of business
2. Description of corporate structure
3. List of officers and directors, their affiliations and background
4. Stock distribution — number, principal holders, etc.
5. Organization chart

6. Policy manual
7. Extent of integration of company — can it expand vertically
8. Philosophy of management on matters such as growth, industrial relations, organizational planning, industrial engineering, merchandising, educational selling, advertising, accounting and budgeting, research, development engineering, product design, etc.
9. Can we evaluate company ourselves or must we hire outside consultants for personnel analysis, market research, or any other factors?
10. Are there any legal problems peculiar to the company, its products, or the industry?
11. What is company's philosophy or policy on dividends, financing expansion, finances in general?
12. What consulting firms have been or are being retained by the firm?
13. How are relations with the community?
14. What is policy concerning patent protection?
15. Are any major capital expenditures authorized at present?
16. Are any major capital expenditures contemplated in the near term, long term?
17. Are company's name and trademark well known? Are they confusingly similar to any other firm's name and trademark?
18. What did company manufacture during World War II?
19. How did company do during depressed times of the 1930's–49?

Financial

1. Financial statements for last ten years
   a. Balance sheets
   b. Profit and loss and surplus statements
2. Projected operating and financial statements
3. Breakdown of inventory as to raw material, work in process, finished goods
   a. Any change in this mix through the years?
   b. How is inventory carried — average cost, Lifo, Fifo, etc.?
4. Details of prepaid expenses
5. Detail of property, plant and equipment
   a. Any buildings partially completed or under construction?

    b. Any machinery or equipment under construction?

    c. Any leased machinery or equipment? (If so, details concerning quantity, terms of lease, contingent liability, etc.)

    d. Any emergency plant facilities? If so, amount and is fast write-off on books or for tax purposes only?

6. Details of intangible assets including cost of patents and method of amortization
7. Short term loans — interest rate, due date, security if any, etc.
8. Is short term financing used which does not show on annual statements? Explain
9. Long term loans — interest rate, payment dates, prepayments penalty, security, restrictions on working capital and dividends, etc.
10. Details of reserves and capital surplus
11. Federal income tax statue — credits, loss, carry-overs, etc.
12. Details of unrecorded or contingent liabilities
13. Sales and cost of sales by product classification
14. Details of nonmanufacturing costs such as selling, advertising, research, etc.
15. Sources of "other income" — royalties, rent, etc.
16. Details of "other deductions" — interest, royalties and fees, etc.
17. Details of any "strange" items on financial statements
18. Extent of management control techniques used — budget, standard costs, etc.
19. Extent of machine accounting — IBM, integrated data processing, etc.

Sales

General

1. List and evaluate sales personnel — management, inside and outside sales people, advertising, etc.
2. Describe methods (channels) of distribution
3. Are any changes in method of distribution contemplated?
4. Complete list of branch offices, warehouses, service facilities
5. Who are consumers; list and give locations
6. What is the company's geographic distribution of sales, salesmen?

7. Breakdown by size ($) of orders received annually
8. Does company formalize market surveys?   Use consultants?

Advertising and Promotion

1. What is the extent, type, quality and media of the company's past and present advertising program?   How does this compare to advertising done by competitors of the company?
2. What is the present status of catalogs, price sheets, sales tools, sales engineering data, service manuals and parts lists?   How does this compare to like material put out by competitors of the company?
3. Does the company participate in trade shows?   Do the company's competitors participate in trade shows?
4. How are publicity and public relations handled by the company?   How does this compare to the programs handled by the company's competitors?

Competition

1. What is the competitive position of the company?
2. Who are the company's competitors?
3. By line, what share of the market does the company hold?
4. To what extent do unrelated products indirectly compete with company's product?
5. Do competitors have any natural advantages over this company (location, shipping facilities, priority to raw materials) ?
6. What recognizable advantages do company and products have over each competitor and their products?
7. What recognizable advantages do competitors and their products have over this company?
8. To what extent is there competition from the so-called "back alley" or "garage" shops?
9. Do competitors' merchandising methods differ from company's?   Explain

International Aspects

1. What is the present foreign market?   What is its potential foreign market?

2. Does the company have any plants or licenses abroad? Where? What are the terms?
3. Has advertising made the company's trade names known abroad?
4. Is foreign competition a threat?

The Product

1. List product lines with description and history
2. Volume of each item or line
   a. Each of past five years
   b. Budgeted for this year
   c. Present backlog
   d. Future outlook (present and new fields)
3. What is the life of the product? Is it consumable?
4. How much of annual sales are supply and repair orders?
5. Are any items or supplies purchased for resale? If so, what is the volume and characteristic markup of each?
6. List patents and licenses giving life and degree of exclusivity
7. What emphasis does the company place on industrial design and packaging?
8. For the past five years how were the sales broken down by industry (chemical, foods, etc.)?
9. Do products and facilities have possibilities in the consumer field as well as the industrial field?
10. Do products and facilities lend themselves naturally to other products and new fields?
11. Are there possibilities of using the company's products in the great "new growth" industries — atomic energy, electronics, automatic controls and materials handling?
12. Will any foreseeable events bring technological obsolescence to the company's industry or any of its products? Review past, current and prospective technological trends with relation to company's products, its customers and its competitors
13. What is the ability of the company to supply present demands — anticipated demands?

Engineering and Research

1. Number and grade of engineers, production and development

2. Evaluation of engineers and their specialties
3. Evaluation of designs (particularly as to possible improvements)
4. What developmental projects are being carried on at present — any new products?
5. Description and condition of facilities — drafting room, laboratory, etc.
6. Research personnel — number, grade and evaluation
7. Applied or basic research?
8. Description and condition of facilities
9. Any research projects contracted out?
10. Any special experimental or test equipment?

Manufacturing

1. List and evaluate the key manufacturing people of the company and their jobs
2. Give a description and layout of the plant and its property
3. What are the possibilities for plant expansion?
4. What transportation facilities are available?
5. Is water or power supply adequate? Is waste disposal a problem?
6. What raw materials are used?
   a. Where are they obtained?
   b. Is supply limited?
   c. What is relation of cost to sales?
7. Give a description of manufacturing facilities and processes in general
8. Extent to which plant and facilities are used — any unused capacity, machines or departments?
9. List of principal machine tools giving age and condition of each
10. List of other company operated equipment (trucks, ovens, welding machines, etc.) What is the condition of each?
11. Are any manufacturing processes patented or licensed? If so, describe as to term of each agreement and exclusivity
12. Are there any changes in production techniques advisable or contemplated?
13. What are hazards of production process?
14. Does the company have any of its work jobbed out?

15. Are sales seasonal or cyclical? If so, does production follow or can stocking and production control smooth out fluctuation?
16. How is production controlled or scheduled?
17. How is inventory controlled?
18. Extent and quality of industrial engineering — standards, methods analysis, quality control, operation sheets, etc.

Personnel

1. Number, sex, age of labor force
2. Breakdown of personnel by direct, indirect labor; by department
3. Breakdown of labor force as to length of service
4. Are employees paid on hourly or piece rates?
5. What is minimum, maximum and average wage?
6. Description and cost of fringe benefits (insurances, vacation and holiday policy, pensions, etc.)
7. Are incentive, profit sharing or stock purchase plans in force? Explain
8. How do wages and salaries compare with competition and other industries in the community?
9. What degree of skill is required?
10. Has there been any difficulty in obtaining labor?
11. Has there been any unusual turnover of personnel in any division of company?
12. What is union affiliation?
13. Is a written labor contract available?
14. What is history of labor relations?
15. What schools, courses, conferences or clinics are personnel sent to?
16. Give salary structure of key personnel (officers, salesmen, engineers, factory management, etc.)
17. Are aptitude or psychological tests used in hiring personnel?

In some situations, particularly where the acquiring management had not had direct business experience in the industry served by the company under consideration, professional consultants were asked to perform the evaluation function and to recommend what decisions should be made. Also, although we encountered this less frequently, the management of a company to be acquired employed a consulting firm to evaluate the potential acquirer. Both acquiring and acquired company executives reported that the analyses done by consultants were excellent, although expensive.

Evaluation, then, of the prospective selling company and the prospective buying company is essential to a mutually attractive acquisition. Sizing up any business organization is difficult and the task is complicated by the many intangible qualitative factors involved. It is easy to become preoccupied with the financial aspects of an acquisition opportunity. But here, too, figures have value and validity only to the extent the people of the organization give them meaning. Both the buyer and the seller must take the time necessary for thorough and careful analysis of the other.

CHAPTER VIII

Some Financial Problems

IN the previous chapter we discussed some of the problems of evaluating the largely intangible nonfinancial factors involved in a company's operations. The problems of evaluating the financial condition and projecting the profit future of an enterprise are equally, but not more, important. As indicated earlier, each company is truly unique and each company has its own distinguishing financial history and potential. All experienced acquirers state that no two situations are alike and that there are great dangers in projecting financial assumptions gained from one experience into a new situation. But from the many detailed financial cases studied, we have extracted what seem to be common financial problem areas. These are stated and illustrated in an effort to be helpful to the managements of acquiring organizations as well as to the managements and owners of companies contemplating sale.

GENERALLY ACCEPTED ACCOUNTING PRINCIPLES

The evaluation of people, organizations, marketing capability, and product acceptance is generally recognized as difficult because of the absence of objective standards and analysis techniques. Many, far too many, executives assume that these uncertainties and difficulties are not found in the financial area. "Here at last in the evaluation of a company we are dealing with concrete facts. Now we can deal with measurable quantitative factors where we have precise measuring techniques. No more subjective judgments. The accounting and financial reports and statements are accurate and we can really find out what a company is worth."

Such executives are especially assured when they learn the financial statements of the company under consideration for acquisition bear an auditor's statement similar to this:

> We have examined the balance sheet of the Archer Company as of December 31, 1961, and the related statement of income and net income retained in the business for the year then ended. Our examination was made in accordance with generally accepted auditing standards and included such tests of the accounting records and such other auditing procedures as we considered necessary in the circumstances.
>
> In our opinion, the accompanying balance sheet and statement of income and net income retained for use in the business present fairly the financial position of the company at December 31, 1961, and the results of its operations for the year then ended in conformity with generally accepted accounting principles applied on a basis consistent with that of the preceding year.

And their assurance is even greater when it is learned that the auditing firm is a well-known national organization rather than a small local enterprise.

Clearly, financial statements are essential for any evaluation of a company's record, and a statement certified by auditors is more likely to reflect fairly the status of a company than an unaudited statement. But even audited financial reports can provide a misleading feeling of certainty and comparability. Sophisticated analysts recognize the value of financial reports and statements but they remember that the auditor's certificate says, "In our opinion, the accompanying balance sheet and statement of income and net income retained for use in the business present *fairly* the financial position of the company at December 31, 1961, and the results of its operations for the year then ended in conformity with gen-

	Company A Col. 1	Company B's Profits	
		Use of Fifo in Pricing Inventory Col. 2	Use of Straight-line Depreciation Col. 3
Sales in units	100,000 units		
Sales in dollars	$100 each		
	$10,000,000		
Costs and expenses —			
Cost of goods sold	$ 6,000,000		
Selling, general and administrative	1,500,000		
LIFO inventory reserve	400,000	$(400,000)	
Depreciation	400,000		$(100,000)
Research costs	100,000		
Pension costs	200,000		
Officers' compensation:			
Base salaries	200,000		
Bonuses	200,000		
Total costs and expenses	$ 9,000,000	$ (400,000)	$ (100,000)
Profit before income taxes	$ 1,000,000	$ 400,000	$ 100,000
Income taxes	520,000	208,000	52,000
	$ 480,000	$ 192,000	$ 48,000
Gain on sale of property (net of income tax)	—	—	—
Net profit reported	$ 480,000	$ 192,000	$ 48,000
Per share on 600,000 shares	$ .80	$ .32	$ .08
Market value at:			
10 times earnings	$ 8.00	$3.20	$ .80
12 times earnings	9.60	3.84	.96
15 times earnings	12.00	4.80	1.20

( ) Denotes deduction.
See explanation of Columns

Magic

accepted accounting principles"

Are Higher Because of

Deferring Research Costs over Five Years Col. 4	Funding Only the Pensions Vested Col. 5	Use of Stock Options for Incentive Col. 6	Including Capital Gain in Income Col. 7	Company B Col. 8
				100,000 units
				$100 each
				$10,000,000
				$ 6,000,000
				1,500,000

				300,000
$(80,000)				20,000
	$(150,000)			50,000
				200,000
		$(200,000)		---
$(80,000)	$(150,000)	$(200,000)	---	$ 8,070,000
$ 80,000	$ 150,000	$ 200,000	---	$ 1,930,000
42,000	78,000	104,000	---	$ 1,004,000
$ 38,000	$ 72,000	$ 96,000	---	$ 926,000
---	---	---	$150,000	150,000
$ 38,000	$ 72,000	$ 96,000	$150,000	$ 1,076,000
$ .06	$ .12	$ .16	$ .25	1.79
$.60	$1.20	$1.60	$2.50	$17.90
.72	1.44	1.92	3.00	21.48
.90	1.80	2.40	3.75	26.85

2 to 7 inclusive on page 180.

Accounting Magic

Explanation of Columns 2 to 7, inclusive

Column	Company A	Company B
2.	Uses Lifo (last in, first out) for pricing inventory	Uses Fifo (first in, first out)
3.	Uses accelerated depreciation for book and tax purposes	Uses straight-line
4.	Charges research and development costs to expense currently	Capitalizes and amortizes over five-year period

(If R & D costs remain at same level, the difference disappears after five years. The difference of $80,000 in the chart is in the five year, where A expenses $100,000, and B capitalizes the $100,000 but amortizes 1/5.)

5.	Funds the current pension costs — i.e., current service plus amortization of past service	Funds only the present value of pensions vested

(Difference in pension charges might also arise where, as in the case of U. S. Steel in 1958, management decides that current contributions can be reduced or omitted because of excess funding in prior years and/or increased earnings of the fund or the rise in market value of the investments.)

6.	Pays incentive bonuses to officers in cash	Grants stock options instead of paying cash bonuses
7.	Credits gains (net of tax thereon) directly to earned surplus (or treats them as special credits below net income)	Includes such gains (net of income tax thereon) in income

erally accepted accounting principles applied on a basis consistent with that of the preceding year." [1]

The significance of financial differences in the application

[1] *Accounting and Reporting Problems of the Accounting Profession,* September, 1960, Arthur Andersen and Company. "Great emphasis has thus been placed on generally accepted accounting principles. However, there have never been any comprehensive and authoritative pronouncements that have been accepted in industry or in the accounting profession as to: (1) What are the underlying accounting postulates, concepts, or standards, or what are the accounting principles referred to in auditor's opinion; (2) what constitutes general acceptance either by whom or to what extent." (p. 1.)

of generally accepted accounting practice has been under-
lined and illustrated by Mr. Leonard Spacek, managing partner of Arthur Andersen and Company.   He prepared the
tabulations of "accounting magic" on pages 178–179.

Mr. Spacek stated:

The chart . . . was prepared to show how the use of alternative
generally accepted accounting principles might affect the earnings reported in a given case. Column 1 shows the profit results
of an assumed Company A that faces economic conditions realistically and so reports them in its earnings statement. Columns 2
to 7 show the effect of alternative accounting priciples that are
also generally acceptable. Column 8 shows Company B's earnings, with no change in operations except the application of alternative methods of accounting followed, yet Company B reports
net profits of over twice as much as Company A.

It is wholly possible to have the stock of these two comparable
companies selling at prices as much as 100% apart, merely because of the differences in accounting practices.

. . . the so-called "dollars" that we use as the common denominators in accounting reports are not common denominators at all
because of the wide variety of accounting practices applied in
arriving at the reported results.

Now I want to mention some of the misleading but accepted
beliefs in accounting. There are times when inventory costs
charged off will produce future profits, and thus are not losses;
when research and development costs shown as expenses (and
thus as losses) are in fact future profit items; when additions to
plant and equipment are made under the guise of expenses, and
thus show up as losses rather than as increased plant and profit
capacity. There are times when no provision is made for deferred taxes, thus in effect, permitting them to be reported as
current profits rather than as provisions for the liabilities they
really are. There are times when write-downs of the goods in
inventory are reported as cost of the goods that have been sold,
and when obsolete items inflate profit because the loss thereon
has not been recognized. Sometimes the obligations to build
plants are shown on the balance sheet, yet sometimes they are not.

It is noteworthy that Mr. Spacek's comments apply not only to small, family-owned audited or unaudited company statements, but also to the financial statements of large companies listed on the stock exchanges. In the Rowley Company, for example, Mr. Terry, the president, stated that differences in reconciling the application of accounting principles were *the* major reason for not acquiring a listed company with sales of over $50,000,000 annually. In this situation the Rowley Company evaluation officer was an executive vice president with long experience in the technology, operating procedures, and accounting practices of the industry in which the company to be acquired was functioning. He studied the company's balance sheet and profit-and-loss statement and then visited the facilities of the company under consideration for acquisition. In his judgment:

1. Over $500,000 worth of tooling for the manufacture of obsolete equipment was carried as an asset on the company's books. These tools had not been depreciated and expensed even though it was unlikely they would ever be used again.

2. The inventory included over $1,000,000 in spare parts for equipment which had been obsolete for many years. These parts had salvage, not market, value and yet they were on the company's balance sheet as current assets.

3. Several million dollars of research and development costs had been capitalized and not expensed as incurred. The Rowley Company never capitalized research and development expenses, and a substantial writedown in asset value of the company to be acquired would have been necessary after the acquisition in order to be consistent with Rowley Company policy.

4. Earnings of the selling company for the six-month period preceding negotiations had been overstated. The Rowley Company executive vice president found that during the six-month period production exceeded sales by a substantial amount.

At the end of the six-month period, overabsorbed overhead had been included in earnings, thus increasing earnings for an interim reporting period. If, in addition, sales for the entire year did not equal production (and the executive vice president believed that sales would continue to fall short), the profit for the year would be substantially less than indicated by the reported profit for the six-month period.

The accounting policies and practices of the Rowley Company were substantially more conservative than of the company to be acquired and the evaluating executive vice president concluded that adjusting the financial statements to make them consistent with Rowley Company policies would result in a purchase price of not more than 60% of the indicated price for the company. The disparity resulting from the application of alternative generally accepted accounting principles was so great that negotiations were discontinued immediately.

Mr. Spacek's tabulation and the experience of the Rowley Company point out the importance of determining in what manner the generally accepted accounting principles were applied. Other accounting and financial reporting areas where the same questions can be raised are:

1. The capitalization or expensing of patents, goodwill, or other intangibles.

2. The reasonableness of reserves for bad debts.

3. The capitalization or expensing of improvements to plant and equipment.

4. The inclusion or exclusion of the figures of foreign affiliated companies or subsidiaries in the consolidated balance sheet and profit-and-loss statement and the extent to which reserves for devaluation and exchange losses have been provided.

5. The establishment of reserves for renegotiation settlements.

6. Provisions for possible back tax liabilities.

7. Commitments for long-term leases, licensing agreements, royalty payments, consulting fees, and other fixed contractual liabilities.

8. Policies on accelerated depreciation and deferred tax provisions.

In some situations the company's policy and status in these areas are disclosed in footnotes or references on the balance sheet and profit-and-loss statement. Since footnotes are integral parts of the certified financial statements, notice is given of some of the areas to be questioned. But there seems to be no standard pattern. Explanatory notes to statements vary greatly due in part to the auditors' determination of materiality and consistency.

The problem of analyzing financial statements was summarized succinctly by one experienced acquiring company president who stated:

> We have studied companies for months before making an acquisition. We have made audits, sent in our controller, paid attention to every financial detail — or so we thought. In each case we found out something after we took over that we did not know before the deal was closed. Some of the differences between what we thought we were buying and what we did buy were major. We have learned. But this we believe sincerely — financial statements don't really answer any questions, they just allow you to ask them.

The analysis of financial statements presents problems in all situations, but the problems are especially acute when efforts are made to examine the statements of small and medium-sized companies whose unlisted stock is owned by a few people. Accounting practices in this type of business tend to vary within wider limits because of the absence of requirements to conform to SEC or stock exchange accounting regulations. Generally, closely held companies take every possible deduction to reduce taxes. They use the fastest depreciation allowances permitted by the Internal Revenue Service, and expense rather than capitalize costs, and take every step to minimize taxable profits. The closely held company has little or no pressure to report earnings to the public whereas the listed company is required to submit periodic reports to the SEC, to a stock exchange, and to stockholders.

One of the difficult problems in the analysis of the financial statements of a closely held company is to determine what adjustments should be made in the figures in order to determine a reasonable basis of value. Many examples of adjustments upward were found, both in balance sheet items and in the profit-and-loss results. Owners and managers of such companies are quick to point out early in the negotiations how completely understated are the figures shown in the financial reports. But it is the task of the potential acquirer to evaluate and reconcile the upward adjustments described as necessary by the prospective sellers.

The management of the Nick Company, for example, reviewed the balance sheet of the Ferranti Manufacturing Company shown below and after considerable discussions and appraisals concluded that the adjustments, as shown, were reasonable and appropriate.

In another situation adjustments to a company's profit-and-loss statement were made in an effort to forecast profits in future years. Here the buying company wanted to acquire the Sherman Company as a diversification move, and since the companies were in quite different industries, it was planned that the Sherman Company would be operated as an autonomous division. The acquiring company intended to purchase the Sherman Company for cash and had a policy requirement that any acquisition should provide a pretax return on investment of 20%. The owners of the Sherman Company were asking $1,000,000 for their enterprise, while

Ferranti Manufacturing Company

Balance Sheet

as of September 30, 1961

	Per Books (Unaudited)	Adjusted to Fair Market Value *
Assets		
Total Current Assets	$ 597,000	$ 757,000
Buildings (Net)	533,000	620,000
Equipment and Machinery (Net)	266,000	1,290,000
Land	20,000	400,000
Total Assets	$1,416,000	$3,067,000 †
Liabilities		
Total Current	$ 214,000	$ 214,000
Notes Payable	150,000	150,000
Net Worth	1,052,000	2,703,000
Total Liabilities	$1,416,000	$3,067,000

* Based on new appraisal reports.

† Includes $160,000 increase in inventory to reflect an estimate of full cost of work-in-process and finished goods. Ferranti values work-in-process and finished goods at raw material cost only.

Note: In this example the balance sheet was adjusted to reflect "fair market value," that is appraised current values. The phrase "fairly presents" in the auditors' certificate does not mean the same thing as "fair market value."

annual pretax earnings for the previous three years had been $150,000.

The head of the acquiring company's plans department analyzed the operations and statements of the Sherman Company and in a memorandum to his president stated in part:

1. *Depreciation:* Sherman writes off assets as fast as permitted. They have improved and added to some machine tools, expensing rather than capitalizing the im-

provements. We estimate that the cost of this has averaged about $30,000 a year. We will however write up the physical assets to their appraised value (our cost) from their present book value when we make the acquisition. The writeup of about $600,000 will add about $60,000 a year to depreciation expense. Adjustments to earnings: subtract $30,000.

2. *Executive expenses:* To understate taxable income, the management has charged personal expenses such as automobiles to the company. After the acquisition, these charges would not be made. Adjustment to earnings: add $10,000.

3. *Officers' salaries:* The salaries of $60,000, $60,000, and $40,000, plus deferred bonuses, drawn by three top managers are out of line with what our division officers receive. The selling managers will have to take a cut in salaries but this should be acceptable to them since our dividend will take up part of the salary slack. Adjustment to earnings: add $50,000.

4. *Pension plan:* Sherman increases or decreases the pension charge to income as profits rise or fall. We will switch to a full accrual current service costs basis. The net effect of the change in accounting practice on earnings is impossible to determine now, but it should be minor. No adjustment.

5. *R & D Expenses:* All charges for Sherman's R and D have been expensed, again to keep down taxable earnings. These costs have increased in the past few years. We would capitalize some of these basic research costs. Adjustment to earnings: add $20,000.

The net adjustment to profits from changes in accounting practice would be an addition of $50,000 ($80,000–$30,000) before tax. We feel that this adjustment should be added to the past average $150,000 to bring the expected base earnings to something on the order of $200,000. We should further adjust this figure for any operating benefits we expect to bring to Sherman after the acquisition and use this figure as the basis for determining value.

During recent years some financial analysts, aware of the problems of interpreting balance sheets and profit-and-loss statements, have used the financial data to compute the cash or fund flow which a prospective acquisition has or may have. A cash flow analysis adjusts reported earnings for major elements of cost such as depreciation and expensed or deferred research and development costs, thus permitting comparisons between companies in an industry where one company's earnings can be distorted by heavy accelerated expense charges. Also, the cash flow analysis is used to calculate how quickly an acquiring company can recover its proposed investment.

OTHER ADJUSTMENTS NECESSARY TO FORECAST EARNINGS

A company's basic accounting and financial reports, after being adjusted, do provide a basis for judgment as to value. But in addition it is necessary to take into account the effects of changes in the acquired company's operations. Many times these changes are considered and anticipated before agreement is reached, but in other cases the impact of change, with attendant costs in time and money, is neglected in the haste to complete an acquisition agreement.

Careful analysis of a company's status may disclose opportunities for remedial action which will make the enterprise much more profitable. Strengths of the buying company (e.g., an effective distribution system) applied to the selling company can add to earnings. In the Mitten Company, for example, the evaluation of a small company under consideration for acquisition disclosed several areas which could be improved. The Mitten Company president negotiated the purchase of the company for $540,000, about nine times the average earnings in the three years prior to the transaction. After the purchase, steps were taken immediately to make profit increasing changes — the operations of the acquired company were moved to the acquirer's plant, the products of the acquired company were added to the Mitten product line and sales organization and the previous use of manufacturers' agents was discontinued. The owner-manager of the acquired company retired, thus relieving the administration cost of a substantial salary expense. These three changes, accomplished within five months of the acquisition, resulted not only in higher sales in the first year following the purchase, but also in an increase in the acquired company's after-tax earnings from $62,000 to $175,000.

In this instance, and in many others, acquirers recognized opportunities for savings and for expanding the selling company's sales to make it more profitable. But in other cases additional costs were not considered, the time necessary to effect changes was underestimated, and the loose talk during acquisition discussions disguised the business facts of life with which the acquirer had to live after the purchase. What appear to be opportunities for changes and increased profits turn out to be illusory. There is more to the problem than is apparent during the first exposures. Generally, acquirers tend to overestimate rather than underestimate the earnings to be derived from an acquisition. This, again, is part of the problem of maintaining a coldly objective, tough-minded, evaluation approach while at the same time establishing and maintaining an atmosphere of "you are dealing with your kind of people."

Some of the significant areas of cost which are often overlooked are as follows:

1. Employee benefit plans. The myriad of benefit plans found in business today and their varying real costs require considerable examination before making an acquisition commitment. Small and medium-sized enterprises, in particular, seem to have elements in their employee benefit plans which a larger acquirer often does not include. The problems of making changes in benefit plans after acquisition are discussed in Chapter IX, but the consideration of the necessity

for such changes and their impact on costs and earnings frequently are overlooked during an evaluation.

A production worker in the acquired company, for example, will become unhappy when he learns that his counterpart in the acquirer gets two more weeks' vacation and has better sickness, accident, and life insurance arrangements. He will forget that his benefits include a pension and a year-end cash bonus. In forecasting earnings in a prospective acquisition, it is essential to plan what adjustments are to be made in the acquired company, and the timing of these adjustments. These are costs and represent important consideration in any projection of earnings with a new owner. Neglecting to take this type of expense into account was a common omission — in one situation the acquired company's earnings in the first year were more than $150,000 below estimates because the costs of additional fringe benefits were not included in the forecast.

2. Savings through the termination of personnel. During the evaluation period several opportunities to perform business functions more economically and with fewer people by centralizing the function at headquarters, for example, appear to be present to the evaluating management. These may include the centralization of the accounting and book-keeping departments, legal staffs, general and administrative personnel, research and development, product development, and so on. These are, of course, important cost reduction areas to consider; but here again, profit forecasts based on broad conclusions as to when and how to achieve these economies can be misleading and costly. The centralization of business functions is not always more efficient and in some cases, while cost reductions can be accomplished by centralizing the jobs to be done, service to customers is impaired. What appears to be logical and profitable may, in fact, turn out to be illogical and expensive in terms of sales and profits. The experience of many companies in reorganizing these

departments and then reverting to the former setup in order to improve service to customers suggests that the requirements of each situation be considered carefully before making changes in an effort to reduce costs.

Also the savings to be made through the elimination of what are regarded initially as surplus personnel are reduced when specific decisions must be made as to which men or women are to be taken off the payroll. The head of the acquired company will be reluctant to terminate key employees of long tenure and will make every effort to find alternative and suitable positions for them.

3. Unanticipated product development costs. Acquirers sometimes assume that a new product or process of the selling company is ready to market, only to find out that additional engineering, tooling, or promotional expenditures are necessary before it can be introduced. In an extreme case of misforecasting profits for an acquired company, one metal fabricating company bought an essentially one-man engineering company for $200,000, invested another $100,000, and got none of its investment back. The purchase price represented the engineering and development work which had taken the product concept from an idea to a prototype. The acquiring company officers discovered after the purchase that the product had to be redesigned before it could be produced and sold. The company then spent an additional $100,000 on reworking expenses, but after one year had to drop the product because sales volume never reached a profitable level.

4. Costs of integrating product line and sales organizations. Forecasts of postacquisition earnings frequently are based on the assumption that the acquired company's products can be added easily to the acquirer's present product line. Careless and optimistic management thinking can oversimplify the problems involved in adding related but new articles. Existing customers of the acquirer may indeed buy the products of the acquired company, but the purchasing agents and the

basis for procurement may be different.   Also, time and money are required to train salesmen in the marketing of the new product.   But most important is the problem of motivating the sales organization to accept the addition to its product line, especially if it competes with an existing product.   For example, a large food processor acquired a smaller food specialty company and the two lines overlapped on several cocktail snacks.   A new product sales indoctrination program was carried on but the acquiring company's salesmen found themselves trying to sell to grocers the acquired company's brand whose reputation they had spent years in tearing down. The time and expense necessary to integrate product lines and sales organizations represent costs which are frequently underestimated or overlooked.

5. The costs of the acquiring company's overhead.   The acquiring company's overhead — headquarters expense or "country club dues" as it is known in some organizations — is a real cost of doing business.   Typically, these expenses are allocated to operating divisions and subsidiaries on some basis which seems reasonable to the headquarters' controller or vice president of finance.   In the evaluation of companies for possible acquisition, the necessity and inevitability of overhead charges are often overlooked.   Companies in some industries are able to earn a reasonable profit as small and medium-sized independent enterprises, but they cannot absorb the additional overhead charges of a multidivision acquirer and maintain their profit standards.   In the case of one diversified drug company, this problem resulted in "disacquisition" after a period of years.   Two acquired subsidiaries, profitable before their purchase, made chronically meager profits after overhead allocations.   Executives of the parent company finally decided to sell the two subsidiaries and to reinvest cash proceeds from their sale in companies holding promise of a higher return on investments after overhead allocation.

The management of another company recognized that the potential acquisitions under consideration did not have the earning capacity to absorb any allocation of headquarters overhead and considered a proposal to organize a separate subsidiary which would have the benefit of headquarters staff services but would not be charged with the costs!

A significant, and less measurable, expense which is part of every acquisition is the cost in executive time devoted to integrating the acquired organization with the acquirer. Working out new relationships, deciding on titles and positions, establishing intercompany controls, and creating a rapport between the personnel of the two organizations takes time and energy. Determining the costs of such efforts is difficult, but the expenses are real and are frequently greater than anticipated. Other often forgotten costs are the legal, auditing, appraisal, and in some cases, registration expenses.

SOME OTHER FINANCIAL EVALUATION PROBLEMS

"Dressing Up a Company for Sale"

Some owner-managers looking forward to selling their enterprises in the next two or three years use a number of accounting and financial devices to make the operation appear more valuable without adding substance to its worth. They recognize, for example, that evaluators frequently look at the last three to five years of earnings. These profit figures may be averaged to give some assurance of the same kind of earnings in the future and then multiplied by a factor to establish an indication of value. And a company with a rising trend of earnings is likely to get a higher earnings multiplier than one with stable earnings year after year.

One executive, who had participated in the purchase of over 20 companies, said that if he owned a company and had three years to prepare it for sale, he would create a rising earnings rate and then negotiate on the grounds that "We are on the threshold of even higher earnings. It would be unfair to average our profits because future earnings will be even higher. If," he continued, "a company can average $200,000 profits annually over a period of three years, appropriate policy and operating decisions can be made to result in an increasing earnings trend from $100,000 to $200,000 and to $300,000 profits each year. This trend of earnings is much more impressive to a prospective buyer than a steady $200,000 per year even though the total profits for three years are the same, $600,000. In the first year more than a normal amount of funds are spent in research, long-term promotions, and plant and machine maintenance to keep the reported profits down. Very conservative accounting practices in expensing charges which could be capitalized, for example, will help achieve the lower profit goal of $100,000. In the following year the company is operated in its historical manner with less expensing so that profits of $200,000 are reported for that period. In the third year, just prior to a possible sale, the accounting practices indicated above are reversed and every effort is made to reduce costs so as to produce a $300,000 earnings rate."

Negotiations to establish a value then proceed on the capitalization of a $300,000 earnings rate rather than an average of $200,000. And the multiplier factor may be 15 or more times earnings, rather than 10 or 12, because of the obvious extrapolation of the earnings curve to $400,000 and $500,000 in each of the succeeding years. Careful examination of the accounting methods may disclose the basis of the earnings trend, but some overeager acquisition evaluators neglect to take the time and effort necessary to get behind the reported figures.

The executive who described the earnings trend evaluation problem said that three years are needed to "create an earnings curve." But much can be accomplished in only a few months to make earnings appear to be higher, thus raising difficult financial problems for the evaluator. In one case, to illustrate, the president and major stockholder of a closely held company with its stock traded over-the-counter called his top executives into his office immediately after a telephone conversation with a potential acquirer. At the meeting the president reported that a possible purchaser had called and that in the next several months while negotiations were going on, "I want you to take every action to make our earnings look good." The advertising and sales promotion expenditures were reduced from a $900,000 annual rate to $150,000, and sales volume was increased by special incentives to salesmen which could not be sustained over a longer period. Other action was taken to reduce costs, and one executive estimated that the continued efforts to enhance profits added about $600,000 to after-tax earnings for the current year which proved to be the basis for the determination of the company's value. He added that the final purchase price was at least $2,000,000 more than would have been indicated through the continuation of its traditional business policies and practices.

In another situation, an owner-manager, anticipating a sale of his enterprise, used a special sales promotion appeal to increase sales and apparent profits. The company's products were proprietary and during a two-month period, salesmen were urged to stock customer shelves with a new item and to assure them that a $800,000 advertising and promotion campaign would commence when the distribution channels were filled. After these were saturated and before the commitment of $800,000 for advertising was made, the enterprise was sold. The representation to company customers that a national campaign would be used to move the new products was not mentioned during the negotiations, but the need for such expenses became clear very quickly after the acquisition. The acquiring company paid far more than a fair price and in addition felt obliged to fulfill the costly advertising commitment.

These two abbreviated examples suggest some of the financial evaluation problems facing acquirers when there have been conscious efforts by the seller to deceive the buyer, to give an impression of greater worth than the usual operations of the company warranted. But even when there is no intent by the seller to deceive, reliance on an increasing earnings trend can be misleading.

The Kramer Drug Company, for example, acquired the White Company for $14,000,000 of Kramer stock. The Kramer company is a well-known manufacturer and distributor of specialty items and its president learned that the White Company owners might be willing to sell. The White Company sales were primarily of a household product which it developed, manufactured, and sold through drugstores with great success. Negotiations were initiated and the White Company financial statements showed steady sales and profit growth for a number of years with a very sharp increase in the year prior to the acquisition discussions. It appeared to the Kramer executives that the improvement in sales and earnings was the result of more effective selling and that these rates could be sustained or increased.

Only after the acquisition did it become evident that a major reason for the higher sales and earnings in the prior year was the White Company's new package which contained six units instead of the two in the former package. As a result of buying the new and larger package, housewives had three times their normal inventories on their shelves when Kramer took over. Sales in the first few months after the acquisition lagged far behind those of the prior year as housewives used up what they had on hand before buying more. Profits of the White division declined sharply. After a year of stepped-up promotion expense and lower sales and profits, the Kramer company management was able to get the White division back on its earlier indicated growth curve. There was no evidence to indicate that the former owners of the White Company introduced the larger package in order to deceive the buyer and to secure a higher price for the company. Financial information was completely available on the White Company operations, but the evaluating executives of the Kramer company neglected to ask the appropriate questions. They forgot the adage, "Financial statements do not answer questions, they just allow you to ask them."

Sales and Order Backlogs

In some industries a critical factor to consider in trying to determine company value is the dollar size of the backlog of orders. This element is especially significant in companies whose business is largely on government research, development, and fixed-price production contracts, but it is important in other types of business as well.

Companies whose primary market is the federal government generally report their current backlog and compare this figure with that of the previous period. A larger backlog is presumed by many to indicate that there is an increasing acceptance of the company's products and services by the government agencies. But in making a financial evaluation of the quality of the backlog, it is most important to examine carefully each contract and to establish the possibility of realizing profits on these contracts at the same rate as that disclosed by historical experience. This is difficult. Research and development contracts, even on a cost-plus-a-fixed-fee basis, may be partially fulfilled and estimating costs necessary to complete these contracts can be difficult, even by the technical personnel assigned to the project. And backlog totals which include fixed-price manufacturing contracts are subject to the same sort of questioning. Many instances of deceptive and misleading backlog figures suggest the importance of careful evaluation prior to acquisition. To be sure, suitable warranties as to run out costs, costs to complete, and profit rates on manufacturing contracts can be included in the agreement to buy. But, here again, reluctance by the buyer to rescind a published report of acquisition and the seemingly interminable discussions and negotiations to secure a purchase price adjustment lead many managements to regret not having taken a more careful look at the real quality of the backlog figures.

High backlog totals can prove to be dangerous in nongovernment industries as well. A large producer of a basic raw material, for example, acquired several intermediate manufacturers in a move to protect the production level of profits for the parent company by performing the next step in production. To appraise the intermediate manufacturers, a formula was constructed which gave greater weight to volume and backlog than to profit. One prospective acquisition showed a sharp increase in sales for the year and a half prior to negotiations. The vice president of the acquirer took a close look at the margins on the new orders and found that some of this new business was not even making a contribution to overhead, much less a profit, and that the company was shipping intermediate products into ordinarily uneconomic marketing areas. Puzzled by this, he asked the company controller if the cost and estimating procedures were satisfactory and the reply was, "Our cost and estimating methods are fine. Salesmen know how to use them. But our boss has told us for a year and a half to get volume and not to pay much attention to price." Recognition that the high volume and backlog represented "dressing the company up for sale" resulted in a lower, more realistic purchase price. Quick changes, however, were made in the application and use of cost and estimating procedures.

There are many other financial evaluation problem areas to investigate: an apparent high return on net worth resulting in part from the liberal use of debt, a good working capital position attained by substantial bank term loans only part of which is included in current liabilities, a highly liquid financial position effected by leasing rather than purchasing equipment, and so on. The need for asking discerning questions suggested by an analysis of financial statements is apparent. Many will think that the few problem areas we have presented and illustrated are limited to the unsophisticated and the amateurs. But this is not the case. The case situations described in this section were provided by experienced executives of companies with several years' exposure to the management problems of acquisitions. Their lessons are reported here to assist others embarking on a growth through acquisition program.

Pre-acquisition Audits

In efforts to find the bases for the determination of comparable values, some acquiring managements insist upon an audit of the potential acquisition before a contract to purchase is signed. Such an audit enables the acquirer's public accountants to ascertain the manner in which generally accepted accounting principles are applied, the significance of disclosed and undisclosed financial adjustments, and the extent to which the reported balance sheets and profit-and-loss statements must be written up or down to make them compatible with the acquirer's methods of accounting.

Theoretically, an audit prior to acquisition appears to be desirable in all cases. But practically, an audit is provided for usually as one of the warranties of the contract and serves as the basis for past acquisition changes in the purchase price. Full audits require considerable time and with a sellers' market, the managers and owners of companies to be sold are reluctant to delay the consummation of an agreement in order that such an audit can be made. They point out that a buyer's insistence on an audit before an agreement to purchase is signed implies that the buyers do not trust the sellers.

Also the presence of auditors who are strangers to the organization is disruptive to the company's personnel. If the sale does not go through, doubts are raised in employees' minds as to "what is wrong." Any attempts to maintain the secrecy of negotiations to acquire are quickly dissipated when unknown auditors begin working on the books. Generally, therefore, audits of the acquired company's books are provided for in the agreement to purchase and are usually undertaken very soon after the acquisition is completed legally.

An illustration of the problems which can arise when an audit is made after the acquisition was found in the Randall Control Corporation's purchase of the Tempo Scientific Company. We found many similar situations but the Randall Control Corporation is typical.

Early in 1959 Randall became interested in acquiring Tempo, a research-based privately owned company with annual sales of about $10,000,000. Tempo had six scattered divisions all working on development and production of highly technical products related to each other and also to Randall's product line. After studying Dun and Bradstreet reports and going over the meager volume of published information about Tempo, Randall's executives met with the president and principal owner of Tempo. They learned from him that Tempo's sales had risen from $3,500,000 in 1952 to over $10,000,000 in fiscal 1958 and that the company had been profitable each year except 1954. The company sold to about 50 major accounts, including the top companies that could use its products. Randall executives were impressed by the president and his record. They were given financial statements for several fiscal years prior to the investigation, prepared by an independent accounting firm, and an interim nine-month unaudited income statement and balance sheet prepared by company accountants which showed nine-month sales of just over $8,000,000, after-tax profit of $270,000, and net worth of over $1,300,000. It was recognized that interim statements are particularly suspect because of the absence of year-end adjustments. Nevertheless, the Randall executives decided that Tempo, because of its complementary products, its record of sales and profit growth, and its projected earnings, should be acquired if mutually attractive terms could be arranged. They sensed that the company's president was in a selling mood and that because Tempo had grown rapidly he needed some of the managerial help that Randall could provide. Because of the owner's mood and the success of his company, they expected some competition from other acquirers and decided to make an offer as soon as possible.

What could be gained by an audit? The Randall executives had been given audited statements for prior years and they had no reason to doubt the competence or honesty of Tempo's president from the discussions they had. They ran a risk of having another buyer make an acceptable offer to him while the audit and its results were being conducted and studied. They expected to pay well over book value for Tempo so that the net worth established by the audit would have little if any influence on price. They also feared that the suggestion of an audit might be interpreted by Tempo's president as evidence of lack of trust; there was the danger that he might think, "If Randall is suspicious now, what is it going to be like after the acquisition?"

Randall executives decided to make a purchase proposal without the benefit of a preacquisition audit. The offer was accepted by Tempo's president and the agreement was signed. It was not until several months after the closing that Randall's accountants conducted an audit of Tempo.

The audit revealed many abnormal accounting and operating procedures. The Randall company's auditor objected to including in the inventory obsolete parts which were believed to be overvalued. Methods of valuing inventory had been left to the discretion of each plant accountant in Tempo's six plants, and among other results of this practice, some of the inventory included general and administrative expenses and some did not. Each plant accountant adjusted burden rates as he saw fit. Overvalued inventory obscured losses over several accounting periods. The cost system was inadequate and, as a result estimates were not realistic. Fixed-fee contracts which appeared profitable were actually taken on at a loss because of inadequate price estimating methods.

These and other procedures, or lack of them, resulted in misstatements which, according to Randall's accountants, overstated Tempo's net worth by at least $700,000. The accountants estimated that Tempo *lost* $277,000 in fiscal 1959 while the company's president had claimed a *profit* in the first nine months of $270,000. Randall's lawyers drafted a complaint charging breach of contract, negligent statements, fraud, and breach of the indemnity agreement. The issues were settled out of court a year and a half later when Tempo's president and his fellow shareowners agreed to pay Randall a sum of cash and canceled part of the original agreement. Several key executives, plus lawyers and accountants, spent months of their time after the acquisition investigating the extent of the difference between what Randall thought it paid for and what it really paid for. Not only was the time of many people expensive to Randall, but also the rancor, doubts, and suspicions aroused by the investigation and settlement had a harmful effect on integrating the two companies.

When a Randall officer was asked if he would purchase another company without a preacquisition audit he replied:

> Yes. We'd take the same risk again; we have to, to get the companies we want. You can bet, though, that we learned from this experience. In the first place we never go though with a deal unless we get a guarantee from the sellers of the statements we base our offer on — we put this guarantee into the purchase agreement. Secondly, we have our auditors move in as soon after the closing as possible.

Experienced acquirers observed that an audit of a company's books by professional and competent accountants is not enough. Unless a representative of the acquiring management familiar with the industry of the potential acquisition spends time checking and validating the figures verified by the auditors, surprises are likely to appear. The president of one company, for example, stated:

> You can't rely on an audit to tell you what the value of finished goods inventory is. You have to know the industry, industry trends, fashions, what have you. Take a product where style is important, a woman's dress for example. An accountant is able to tell you that the costs of making a purple dress are properly carried on the books and that the appropriate expenses totaling $10.34 ended up in finished goods inventory. But he doesn't tell you that the purple dress is yesterday's news and not worth $2.00 now. No matter what it cost to make, no one wants this kind of a purple dress this year except perhaps some woman in the sticks who is still reading last year's catalogue.

Determination of Price

The careful evaluation of the nonfinancial considerations of a potential acquisition as indicated in Chapter VII and an analysis of the company's financial statements, with required adjustments, provide the basis for negotiations as to the value to be placed on the assets or stock of the company to be acquired. We noted earlier that each company situation is truly unique and that the relative negotiation strengths of the buyer and seller vary greatly.[1] Also, it should be noted

[1] "It must be remembered . . . that in mergers and in some other valuation situations, the final determination of value is a part of a bargaining process and that a compromise value is therefore likely to result. In such cases it would be largely a matter of coincidence if the agreed-on value corresponded exactly to that indicated by any of the objective approaches. This does not mean that they are therefore of no value in practical situations for they will normally play a significant role in setting rational limits within which the negotiated value will fall. It is not surprising to find that each party to the

again that evaluation of financial and nonfinancial factors may proceed concomitantly with negotiations, but we have separated the process into elementary parts for ease of discussion.

Negotiations between the managements of the buyer and the seller generally extend over weeks and sometimes months. In one unusual case, the president of an acquiring company went into the offices of a potential acquisition in the morning, studied the financial statements quickly, walked through the offices and the adjacent manufacturing facility, made an offer to buy the company for over $1,000,000 in cash, reduced the offer to a contract to buy in the late afternoon, and both parties signed the agreement before the day was over. In another situation reasonably active negotiations continued over a period of two years before agreement was reached by the owners of the buyer and the seller.

When the stock of a company to be valued for acquisition is listed, widely held and traded actively on an exchange or over-the-counter, the minimum total price for such an enterprise is generally greater than the total value determined in the market place. The primary task of the acquirer, then, in these situations is to determine through careful evaluation whether the market values are real and what, if any, premium must be paid to persuade the directors and stockholders to exchange their company's securities for the cash or stock of the acquirer. To stockholders the quoted price on the market constitutes value and any offer less than what is believed to be value usually will be rejected.

In the Rowley Company, cited earlier,[2] the executives of the acquirer concluded that for them the market price of the

---

negotiation will champion the method of valuation which is most favorable to its interests." Pearson Hunt, Charles M. Williams, Gordon Donaldson: *Basic Business Finance: Text and Cases.* Revised Edition, Homewood, Richard D. Irwin, Inc., 1961. Chapter 26, pp. 556, 557.

[2] Chapter VIII, page 182.

stock of the potential acquisition was higher than appropriate because of the different application of generally accepted accounting principles. In other situations, the market price was deemed too high because of lags in technological achievement, the unrecognized loss of position because of expiring patents, largely responsible for the company's success to date, and market delays in accepting the impact on profits of competition from abroad. The value established by the market does not necessarily equal the real values of the enterprise. In many cases the market overvalues the company and in a few, undervalues it, and it is the task of the acquirer to discover which is the case.

If it is concluded that the market value is reasonable, premiums over that amount are the results of negotiation. In the Wilder Company, for example, the president, Mr. Henry, approached the chief executive officer of the Scott Company, Mr. Davies, and after general discussion about the benefits Scott would gain by selling out to the Wilder Company, Mr. Henry asked what price would be interesting to Mr. Davies. He replied facetiously that the present over-the-counter market price of his company's stock was about $20 a share and any offer at least twice this would be considered. Two weeks later Mr. Davies received a letter from Mr. Henry offering to exchange Wilder Company common stock selling on one of the exchanges at $38 per share for Scott Company common stock on a share-for-share basis. Because the exchange rate seemed so favorable for Scott Company stockholders, Mr. Davies decided that it was mandatory for him to pass the offer on to his directors who approved seeking stockholder approval for the exchange. This was done and the exchange was made. The Wilder Company acquired the Scott Company for a market premium of 90%.

An interesting element in this situation is that Mr. Davies, the president of the Scott Company, was opposed to the sale because he believed that the Scott Company sales and profits would increase sharply in the next three years and these financial results would be reflected in a much higher market price for the company's stock. He decided, reluctantly, however, that the task of persuading his directors and stockholders to turn down an immediate apparent premium price of 90% was virtually impossible and endorsed the proposal to accept the offer of the Wilder Company. Three years after the acquisition, the earnings of the Scott Company, operating as an autonomous division of the Wilder Company, had quadrupled from $2 per share to what would have been $8 a share if the decision had not been made to sell. And if the same market price earnings ratio of 10 prevailed at the end of the three years, a not unlikely possibility, the Scott Company stock would have sold at $80 a share versus the $20 a share when the company was sold. The Wilder Company stock continued to sell for about $38 per share, even with the increased earnings of the Scott division.

The determination of the value or the price to be paid for a company with listed or actively traded over-the-counter securities is difficult. But the minimum acceptable price is generally established by the market value. In the case of closely held companies with no market value set for its stock, the problems of determining value and price are even more difficult. And in addition to the evaluation problems resulting from the different application of generally accepted accounting principles, there are all the problems of making adjustments in the balance sheets and profit-and-loss statements resulting from many years of efforts to expense all possible costs in order to reduce taxes.

For unlisted, closely held companies there is no single standard for the determination of value. In October 1961 the owner of a medium-sized and profitable New York company asked a consultant for a formula to apply to his wholly owned company. "Surely," he said, "there must be some scientific basis for putting a price on my company." When it was suggested that no single method would be appropriate and that capitalized earnings, net worth, and asset valuation approaches could all be used as preliminary determinants, he seemed shocked that financial experts could not tell him exactly what his company was worth.

Many owners of unlisted companies have attempted to place a value on their enterprises by negotiating with prospective acquirers for the purpose of getting some kind of a financial offer. The owners have no intention of selling to the possible acquirer, but as one stated, "I will at least have one bench mark when I start negotiations with the management of a company I really want to sell to." Other owners, seeking an outside and objective approach to value, have discussed the possibility of a public offering of their stock with underwriters. Some underwriters, especially those who have worked with small and medium-sized companies before, can indicate what the market might be willing to pay for a previously unlisted stock. If the underwriters' estimate of a market price is sufficiently high, the figure is used by the owner as a negotiating gambit. "The Wall Street people tell me our stock could be sold at $30 a share. And I could still keep control. Control of the whole enterprise is certainly more valuable than a minority interest and therefore a price of $45 a share seems reasonable." The negotiating position of the acquiring company management is weakened further by the interest of the underwriter who will be urging the owners to have a public offering as an alternative to selling the entire company.

Another method of determining value of an unlisted company is the market value of a comparable company. A determination of other price earnings ratios and application to the stock of an unlisted company does provide a bench mark of value.

All the usual financial yardsticks of corporate values of unlisted companies are used in negotiations by buyers and sellers, each stressing the approach or approaches which benefits their positions most. The ultimate purchase price or value of such enterprises then is determined largely by the skill and persuasion of negotiations. In one case the single owner of a company arrived at a cash price for his enterprise by stating and finally getting enough cash to pay his taxes on the gain and have $1,000,000 remaining. His goal was to be a "millionaire."

The relative bargaining positions of the buyer and seller are different in each situation, and the skills with which negotiations are conducted vary enormously among the managements of the acquirers and the acquired. The effect of the buyers' needs, the personalities and motives of the sellers, and the effect of the other relative bargaining positions on the price and eventual consummation of a transaction is illustrated by the acquisition of the Northwest Lumber Company by the Western Paper Company.

The Northwest Lumber Company owned a large timber property in the Pacific Northwest. It had been in business for 65 years, and as a result of continuing growth in value of land and forest products, it had prospered. The company was closely held by the descendants of the two original founders, and had provided a comfortable income for them. Accumulation of additional timber land and growth of the forest had built up a book value of over $20,000,000 by the early 1950's.

The grandson of one of the founders of Northwest Lumber owned one-third of the stock; the remainder was scattered among 20 descendants of the other founder. The president lived in the town where Northwest was located, while the other stockholders were widely scattered over the United States. Although Northwest Lumber was producing steady dividends, earnings had not grown, and the market for lumber was declining. The value of the timber land had increased faster than earnings from the lumber business because of the increased demand for timber land by paper companies.

The president of Northwest was content with the situation because of the prestige of his position in the community and the fact that his ownership of one-third of the company produced a substantial income for him. However, many of the other stockholders were uneasy, because they were receiving small return on what seemed to be the true value of their investment. In addition, they were getting a smaller voice in the policies of the company as their two-thirds' portion of the company passed by succession into smaller blocks held by a rapidly growing number of children and grandchildren.

In addition, since there was no market for Northwest Lumber Company stock, several major stockholders had no way to realize the cash value of their investment for estate or other purposes. Some of the directors realized that this ownership problem would not solve itself with time and that the company was too small and did not have the necessary depth to handle the required substantial investment of going into the paper business itself.

Meanwhile the Western Paper Company realized that it was faced with a shortage of raw material for its recently constructed pulp mill. The Northwest Lumber Company tract of timber was the only stand located near the Western Paper Company mill. The Western Paper management approached Northwest to discuss a possible acquisition and indicated willingness to pay the going market prices for both land and timber, plus fair values for the saw mill and other assets. Based on these values, Western Paper offered to acquire the company by means of a tax-free exchange of stock or assets. At the exchange ratio offered, Western Paper dividends would amount to three times the rate presently paid by Northwest Lumber. At the same time the Western Paper Company stock would provide a marketable value to the Northwest stockholders since it was a widely-held company listed on a major stock exchange. In addition, it would provide a suitable "blue chip" investment for the other stockholders who could continue to hold it as an investment.

A special meeting of the Northwest Lumber Company stockholders was called to vote on the offer. The directors who were in favor of the sale held proxies for exactly two-thirds of the outstanding stock which was the amount required for statutory approval of such a sale of assets.

The night before the stockholders' meeting, it was learned that one of the stockholders had been approached by the president of another paper company, Green Paper Corp., which was a closely-held, multimillion dollar company. Green Paper had a mill about 50 miles away from Western's and Green was also dependent to some extent on timber reserves and pulp produced in the same local area. The president of Green Paper Corp. had induced the stockholder to sell her stock to him for cash, at a price 25% higher than the market value represented by the Western exchange offer. It was apparent to the directors who wished to sell to Western Paper that the cash purchase of the shares critical to approval of the merger had been engineered by the president of Northwest in order to block the sale he opposed. The transfer of shares left the Northwest directors with less than the two-thirds' vote needed for approval of the merger.

This development seemed unfavorable for both the Western Paper Company and the stockholders of Northwest Lumber who wanted to sell. There was a risk that Green Paper would purchase some additional stock and the company was strong enough financially to do so. Green Paper would thus be able to block any future sale of Northwest.

The directors of Northwest who favored the sale met secretly with representatives of Western Paper. Since Western officers were still eager to acquire the property, they offered to buy stock of Northwest Lumber for cash, provided they could purchase majority control, 51%, of the outstanding shares. They offered a price that was nominally higher than the cash terms that Green Paper's president had paid. This price resulted in slightly more after taxes to Northwest shareowners than the market value of Western Paper stock originally offered. An invitation for tenders was prepared by Western Paper in great haste and secrecy, lest the Green Paper Corporation learn of the plan and purchase the additional shares required to break control. With the cooperation of the major stockholders who favored selling to Western, the required number of shares were speedily assembled. Most of them were deposited before the invitation for tenders even had been put in the mail. Faced with the fact that Western Paper would control Northwest, the reluctant president chose to sell his stock also, and the acquisition was effected.

The final purchase price reflected both the needs of the acquirer and the strong bargaining position of the sellers. Because Western needed to make the acquisition to protect its mill investment and because of the reluctance of Northwest's president to sell, the purchase price seemed high in relation to "normal" financial yardsticks of capitalized earnings, book value, or even underlying asset value. In this instance, the purchase price represented about 50 times Northwest's average earnings for the five years prior to the acquisition, about 7.7 times book value, and over 125% of appraised market value of Northwest's assets.

In some acquiring companies, efforts are made to forecast earnings of the potential company to be acquired, decide on a minimum return on investment, and thereby establish a maximum price for the company under consideration. In 1959 Wilson Industries, for example, used this method in valuing the Crawford Products Company.

In 1959, Wilson Industries, a manufacturer of parts sold to the automobile industry, netted only $81,000 after taxes on sales of over $4,800,000. Chronically low profit margins were the result for the most part of two factors: First, the company's principal plant was located in an area where labor costs were extremely high in relation to most other industrial areas. Second, the plant was an old two-story building which caused many material-handling problems. The company management had considered building a new plant in an area where labor costs were lower, but in appraising each possibility had come to the conclusion that the expected return did not warrant the investment. The Wilson management then turned to the possibility of acquiring a company with a complementary product line.

They approached the owners of Crawford Products, another supplier to the automobile industry. Crawford had moved operations to a new plant built in 1957 in a location where labor costs were substantially less than Wilson's. The plant was operating on a one-shift basis, well below its capacity, when the Wilson management began discussions with the Crawford family. Wilson's management recognized that they could move their entire production volume into Crawford's plant and on a three-shift basis still have unused capacity after selling the old plant. Combining the Wilson and Crawford operations under one roof would increase profit margins for both activities.

Based primarily on the past earnings of Crawford which was privately owned, Wilson executives planned to pay Crawford's owners between $1,500,000 and $2,000,000. Their first offer was rejected because Crawford's owners also recognized the savings that would come from the acquisition and demanded a price closer to book value of $2,800,000.

To determine the maximum Wilson should pay, the vice president of the Wilson division which would take over Crawford, plus a member of the company's acquisition staff, began the painstaking job of determining the expected future profits from the combination. They estimated future sales of the combined entity, anticipated margins, moving expenses, equipment additions, and hiring and start-up costs.

After making these forecasts, a memorandum was sent to Wilson's president which stated in part:

> . . . the decision of how far we would want to go on price is a matter of establishing a minimum return that would be satisfactory to Wilson. This would involve an appraisal of the risks involved in this kind of venture and also an appraisal of the reliability of the figures leading to the percentage return figure. . . .
>
> I would think that Wilson would want a rock bottom minimum of 12% return on this kind of an investment, if the estimates were considered reliable. This would point to a top price of $3,608,000.
>
> If it was felt that there were enough question marks in the forecast of added savings and income, we might deduct up to $100,000 from the income forecast of $500,000, leaving $400,000 for the added annual income from this investment. On this conservative basis, a price of $2,775,000 would provide the 12% return on investment. If we accept the added income figure of $500,000 but want a 14% return on added investment, a price of $3,013,000 is tops.
>
> * * * * * * *
>
> From the above analysis, I would think that an upper limit of $3,600,000 should be placed on any price consideration. Further, I would not think it unreasonable if Wilson were to require a somewhat higher return than 12% and/or reduce the estimated savings somewhat to be on the conservative side. These would be questions of management judgment. Such treatment would probably result in some figure of $3,000,000 plus. If paid in stock, there will be no dilution in Wilson's earnings per share.
>
> After establishing an upper price, it then becomes a question of how much under this price you can go in negotiation so as to make an added return for Wilson beyond the established minimum.

The staff analyst in this instance arrived at an upper limit using the discounted earnings approach. First he worked out an estimate of after-tax profit for the life of the company and the price $3,608,000 is the present value of the stream of estimated future income discounted at a rate of 12%, after adjustments for the required investment other than price.

Another approach in determining the value of a possible acquisition to the acquirer is to estimate the cost of starting a similar situation internally and from scratch. In the Western Corporation, for example, the vice president for plans prepared a memorandum for his chief operating executive outlining some of the elements to be taken into account on a decision to acquire a going concern rather than expend the time and money to build up the same type of business within the organization:

> The price we should be willing to pay for Thacher has to be measured against what it would cost us to build a similar business of like size and profitability.
>
> *Our* cost would consist of capital assets and working capital, losses incurred during the start-up period, and in my opinion of profits foregone during the years it will take to catch up with Thacher. (Thacher is not going to stand still.)
>
> As to capital assets, it will cost us considerably more than Thacher's book value to acquire equivalent productive capacity. We could afford to pay them that excess over their book value. This could amount to $150,000; an appraisal would not cost much and would establish this figure for us.
>
> If we should start a unit to produce a comparable product, a considerable period would elapse before it would be self-supporting. How long this period would be and the amount of the loss that would be suffered are matters for guesswork. We can do some speculating as shown below.
>
> Conceivably, we could start with little or no additional plant. Two of our divisions are making small amounts of a comparable product now. Presumably they could take on some more business with existing equipment. However, it would have to be limited to formulations for which their

equipment is suited — which would seriously restrict sales efforts.

We would have to have, as a starter, a sales-technical group. It would probably be split into two teams. One of these teams would look for business in and devise products for customer uses. The other would study the general industrial field, select likely segments of it for intensive treatment, work on formulations for these segments, and do sales missionary work in them.

It seems to me that a minimum group would consist of a sales boss, two salesmen, a technical boss, two chemists, and clerical assistance. It might very well look like this for the first year:

General manager	$15,000
Salesman — Industrials	7,500
Salesman — Packaging	7,500
Technician	10,000
Chemist — Industrials	6,500
Chemist — Packaging	6,500
Secretary	3,900
Stenographer — clerk	3,380
Travel expenses — Sales and Technical	20,000
Accountant	4,680
Accountant — clerk	3,640
Miscellaneous office expenses	1,200
Miscellaneous laboratory expenses	5,000
	$94,800

I can conceive of first-year sales of $100,000 at 25% gross. This would yield $25,000 of gross profit against expenses of $94,800, leaving us a deficit of $69,800. Tax credits would absorb half of this, leaving a figure of $34,900 as our loss for the first year.

In the above computation I have included no such expenses as rent, freight out, telephone, etc., assuming that during the first year or two this would not be an independent unit but would, to a degree, "live off" its host.

In the second year we might still get by with equipment now owned and continue to operate this venture as a part of some existing division. Even so, it would be necessary to add to sales coverage. I would expect that at least two more salesmen would have to be added. Their sales and travel would come to about $25,000, bringing our expense budget to $119,800.

Our second-year sales might reach $300,000 yielding a gross of $75,000. This would leave us with a deficit for the year, after tax credits, of $22,400. Our cumulative deficit would be $57,300.

At this point our cumulative deficit is not too serious, $57,300 by my example. However, we still do not have a business, really. Volume is not large enough to support a plant — and we must, about now, have one. If we do not, if we continue to limit our output to the kind of equipment already in use by our sponsoring division we shall almost fatally restrict our chances of building a real business.

So we set up a plant and staff it. At once we will pick up the full costs of an operation, albeit a small one. It is inevitable that we will have underabsorption in our plant. We will have a foreman, a shipping clerk, a cost clerk, etc., and not have at once an increase in sales proportionate to the addition of expenses.

In an effort to eliminate underabsorption we will naturally add further to our salesforce. We could easily, I think, sink after-tax money of $50,000 in the third year and $25,000 in the fourth year.

By the end of the fourth year we might be doing $750,000 to $1,000,000. This is still not enough to make a really self-supporting unit, one which can carry on or pay for research and development, of our venture. It has cost us, by the rough calculation above, some $135,000 after tax credits.

Our plant has cost us at least $125,000 more than Thacher's price. We have sunk $135,000 in expenses. In total we have paid out $260,000, are at a break-even as far as profits are concerned and have a business about one-third as large, if that, as Thacher will then be. We will have foregone at least $250,000 of profits through failure to employ funds presently idle.

It seems clear to me that we could easily afford to pay something over $600,000 for the company on the basis of:

1)	Plant	$125,000
2)	Expenses	$135,000
3)	Foregone past profits	$250,000
4)	Differential between profits, when we get to the $1,000,000 sales level and profits we will get from Thacher, then three times our size	$200,000

Determining Price for the Aquisition of Key Peopli

The traditional bench marks of company value are of little use when the primary objective of the acquisition is to secure the services of a team of talented scientists, a brilliant marketing executive, or a highly competent chief operating executive. The Tracy Company, for example, developed, manufactured, and sold a variety of chemical intermediates. The company's research staff had been unable to develop a workable process for making economically a complex product for which there seemed to be great profit potential. The president of the Tracy Company learned of a small company owned and operated by five scientists who had developed a process for the desired product. In the previous fiscal year, the small company had sales, royalties, and consulting revenues of $400,000, net income of $2,700, and a year-end net worth of $75,000. The Tracy Company exchanged its stock with a market value equivalent of $600,000 for the stock of the acquired company and agreed to pay an additional 2% royalty on the sales of the product resulting from the five scientists' process. The purchase price represented one and a half times sales, over eight times book value, and well over 200 times earnings after taxes.

The acquisition of companies for the purpose of securing

key people is fraught with risks. Employment contracts may be exacted as part of the agreement to purchase, but employment contracts are of little value when key people become disenchanted, unhappy, or their incentives change as a result of the acquiring of tangible wealth. Many companies include in the employment contract an agreement that the persons so hired will not accept employment with a competitor if they leave. Such an agreement is enforceable, but it obviously does not ensure that the acquiring company will have the benefit of the abilities of the key people they have sought to obtain.

OTHER FINANCIAL PROBLEMS

Two other common financial problems are:

1. The method of accounting for acquisition — pooling of interests or purchase; and

2. Policy of nondilution of earnings.

When one company acquires another, the method of accounting for the transaction affects book values, net worth, taxes and earnings; the choice of the accounting method to be used is therefore exceedingly important. One of the most interesting accounting concepts is that of pooling of interests. *The Accounting Research Bulletin* of the American Institute of Certified Public Accountants describes it as follows:

> When a combination is deemed to be a pooling of interests, a new basis of accountability does not arise. The carrying amounts of the assets of the constituent corporations, if stated in conformity with generally accepted accounting principles and appropriately adjusted when deemed necessary to place them on a uniform accounting basis, should be carried forward; and the combined earned surpluses and deficits, if any, of the constituent corporations should be carried forward, except to the extent otherwise required by law or appropriate corporate action. Adjustments of assets

or of surplus which would be in conformity with generally accepted accounting principles in the absence of a combination are ordinarily equally appropriate if effected in connection with a pooling of interests; however, the pooling-of-interests concept implies a combining of surpluses and deficits of the constituent corporations, and it would be inappropriate and misleading in connection with a pooling of interests to eliminate the deficit of one constituent against its capital surplus and to carry forward the earnings surplus of another constituent.[3]

Thus, in a pooling of interests all the assets and liabilities of the combined companies are cross-added and brought forward at their book values on the acquiring company's books. The stated capital of the acquirer is increased by the par or stated value of the new shares issued to the selling company's owners and the capital surplus and earned surplus accounts are cross-added. The amount by which the total par or stated value of the stock outstanding after the transaction exceeds (or is less than) the total capital stock of the combined companies is subtracted from (or added to) the combined capital surplus of the surviving company to the extent capital surplus is available. Any remaining excess is subtracted from earned surplus.

In today's typical situation in which the buyer pays more than book value for the seller, no goodwill item is created if the combination is accounted for as a pooling of interests rather than a purchase. Subsequently, the reported earnings of the combined company do not have to be decreased by amortization of goodwill of course. An additional benefit of pooling-of-interests accounting is that the income statement of the surviving company for the period in which the combination occurs includes the combined results of operation

[3] Committee on Accounting Procedure, American Institute of Certified Public Accountants, *Accounting Research Bulletin, No. 48,* January, 1957. Copyright American Institute of Certified Public Accountants.

during the preceding part of the fiscal period in which the combination takes place. In other words, if the merger or acquisition takes place on December 1, the eleventh month of the fiscal year for the surviving corporation, the buyer can report its own earnings for the 11 months prior to the closing, the seller's 11-month earnings, and the combined company's December earnings on its income statement for the year of the combination. Also, since no goodwill with its offset to surplus is recorded, the dollar return on net worth of the surviving company may appear higher than it would if goodwill were included on the balance sheets.

The requirements for an acquisition to qualify as a pooling of interests are vague, indefinite, and constantly changing — another example of the problems resulting from the absence of "sound accounting principles to be used as objective standards." [4] The Securities and Exchange Commission makes the final decision as to whether a transaction in which listed securities are involved can be considered a pooling. For unlisted companies, the accounting profession applies and interprets the Securities and Exchange rulings.

At the present time four criteria seem to be applied in determining if an acquisition can be treated as a pooling of interests:

1. Continuity of Ownership: If the owners of the selling company receive voting stock in the surviving company in proportion to their former interest, a strong case can be made for a pooling. Conversely, when material payment in cash, debt securities, or nonvoting preferred stock is issued in exchange, there is an inference that the transaction is not a pooling. Also a change in ownership of either company before the transaction takes place, or the sale of substantial amounts of stock by the owners of the selling company soon after the transaction, prevents accounting treatment as a

---

[4] *Accounting and Reporting Problems of the Accounting Profession,* September, 1960. Arthur Andersen and Company.

pooling. A conservative estimate of what substantial means here is 15% to 20%; some concerned with the problem suggest that sale of 33⅓% of the stock issued to the sellers does not militate against a pooling.

2. *Continuity of Management:* Indication of a continuity of management is given by the election of directors and officers from each predecessor company to the management of the combined organization in general relationship to size, ownership, and other business factors. Representation on the board may not be essential. In several cases a transaction has been considered a pooling where the top officer of the selling company did not continue in the business after the acquisition but second-level management did stay on.

3. *Business Reasons:* As both of the preceding criteria imply, there should be interest on the part of managers and owners of both companies to combine for business reasons. These often include the desire of one party to strengthen certain areas, such as operations, purchasing, marketing or administration, while providing strength in another of these areas for the other party. An illustration of this would be the merger of a company whose research engineers had developed products that needed an extensive sales and service organization with an established company looking for new products and with a staff of proven research engineers. An acquisition made for such purposes as getting tax benefits, solving estate problems, or liquidating one of the entities usually would not qualify as a pooling.

4. *Comparability of Size:* Probably the least important criterion is that the two companies should be of similar size. Originally it was suggested that the two companies should be of equal size, but later the Securities and Exchange Commission approved a pooling treatment in 80–20 situations. Subsequently, a pooling of interests was approved when the smaller companies were 8.3%, 6.5%, and 2% of the merged entities.

PURCHASE ACCOUNTING

If the acquisition of one company by another cannot meet the criteria qualifications for treatment as a pooling of interests, the traditional purchase accounting method must be used:

> When a combination is deemed to be a purchase, the assets acquired should be recorded on the books of the acquiring corporation at cost, measured in money, or in the event other consideration is given, at the fair value of such other consideration, or at the fair value of the property acquired, whichever is more clearly evident. This is in accordance with the procedure applicable to accounting for purchases of assets.[5]

In cases where the acquiring company pays (either in cash or in other property or securities) more than the book value of the seller, the excess must be reflected in the balance sheet of the surviving company. Sometimes some of the excess over book value can be assigned to certain assets. For example, the seller's plant may be fully depreciated yet have a fair value of $100,000. In such a case, the asset will appear on the books of the survivor at $100,000 and can be depreciated by the surviving company. This write-up in assets results in additional cash flow since the depreciation is an offset to income for tax purposes. More frequently, the assets of the selling company cannot be written up to the full extent of the increase over book value paid by the acquirer. The excess is then recorded on the buyer's balance sheet as "goodwill."

The Securities and Exchange Commission requires that goodwill be amortized through the income statement over the "estimated useful life." The Treasury Department rulings, on the other hand, provide that the amortization of goodwill cannot be deducted as an expense for tax purposes. Also,

---

[5] *Accounting Research Bulletin, No. 48, op. cit.*

when an acquisition is accounted for as a purchase, the acquirer can include only the profits of the acquired company from the date the transaction is completed.

To illustrate the distinction between accounting for an acquisition as a pooling of interest or as a purchase, we assume in the following example that Company B buys Company S, that Company S's tangible and depreciable assets are not written up through an appraisal, and that the goodwill will be amortized over a ten-year period.

Balance Sheet	Company B	Company S
Net Assets	$4,000,000	$1,000,000
Capitalization:		
Common Stock	250,000 sh. $2.par	100,000 sh. $1.par
	$500,000	$100,000
Earned Surplus	$3,500,000	$ 900,000
Book Value	$4,000,000	$1,000,000

Income Statement Year of Combination:		
Net Income	$1,000,000	$ 200,000
Earnings per Share	$4.00	$2.00
Market Price per		
Share Closing Date	$120.00	Price paid $30.00
		(S was privately held)

Company B pays owners of Company S a total of $3,000,000 worth of B stock, or 25,000 B shares.

If the merger is accounted for as a purchase, the balance sheet would be:

Combined Company:

Assets	$1,000,000 + $4,000,000	= $5,000,000
Goodwill		= $2,000,000
	Total net assets	= $7,000,000
Net Worth: Common (275,000 @ $2 par)		= $ 550,000
Capital Surplus		$2,950,000
Retained Earnings		$3,500,000
		$7,000,000

(Assumes B issued 25,000 new shares of $2 par common stock.)

If the merger were accounted for as a pooling of interests, the combined balance sheet would be:

Combined Company:

| Combined Net Assets | $4,000,000 + $1,000,000 = $5,000,000 |

Stock and Surplus:

Common (275,000 shares @ $2 par)	$ 550,000
Capital Surplus	$ 50,000
Retained Earnings	$4,400,000
Net Worth	$5,000,000

If Company B acquires Company S in the last month of Company B's fiscal year, Company S's earnings for the year can be included in Company B's combined earnings for the year. Accordingly, Company B's earnings per share would be:

Company B earnings	$1,000,000
Company S earnings	200,000
Total	$1,200,000

$$\frac{\$1,200,000}{250,000 \text{ shares} + 25,000 \text{ shares}} = \$4.36 \text{ per share earnings}$$

instead of the $4.00 per share earnings which would have been reported if the acquisition had not been made.

Also assume that the combined company earns $1,500,000 before amortization of goodwill in the year after the merger. The earnings per share of the combined company the year after the merger with purchase accounting would be:

Net income after taxes but before amortization	$1,500,000
Less amortization of goodwill	= 200,000
Net income	$1,300,000
Number of shares outstanding	275,000
Earnings per share	$4.73

If the combination were acounted for as a pooling, the earnings per share would be:

Net income	$1,500,000
Number of shares outstanding	275,000
Earnings per share	$5.45

If the market is capitalizing the earnings of this company at between 10 and 30 times, the effect of the accounting distinction between a purchase and a pooling would be:

		Market Price		
Price earnings ratio		10 ×	20 ×	30 ×
Pooling of interests	$5.45	$54.50	$109.00	$163.50
Purchase	$4.73	47.30	94.60	141.90

The wise management decision of the acquiring company as to whether to apply pooling of interests or to use a purchase accounting concept takes into account:

1. The incremental addition to earnings per share;

2. The amount of goodwill to be included on the balance sheet;

3. The extent to which tangible assets can be written up thereby reducing or eliminating goodwill; and

4. The capacity of forecasted earnings to absorb higher depreciation rates on assets written up without reducing the reported earnings per share of the combined company.

If an acquisition does meet the criteria to qualify for accounting treatment as a pooling of interests, the acquirer's management is not required to apply the pooling concepts, but may, if it elects, regard the acquisition as a purchase. The pooling-of-interests principle is permissible, not mandatory.

Company Policy Not to Dilute Earnings Through Acquisition

The managements of some companies, particularly those with relatively low price earnings ratios, have adopted strict policy standards that the acquisition of another company must not reduce, even for a short period, the earnings per share. Clearly, the reports of earnings per share by period is an important factor to financial analysts, stockholders, and the management. But strict adherence to this policy does eliminate many candidates for acquisition with sales and growth possibilities greater than the acquirer has presently or can foresee in the next several years. One vice president of finance, for example, was influential in rejecting an acquisition when the negotiated exchange of shares would have resulted in a dilution of earnings of 2 cents per share.

A management which holds strictly to a no dilution of earnings policy as a prerequisite to any acquisition is short-sighted. The purchase of a company with good sales and profit potential at the cost of diluting the earnings per share only a few cents for the time being may over a longer period result in the addition of considerably more than the acquired company's proportionate share of total corporate earnings. And in many situations, the public announcement of the acquisition of a company in a business different from that of the acquirer increases the market confidence in the acquiring company.

As indicated earlier our report does not include consideration of the many technical, financial, accounting, and legal factors involved in acquisitions. These are complex matters, requiring the attention of financial, accounting, and legal specialists, and are beyond the scope of our study. In this chapter on financial problems, we have attempted to discuss some of the common problem areas found in all acquisitions.

CHAPTER IX

Some Problems of Integration

A JOINT announcement that the Jones Company has acquired the Smith Company usually appears in local and national newspapers, and the management of each company arranges to put the news on company bulletin boards. Until such an announcement is made, secrecy has usually been observed and relatively few people in each organization have been aware that negotiations were going on. When an agreement has been reached, employees of both groups involved must of course be advised.

IMPACT ON PERSONNEL

However the news is transmitted in the acquired organization, the impact on all company personnel is sharp and real. The workers in the plant and their foremen wonder what will happen to them. They ask: Will the plant be closed or moved? Will I be asked to move? Where else locally can I look for a job? And upward through each level of the company similar questions enter people's minds and become topics of discussion and rumor. Existing work anxieties are compounded by the uncertainty of possible changes and the entire organization may be diverted from its everyday tasks. One executive of an acquired company in Boston was in New York for a labor negotiation meeting when the news that his company had been sold came over the ticker at noon. He described his first reaction as "like a small boy waking up in the dark wondering where he was. Until you have gone through the experience personally, it is hard to realize that the business environment you thought you knew is now different. And different in ways you cannot define."

The *Management Psychologist,* a publication of Rohrer, Hibler, and Replogle, stated:

> The behavior of key people in a newly purchased company is sometimes very puzzling. Occasionally what they do or don't do doesn't make sense to the purchaser. Later on he finds that what appeared to be stupidity or resistance was in actuality anxiety.
>
> When men are afflicted with deepseated anxieties, they tend to backslide into earlier work habits. One man will freeze onto his files and won't let them go when a new computer system is being installed. Another man will play very cozy in controlling his customer contacts. Old-timers who have been at swords' points for years suddenly become chummy when the "house dicks" from the home office come to visit.
>
> The anxiety generated by change of ownership goes much deeper than the fear of losing a pay check. Without putting it into words, many key people feel that that which has made life worthwhile for them is being questioned, and their weekday faith is being threatened. Who they are and what they are here for can no longer be taken for granted.[1]

Responses to the threats to the employees' way of life take many forms. Some resign without waiting to determine what will happen; others begin plotting how to achieve personal goals long subdued in the old structure. One employee of an acquired company wrote a letter to the president of the acquiring organization stating:

> My name is John Peterson. I am employed by the King Company as a technician in charge of a section in the quality control department. I am writing this letter in your interest. Many things are wrong here:

[1] *Management Psychologist,* Rohrer, Hibler, and Replogle; February, 1960; Number 5, page 1.

1. Orders are not coming in because of poor relations.
2. Many key personnel have left for one reason or another.
3. Waste is everywhere.
4. You have the conditions of a three-ring circus and a comic opera, all in one. Although this may sound a bit funny, nevertheless it has caused a big fall in business.
5. I feel new business can be captured.
6. I have the dynamic ability and no-how to manage this company back to life and give it the spark it needs. Not because I say so, but because I have the experience in dealing with customers and labor, I am especially familiar with the problems of the King Company.

I would gladly cooperate in any further correspondence on this matter and most certainly would except the challenge of managing the King Company.

Sincerely your's,

Anxiety exists, also, at the top level of management. The president of Trail, a West Coast company, recounted the problems involved in the personnel management function when his company joined with another. Each of the two companies had a vice president of personnel. The Trail vice president of personnel, believing that as a result of the combination there would be one personnel vice president instead of two, stated strongly and loudly that the personnel function should not be centralized but rather could be performed most effectively by keeping separate personnel departments in the two companies, even though they were now part of a corporate whole. He was afraid that the other vice president of personnel would be named to the top job and that he would have to report to him. Backing up his convictions, he resigned to look for another job. Shortly thereafter, the other vice president of personnel resigned to accept a position in Washington, D. C. By then, the Trail vice president of personnel, whom the Trail president had considered to be well qualified, had accepted a position with another,

much smaller, company as the centralized director of personnel. Both vacancies at Trail were filled on a decentralized
divisional basis, but after further study a corporate personnel
job was set up, and a new man hired to fill it.

These are only two examples of many impulsive and petu-
lant actions taken in response to the news that an organization has been acquired. They illustrate dramatically, however, the truism that the acquired organization is composed
of people — people with fears, ambitions, anxieties, insecuri-
ties, abilities, and potentials. Frequently this underlying
and basic fact of business life gets overlooked. Preoccupation
with the financial figures of "the deal" often results in the
neglect of planning to maintain and strengthen the going
concern values of the acquisition. If the financial figures look
"good," the acquisition must be good. But clearly what
makes the numbers look good lies substantially in the hands
of the acquired organization.

The values to be derived from an acquisition depend
largely upon the skill with which the administrative problems of integration are handled. Many potentially valuable
acquired corporate assets have been lost by neglect and poor
handling during the integration process. Each organization
acquired is composed of a unique combination of human and
physical assets, and it is the job of the acquiring company
management to motivate and administer the unique group to
achieve the objectives which made the arrangement appear
to be a good deal in the first place.

In some situations the integration of an acquired organization was found to have been handled very badly. A midwestern company, for example, acquired a small technical
development organization in San Francisco in the summer of
1957. Although the acquiring company's organization included a president, executive vice president, vice president
for engineering, vice president for manufacturing, and vice
president for finance, it was decided to have the president of

the acquired company report to the vice president of finance, a nonengineering executive. The financial vice president was busy, and his only real management of the new company consisted of signing checks to finance its growth. During the months following the acquisition, the president and executive vice president, but not the financial vice president, stopped in the San Francisco office, but their visits were usually hurried and they achieved no insight or appreciation for the problems of the growing company. In the first year over $750,000 in working capital was added to the acquired company, its sales backlog increased to about $1,000,000, and profits were reported each month and quarter.

Late in 1958, the midwestern headquarters management decided to organize a home office engineering and development section to concentrate in the same technical area as the San Francisco based group. Competition developed between the two technical groups, and the president of the acquiring company called a meeting at headquarters to discuss and conclude how best to relate these competing activities. The discussion became heated when the acquired company president learned of the intention to name the headquarters engineering section head, Mr. Gove, as the manager of both operations. The decision was accepted, however, and Mr. Gove accompanied the acquired company president back to San Francisco to learn more about its operations.

Mr. Gove discovered very quickly that the San Francisco company had purchased an airplane without headquarters approval and provided company-paid vacation trips for several key employees to Hawaii and Las Vegas. Mr. Gove asked the headquarters controller to come to San Francisco. It then became apparent that there was no cost system for pricing contracts, there was no accounting system for reporting profits accurately, and employees were charging to the company $80 a day for food and drinks at a restaurant nearby. Further investigation revealed that inventory was overvalued by $200,000, the president had had his home air-conditioned at company expense, most contracts on the books had substantial overruns and instead of the $137,000 profit before taxes reported for the period, the real results showed a loss of $218,000. Much of the company's costs had been capitalized into inventory which later turned out to be worthless.

While the acquiring company management was critical of the president of the acquired company, "he totally lacks integrity," it should be observed that the acquiring management failed to take even reasonable steps to determine what was acquired and to initiate prompt administrative action which could have reduced the substantial losses incurred.

Other examples of poor beginnings in the integration of newly acquired organizations were found. For instance, a Philadelphia company acquired a Boston organization, and the vice president of the acquiring company arranged a dinner party at the Waldorf-Astoria Hotel in New York to which 15 key people of the acquired company and their wives were invited. The president of the acquiring company agreed to attend but at the last minute canceled the engagement. His absence was reported to the assembled group during cocktails, and when the group moved to one of the main dining rooms he was already seated at a nearby table dictating to a secretary, eating his dinner, and smoking a large cigar all at the same time. The doubts and misgivings which crossed the minds of key personnel of the acquired company were not reported, but a less auspicious integration beginning could not have been accomplished.

In contrast to the unfortunate beginning in these two situations, the approach followed by a New York management showed an appreciation of the early problems involved in taking over an enterprise. When the agreement to sell was completed, the president of the acquired company returned to his home office in Boston accompanied by the president of the acquirer. A meeting of the top 75 people was called immediately and the new organization relationship was explained openly and frankly. All questions from the group were answered and the president of the acquired company explained that with his new title, vice president of the acquirer and general manager of the division, his functions would remain essentially the same as before. The confidence and enthusiasm so clearly indicated by the president of the acquired company in the acquisition, and his new position in it, the evident rapport with the acquirer's president, and the sincerity with which the new relationships were discussed by the two top executives did something to reassure the acquired group's obviously anxious employees.

When the chief operating executive of an acquired company stays on as the top executive, he can play a critically important role in putting to rest the many rumors which arise and can by his behavior indicate his confidence that better, not worse, consequences will come about. Clearly, early statements must be confirmed by consistent administrative actions thereafter, but it is crucially important for the president of the acquired company to establish early that he is staying on the job with great enthusiasm and that he will be there to represent the interests of the group as the integration process takes place. He is the real symbol of security to all the others in the acquired organization.

Mr. Nathaniel, vice president and general manager of a division of the Clark Corporation, stated that he has a set program to follow with each acquisition. Shortly after the chief operating executive of an acquired company has had a meeting to explain the acquisition to his key people, Mr. Nathaniel arranges a cocktail party and dinner to be held in a hotel or country club for as many of the key personnel of the acquired company as practicable. Often foremen, salesmen, and office workers are included. Mr. Nathaniel arranges to have four or five of the top executives from the main office attend the dinner and describe the Clark Corporation, its method of operations, its benefit program, and its plans for continued growth. Most of the evening, however, is devoted to informal conversation in small groups whereby each begins to know the other and the "acquiring group of executives soon loses the attributes of ogres." Mr. Nathaniel closes the social affair with the remark, "Metal castings are our product, but people are our business."

In another instance, a West Coast manufacturing company acquired a New York operating division of a large eastern corporation. The West Coast company's president arranged a cocktail party at the Plaza Hotel in New York for the key personnel and their wives of the acquired division, the selling corporation, and the acquiring company. The obviously friendly and cordial relations between the buyers and sellers became apparent to the personnel of the acquired division and the initial response to the change was strongly affirmative. The beginnings of a climate of constructive and worthwhile new relationships were established.

The same West Coast company acquired another organization in the East shortly thereafter. In this case the rumors among the employees in the company acquired ranged from dissolution of the enterprise to consolidation with a competitor up the street. Here a vice president of the acquiring company stayed at the eastern plant for several weeks, holding meetings with the employees and attempting to assure them that the enterprise would be continued as an independent, autonomous operation. Many questions about benefit plans, seniority, wage and salary administration, possible promotion transfers to other divisions, and company plans for further growth were raised. The presence of an executive from the acquiring company and his sincerity in answering all issues raised did contribute to the orderly and nondisruptive process of integration.

EXPLANATIONS OF CHANGES TO BE MADE

In some integration situations it is clear to the acquiring and the acquired organizations that changes must be made if the believed advantages of joining forces are to be realized. Mr. Donald A. Gaudion, president of Pfaudler Company, Inc., accepted the necessity for making changes in one situation and in a carefully worded presentation faced the issues involved and attempted to describe his company's approach to handling such problems. His comments are given at some length as they clearly indicate many points that need to be covered:

You have been told of some of the hopes and aspirations for our two companies. It is my job to discuss the plans for bringing these fond hopes to fruition.

It would be very nice if I could stand up here and lay out a clear blueprint in the next few minutes of how this was all going to come about. How, by putting these two companies together, we were going to immediately solve all of our individual and company problems and multiply our combined profits. It would be nice if there was a "magic formula."

I hope you won't be too disappointed if I state, quite frankly, that we *do not* have a manual and report all blueprinted as to how this will come about. We were anxious to bring about a merger because of some of the "academic" reasons for bigness but more importantly because we saw in your company a background and personnel quite similar to ours, with many problems quite similar to ours, that we understood even if we didn't have all the answers, in a field that we had studied and moved into on the fringes and that we felt had a great growth potential.

We felt confident that once we were together we could *collectively and cooperatively* develop a plan of action that would capitalize on what we think is the terrific potential of these two combined companies. And now that the stockholders have taken action we're anxious to get going immediately and without further delay.

We recognize the fact that the word "integration" is a "scare" word today to many people in merged companies. They see jobs duplicate to theirs in the partner company and start trying to figure out which of the two is going to be dropped. I could stand up here and tell you that the two divisions were going to be operated entirely independently and that therefore everyone's job was going to be forever intact and perhaps that would make some of you happy. Or I could duck the question entirely and hope that no one asked it in our discussion. But as you will come to see, we don't operate that way!

We honestly believe that over a period of time this merger will make sense only if there is some integration together with the economies that go along with it. But there is no reason for you or the people working for you, any more than the people we've discussed this with at home, to start getting jittery or lose any enthusiasm because of this. Integration will take place only at times and in a way that will build greater strength in the overall picture and then only after very, very careful analysis. And I think any independent discussions you want to have with any of our employees, as you meet them, will confirm the fact that any individuals involved are given every possible consideration and are treated fairly. Furthermore, if this combined company has the dynamic growth we expect, any integration moves are going to be lost in the shuffle because we hope to be always in a state of vibrant forward movement.

Immediate Future:

In the immediate "get-acquainted" period we intend to:

(1) Combine both Boards of Directors as now constituted.

(2) Add together the slates of officers of the individual companies with the minimum changes necessary.

(3) Establish an Executive Committee made up of representatives of the inside Board members of both companies. The minutes of this committee will be presented to the Board for approval and will have the usual functions of an Executive Committee. This committee will meet once a month in an all-day session the day before the regular Board meeting.

(4) A separate Management Committee will be established for our division as previously operated and for your division. This Management Committee will be made up of representatives from the various functional departments of each division. It is expected that they will meet once a week at times most suitable to them and that the minutes of their committee will be referred to the Executive Committee for review.

(5) Both organizations will be kept functioning in the way they have in the past with the minimum number of changes, and therefore it is hoped and expected with minimum disruption. We confidently expect to build both organizations from their present levels and we do not want either of them to go through a period of slump because of the problems of integration.

(6) One or two people from our company will go to yours in a staff capacity as assistants to your president to begin to learn the organization and policies. By taking part in the day-to-day functioning of the operation, they will attempt over a period of time to transmit our ideas helpful to you and also give us the benefit of your thinking. They will also correlate interdivisional travel plans of people on all levels as necessary and desirable to further the get-acquainted process.

(7) If possible, one or more of your people will move to our offices on a similar basis.

(8) Further organizational changes will be made only after both organizations get acquainted with one another and appraisal can be made on a combined, over-all basis. In such appraisals in the future no weight will be given to the antecedents of any individual being considered for different responsibilities. Changes will be made strictly on the basis of capability for the particular job. In order to do this, it will obviously take time since each group currently knows its own organization and not the individuals in the other.

We have a strong feeling that sometime in the future we will be organized on a product divisional basis rather than our present functional divisional basis. In other words, that we will have a Vice President and General Manager, or perhaps a President, in charge of a cohesive group of products. It will be his responsibility to develop his product line into the largest division of the company and he will be given a lot of authority to do so, probably covering the fields of production, sales, engineering, etc. Probably where a separate salesforce is necessary for any product line, then serious consideration should be given to setting up a product division in that area. But this is probably years away and right now I couldn't even guess at how these product lines would be split out.

But in a broad sense we will probably follow a pattern something like this. In the past we have operated as two separate companies. In the immediate future we will continue to operate pretty much as in the past. As time goes on, and we get better acquainted, we will see ways that we can more efficiently and economically combine certain functions and work more together. After this blending operation has taken place we will probably then decentralize or separate again but in a form quite different from what we are today.

Uppermost in most people's minds in a merger such as this are questions as "Where will I stand promotion-wise in the combined operation?" "Security — will I lose my job or my position?" "What will be the personnel policies — wage and salary administration, fringe benefits, etc.?"

Let's take a look at some of these policies as we have been trying to develop them.

What kind of guys get ahead? The guys who produce! Not just their own individual output but what evolves from the team working with and for them — the people who kindle enthusiasm for the company and the growth and improved benefit program on which we are embarked — the people that are just *so far* above the rest of the organization that the *organization itself,* recognizes as being *so* good that when the management promotes them it is a foregone conclusion that comes as no surprise to anyone.

What about salaries and fringes? I usually tell job applicants that if they expect to make a million dollars they'd better go elsewhere. But through constantly improving salary administration we try to keep salaries in line with area rates for comparable jobs. We also try to keep them in line within the company as between individual jobs, keeping in mind such factors as output, responsibility, seniority, etc.

On top of this wage policy a solid and constantly improving fringe benefit program is being built. We have no intention of immediately upgrading the fringes at both divisions to the maximum of either or we would go broke which would help no one. Over a period of time, however, we hope to bring them together into greater uniformity. We have one of the best pension plans in the country. But it has been built over a period of more than ten years as the earnings of the company improved and with the last improvements instituted only about a year ago. We would hope to build a similar program here as fast as the earnings can be built up to pay for it.

What about security?

As far as individuals within the company are concerned, we try to handle cutbacks primarily on the basis of performance, but we give considerable weight to longer-term employees. We try to move older employees around, if necessary, in order to fit them into jobs more suited to their capabilities but we try not to be ruthless. Only when individuals refuse to cooperate and impede progress do we have to take decisive action in the interests of the hundreds of other employees whose lives they may be affecting. In this connection we feel it is extremely important first to be very careful in our new hirings and then to appraise a new employee as quickly as possible so that, if it is felt strongly that he does not have a future in the company, he can go elsewhere before his career is ruined and we are saddled with an employee who is not up to our expectations.

Obviously I could go on the rest of the evening on personnel policies alone. But this should give you some idea of the pattern of our thinking and, again, you can ask us the more specific questions that may be in your minds either now or later.

Atmosphere and Communications

What kind of atmosphere do we try to create? How do we interpret this horribly overworked word — communications? Basically we believe in the "open door" policy. If you have any questions about our plans or policies, ask them. Or ask any of our people you happen to meet. We will try to answer them. If we have to dodge the question we'll try to tell you why we're dodging — it may be for the very simple reason that we don't know the answer.

We are great believers in the principle that *many* of the ideas for the solution to our problems come up through our organization to the top — not down from the top.

In other words, we believe in decentralized authority with the decisions being made as far down in the organization as possible — the first point at which the person making the decision is in a position to have all of the factors involved. To make sure all of our policies are known all the way through the organization so that these decisions can be made intelligently is a matter of communications.

One of our major efforts in the immediate future will be in the direction of improving communications. This meeting is the beginning and we hope that you will carry our message to the rest of the organization and that we may do so in person as time goes on.

In conclusion let's come back to the "magic formula" which we pointed out earlier we didn't have. Actually, the only magic formula we have is maintaining and developing the enthusiastic co-operation of you and your fellow workers. If you look upon this merger as the end of the road and slacken all your efforts that have developed our company into the leader in its field, we are done! If you look upon it as a large step in the further growth of your company which literally doubles your personal opportunity for growth, the sky's the limit! As you meet people you will find plenty of differences of opinion as to how the company should be run. But you'll find *no* difference of opinion as to the direction it should run, namely, *up*. This, then, is the "magic formula."

This statement by Mr. Gaudion was an effort to be completely honest and forthright in facing changes which all parties to the acquisition knew had to be made. The facts and the proposed methods of solution were far less offensive than the rumors in the acquired company had projected them to be.

It was found in other cases that some acquiring managements attempted to hide, disguise, or soft pedal impending changes with the apparent hope that with time the problems would disappear. We doubt whether this is a useful approach in that it discounts the capacity of the organization to recognize and to adapt to what everyone knows really needs and has to be done.

REPRESENTATIONS BY ACQUIRERS

Considerable care must be exercised by any representative of the acquiring organizations in making statements to groups or to individuals in the early stages of the integration process. The uncertainties and anxieties of the listeners result in subjective translation and in efforts to find in the statements some confirmation of their hopes or fears. Chief operating executives frequently were aghast at the conclusions reached from comments they made to such groups and generally reacted, "But I didn't say that!" But the organization heard *that* and any deviation from what was heard was regarded as the work of a false and misleading representative of the acquiring company.

If the management of the acquiring organization does not intend to apply its benefit programs to the newly acquired group, it is better not to say that it will. If there is no intention of permitting the group to operate as an autonomous, profit-and-loss measurable entity, it is better not to indicate directly or indirectly that this is the intention. If the old bonus plan's discontinuance is planned, it is far better to make this plain before those who had received the bonus previously have made commitments or spent the amounts before they were to be received. It is very easy and tempting, especially during the early days and weeks, to say things which will be appealing, gratifying, and expedient to the new organization to be integrated. The inclination to please should be tempered, however, with the forecastable assurance that if the pleasing statement of policy is not fulfilled later by performance, the confidence of the organization will be substantially shaken and any future statement will be largely discounted.

The president of the Board Company, for example, met with the key executives of a relatively small acquisition and stated explicitly that the organization would operate essentially as it had in the past as an autonomous unit. Within one year the new acquisition was merged into one of the acquiring company's operating divisions without any discussion with the people affected and to whom the verbal commitment had been made. The president of the acquired company, who resigned shortly thereafter, said: "The purchasing management should never say things they cannot deliver on, either during negotiations or after the deal is completed. If representations are made, they should be prefaced by saying that 'This is our intention at the present time. Conditions may change, and people in business know this and can adapt, and if changes do become necessary, we in headquarters must rely upon you and our people to work out the best solution under the circumstances.' The key," he continued, "is that the management of the acquirer should say, 'You must have confidence in us' and then live up to it."

A vice president of the same acquired company stated that the acquiring company must instill in the acquired organization the basic correctness of any decisions that are made. He added that the joining of two organizations is an act of faith and it is not until the two groups have lived together that the genuine facts come clear. "Impressions are made during these early days and because this is a new experience, you have to remember that there is an extreme sensitivity to what is said and done. People are going through a relationship, typically for the first time, and they are necessarily uncertain, sensitive, and looking for implications. No union is ever easy and both sides have to learn to adapt if the joint values are to be realized."

INTERORGANIZATIONAL RELATIONSHIPS

Another shortcoming found in the integration programs of some of the companies we studied was the failure to make absolutely sure that the president of the acquired company understood and accepted a clearly defined organizational relationship. Unless it is made clear early that the acquired company head reports to a headquarters or division executive, there can be confusion and unpleasantness. It is equally true that the headquarters or division executive to whom he reports must accept the responsibility and take an active, and time-consuming, interest in seeing that the newly added company becomes part of the total operating structure. Here again, the acquiring company's executives may be tempted during the early weeks of the integration process to continue the wooing process to indicate what a reasonable group of people they are. As one said, "Let's maintain the *status quo* for the time being — things will work out." Maintaining the *status quo* really is allowing the organization acquired to drift away — *status quo* is a euphemism.

Two cases illustrate the unfortunate results of the lack of clear organizational responsibility. A large East Coast company acquired a midwestern paint company largely through the efforts and personal involvement of the president of the acquiring company. He was a well-known, successful executive, and early in the negotiations he asked the owner-manager of the paint company to "please don't call me Mr. I'm just Bill to my good friends." The paint company's president was pleased to be on a first name basis with a distinguished businessman. When the issue of "Where does our company fit in your over-all organization" came up, the answer was, "At all times you have access to me — my door is always open." Agreement was reached on the purchase terms and the acquisition was completed. For a period of several weeks the paint company's president made daily telephone calls to his good friend Bill concerning business problems. The acquiring company's organization included a vice president responsible for paint and related products and Bill concluded that the insistent midwestern paint company's president should be adjusted to reporting to the logical company officer. When the next call was received from the midwest, the acquiring company's president stated that hereafter all calls should be made to the paint vice president. This change in signals, while logical and sensible to the acquiring company's management, was regarded as a breach of faith by the acquired company's president and he resigned shortly thereafter.

The second case is equally dramatic. The president, who was a minority owner, and the nonmanagement owners sold their Connecticut-based metal fastener business to a much larger New York company early in 1956. During the eight weeks of mutual evaluation and negotiations, the Connecticut company's management was greatly impressed by the proposed purchaser's product research and development and market research which would provide an entreé to new markets not previously approached by the fastener company. Acquisition terms were agreed upon and what happened?

> Nothing, said the original company president. We went along as before, nobody bothered us but at the same time nobody helped us. There was no real liaison with headquarters. We thought the New York company research labs would come up with new technical products or improvement of our line, but they did not. Headquarters did remember to soak us on the first of each month with a home office allocation of overhead including the research labora-

tory costs. Our sales and profits in 1956 were not good and
they looked even worse after deducting the overhead allocation. Incidentally I sure would like to know how who
decides what to allocate to each operating division.

I began to lose faith in the New York headquarters and
my feelings became apparent to my organization. Three
people resigned from our technical lab and morale was getting lower and lower. For two years no one paid any real
attention to us and then came 1958. That was a miserable
year. Sales and profits were off even more because of the
recession. The New York president insisted that I reduce
the selling and administration expense by firing 20 people
out of 125. I did, and then rumors and counter-rumors
swept through the plant. It was like a buzzing tomb.
About this time my controller began secretly feeding bad
news to headquarters. When they proposed to make the
controller plant manager, I finally blew up. All our top
people threatened to quit so we killed the idea.

When we did hear from the home office, they wanted to
know what had been done to develop products for sale to
the automobile industry. We thought the company research
and development labs had already done this job, but they
knew as much about the problems involved as we did —
namely nothing. This has been a miserable experience and
never again for the rest of my life would I be willing to
spend such a period of two years.

The president of the Connecticut fastener company, when
asked what he would have done if he had been chief operating executive of the acquiring company, said:

> I would have named a vice president as responsible for
> our operations and then he should spend enough time im-
> mediately in our plant to understand what our real strengths
> and weaknesses were. He should work out with us what
> product line and other goals made sense in terms of the to-
> tal corporate situation. He ought to take time to educate
> Joe, our technical director, on what goes on in the com-

pany labs and help him learn what assistance can be expected from that source. The vice president also could help the headquarters' people understand our problems so that they won't listen to a traitor-type controller.

It seems rather obvious that the acquisition of a company requires establishing early and clearly where it fits in the total organization and requires the designation of a specific person in the acquiring group as responsible for the integration and operations of the acquired company. Sometimes, it is true, acquired companies have been neglected and left on their own with less unfortunate results than found in these two cases, and in others encountered in our study. But if the organizational relationship is not defined clearly, successful results are products of fortuitous circumstances rather than sensible management.

In order to assure early close liaison and effective working relationships, the managements of some acquirers transfer a key executive to the acquired company's organization as soon as the legal agreements have been made. Usually, in these cases, the intention of adding an executive to the company is discussed and agreed upon during the negotiations. The Pace Company, for example, purchased the Rice Company in the fall of 1957. The purchase agreement included the assignment of a Pace Company's vice president, Mr. Stan, who moved to the Rice Company and became assistant to the president. His mission was to help the Pace Company management understand the operations of Rice, to evaluate the several levels of management in Rice, to define and reconcile the different modes of operations, to conclude how best to integrate the two organizations, and to help the Rice personnel understand the management philosophy, policies, and decisions of the Pace management. The Rice Company's vice president of sales died unexpectedly and the president of Pace asked his newly assigned assistant to perform both functions. He agreed and was able through his line and staff positions to learn a great deal about the enterprise in a relatively short time and to contribute to the orderly absorption of an independent company into a much larger organization.

In another case, the Gable Company, a very large eastern company, bought the Trade Company in 1958 from the heirs of the four founders. The owners of Trade were not active in the management, they lived in Florida and relied upon a salaried president, Mr. Bock, to operate the company profitably and to provide the regular dividends necessary for their living. Sales of Trade were about $20,000,000 a year with profit after taxes ranging from $8\frac{1}{2}\%$ to $10\frac{1}{2}\%$. Soon after Gable acquired Trade, it became apparent that Trade was losing its competitive position to a relative newcomer to the industry, and the Gable president transferred a vice president, Mr. Hart, to Trade to work as assistant to the president of Trade. Within four months, Mr. Hart discovered that the Trade position was much weaker than anticipated and Mr. Hart, with Mr. Bock's concurrence, took over as chief operating executive.

Mr. Hart discovered that the two manufacturing plants, producing the same products, had wide differences in costs, that less able people had been transferred to one of the plants, and that considerable resentment and enmity existed between the two groups. One of the facilities was large enough to house all employees so he proposed bringing the two production lines together. With the background of hostility, the production personnel became even more disgruntled and representatives of a national union were able to get an election scheduled. Mr. Hart responded by writing a series of four letters to each employee and the efforts of the union to organize the employees failed. He then hired a personnel consulting firm to make a study of employee attitudes, and the results of the questionnaire isolated problem areas for management attention. With some of the problems defined, Mr. Hart installed a clean and attractive cafeteria for all employees and established a small medical center with a full-time nurse and half-time doctor.

In addition to actions taken on personnel problems, Mr. Hart organized a product development section to try to recapture sales lost to competition, reorganized the marketing structure, reduced the number of foremen from over 40 to 12, and resumed a program of television advertising. Mr. Hart's suggestion to speed up the production line by the use of new machine drives was rejected by the manufacturing department head. "We tried it before and it didn't work." Mr. Hart ordered new drives, had them installed, and was on the plant floor when the machines were started. The output of the initial processing step was doubled with the new drives and affirmative action was taken in overcoming the old management attitude of "Let's not try anything; let's ride along with what we have." As a result of the steps taken, the downward sales trend was reversed immediately, sales increased rapidly to a point where, with the exception of an unusual year of trade stocking of a new pack, the profits on the main product item were the highest in history. Mr. Hart said that when he came to the Trade Company he was shocked by what he found and immediately started corrective action by taking the following steps:

1. Holding more than the usual number of staff meetings. He observed and evaluated key people this way and at the same time communicated his company's management philosophy to the group.

2. Coaching key personnel. He did much of this informally at meals, noting, "It is important to catch people when they are receptive."

3. Holding department heads responsible for decisions in their function areas. When there was uncertainty or conflict between departments, Mr. Hart called in everyone involved at the same time to discuss the issue.

4. Trying to get his personnel to identify problems, not side issues, and asking for alternative solutions.

5. Treating each person with dignity and respect.

The two-year program of corrective action followed by Mr. Hart has been described at some length to illustrate the magnitude of problem areas which he found. Had he not been transferred to the Trade Company very soon after the acquisition was completed, the problems probably would have been compounded by the inaction of the old management. Lack of interest by the acquiring management in the operations, other than periodic sales and profit figures, sometimes results in situations far more serious and complicated than would have come about if they had been analyzed earlier. Again, we emphasize the critical significance of the acquiring management's early and active participation in integrating the newly acquired company into the total organizational structure.

The assignment of personnel from the acquiring company to the organization of the acquired can be handled with tact and effectiveness. In some situations this was not done, and the position of the headquarters employee was difficult and in a few cases completely untenable. He was regarded as the spy from the home office, unasked for, unwanted, and resented by the group newly acquired. With assurances during negotiations that the company would continue to operate independently as it had in the past, acquired managements found in the assignment of headquarters people to their plants the evidence on which to build a strong case for the acquirer's lack of confidence in them.

The decision to transfer key people from the home office to a newly acquired company should take into account representations which were made during negotiations, the functions the man is to perform, the needs and willingness of the acquired organization to accept help, and the personal and professional competence of the man transferred. In many situations we found that representatives of acquiring companies had made explicit statements, or by their phraseology implicit statements, which although not included in any written agreements, became basic planks in the platform of company relationships — forgotten by the maker of the statements but not forgotten by the listeners. In attempts to persuade key people that their careers and the future of their company would be strengthened through acquisition, persuasive representatives had led them to believe promises which were never intended to be kept. When later action indicated a clear breach of the representations, the acquired management concluded that they were the victims of fraud.

If subsequent circumstances indicate that action needs to be taken which is in conflict with earlier representations, an executive of the acquiring company should discuss the problem with the chief operating executive of the acquired group and get his approval before the decision is put into effect. We found many situations in which this was not done, and this administrative failure in effective administrative practice jeopardized rather than helped the acquired company's president to administer his organization profitably through the transition period.

It is essential, also, to discuss with the acquired president what the man assigned from headquarters is to do. A blanket charter "to be helpful in any way he can" raises many questions among the group acquired. Inevitably during the conversations leading to acquisition, areas of weakness in the acquired company operations are defined, and any one of these can serve as the locus of help from the home office.

But the man assigned must have the professional background and experience needed to be helpful in solving the problem that has been isolated, or his presence will be suspect from the beginning. Considerable care needs to be exercised in selecting the executive who is assigned to assist the acquired organization. We observed that in some cases people were transferred to an acquired operation because they happened to be available or because a suitable position could not be found in the home office for them. Clearly, such executives are not likely to be welcomed in the acquired company. Men assigned should have the professional capacity to contribute to the solution of the problem areas that have been defined as well as the ability to make themselves personally acceptable. These two essential characteristics are basic, and the absence of either will jeopardize rather than contribute to the smooth and effective integration process.

Knowledgeable men with the capacity of relating themselves to the new organization can be of immeasurable help. Sometimes the home office representative manifests by his behavior that he is "a rather superior executive from headquarters who has come down to straighten out the operation." Such a man is not likely to be effective. Top executives of most organizations are aware of the varied capacities of their key personnel and can assign those with the desired characteristics to the acquired company. Our observations on the importance of the personal and professional traits of the man to be assigned to an acquired company may appear to be elementary and pedestrian, but the number of poor assignments encountered during our study suggests the value of elaborating the obvious.

To illustrate the sensitivity of the personnel in an acquired organization during the early integration period and the importance of selecting qualified men to be transferred to the acquired company, a Chicago company producing highly technical products, was acquired by a New England company in February 1960. The two owner-manager scientists of the Chicago enterprise recognized that their substantial financial success was attributable, in part, to strong intuitive judgments. They believed that a principal need for future competitive conditions was to bring in logic and thought-through management programs. One of the main reasons for their willingness to sell had been the desire for what was described as "modern management methods to make the company more successful and profitable."

Knowing the kind of assistance desired by the scientist managers in Chicago, the president of the New England company suggested the assignment of one of his key employees, Mr. Dowd. With a Master's degree in Physics, Mr. Dowd would have the technical respect of the two scientists and with a Master's degree in Business Administration and several years of experience, Mr. Dowd could contribute to the solution of the management problems. His transfer was approved by the Chicago executives who sincerely wanted sounder analyses of their business problems.

Mr. Dowd went to Chicago, and in his first interview with the former owners, he announced that he had been sent to become the new assistant to the president. This created an immediate crisis, and the Chicago president called the New England company president and expressed great concern that Mr. Dowd apparently had been sent to Chicago to take over the management of the company. The tension was so great that the New England president caught an early plane to Chicago to try to repair the damage done. He offered to withdraw Mr. Dowd, if that was desired, but explained again in detail what he thought had been agreed was to be Mr. Dowd's role. With some reluctance the Chicago president agreed to let Mr. Dowd stay on, and between March 1960 and May 1960 Mr. Dowd had related himself effectively to the Chicago group. He became an effective member of the technical sales group and the acquired company's president sought his advice more and more. Early in 1961 when a proposal was made to move Mr. Dowd to a new situation, his transfer was resisted and stopped by the plea that he was an indispensable member of the Chicago team.

The New England company's president, after recounting this experience, noted: "I learned how delicate the feelings of an acquired management are. Because of his high sensitivity, the Chicago president extrapolates from very meager evidence, but his problem was not any different from those of all the other chief operating executives of companies we have acquired in the last three years."

ESTABLISHMENT OF MANAGEMENT CONTROLS

During our study we found considerable discussion about how much and what management controls should be established by the acquiring management over the acquired operations. In almost all cases an accounting audit had been made of the acquired company's books to verify the balance sheets and profit-and-loss statements used during the negotiations. In a few cases the audit had been delayed, sometimes with unfortunate results. One company, for example, was acquired in August 1958, and an audit by the acquiring company's public accountants was not made until June 1959. Agreement warranties and a partial deferred payment plan protected the purchasing company; but during the delay of ten months, a bad accounting situation degenerated into an emergency crisis. The acquired company, with inadequate general and cost accounting methods, had shown false profits for several years, obsolete inventories were carried as current assets, and pricing policies were based on cost estimates which have little relationship to actual figures. The monthly and quarterly financial statements submitted to headquarters began to provide clues to the basic problems, but it was not until the spring of 1959 that the magnitude of the problem was recognized. Confronting the acquired president with the so-called facts of financial statements resulted in many unanswered questions. The tragic concealment of the true condition of the enterprise required months of headquarters' management time at first to salvage and then to reorganize the company into a profitable position.

In another company control of the acquired enterprise, which was in an industry quite different from that in which the acquirer was engaged, was almost exclusively through capital and operating budgets, in addition to the usual financial statements. At monthly meetings of the acquiring company's board of directors, including the acquired company's president, the budget status was reviewed and provided the vehicle for discussing questions by the company's board and top management. In another case, the president of the acquiring company worked out budgets with the acquired chief operating executive who was then charged with "meeting these goals and if you do not achieve the objective or come reasonably close, you will be relieved and we will find someone who can."

But management control through limited or even complete financial statements has two major shortcomings: (1) The wide variations of figures permitted by the application of generally accepted accounting practices make analyzing the financial results of any stated period difficult; [2] and (2) the time-consuming collection of financial data and preparation of reasonably useful reports causes a time lag which further delays the application of appropriate remedial action if it is required. Something more is needed. And as indicated earlier, this may include the personal and continuing interest of a designated home office executive responsible for the operation, the assignment of an executive from the home office to the acquired organization, or any of a wide variety of methods of knowing what is going on in the acquired company.

Of course there were situations where nothing more than financial controls were exercised and the integration process

[2] See Chapter VIII, "Some Financial Problems."

was accomplished successfully. Such an approach does run the risk, however, that major problems will result from minor ones which would have been disclosed by closer, more intimate working relationships. It is not possible to generalize on the conditions which need to be met that might permit taking the risks of using limited or complete financial controls as the exclusive method of management controls. Our case studies indicate that from the point of view both of the acquiring management and of the acquired management, financial controls by themselves are not sufficient to enable the realization of the anticipated benefits of acquisition.

INTEGRATING MARKETING

Most of the administrative jobs of integration involved in acquisitions were described as difficult, but one area which seemed particularly perplexing was the integration of the marketing activities. Sales-oriented executives explained that this was due to the fact that the problems involved the heart of any business, namely, sales. Others, however, attributed the complications to the prima donna characteristics of salesmen. The reason for the relative qualities of complicated and entangling factors is not clear, but, nevertheless, many presidents in recounting their experiences of integration would state: "Sales, of course, was the most difficult."

In one company, for example, nine fabricating enterprises throughout the United States were acquired in a period of six years. Before any attempt was made to combine the nine marketing policies into a unified company-wide policy, a study was made of the varying kinds of compensation plans. The investigation disclosed that there were four broad compensation methods, with minor variations in addition. Some companies used straight salary, others straight commission, others paid according to the profitability of the sale, and still others paid salesmen on the basis of volume. Also, variations in the kind of company cars, expense accounts, and entertainment allowances complicated a company-wide solution to the problem.

After considerable study, a plan was worked out. Salesmen were to receive a base salary, a commission based on volume, an override commission based on profitability, travel expense, and a Chevrolet automobile. When the plan was announced to the 150 salesmen, they were guaranteed that in 1960 they would earn as much as they did in 1959 if their volume was equal to 1959. Shortly after the new plan was announced, three salesmen resigned, but by early 1961 the top management believed that the sales group was reasonably satisfied.

In some acquired companies, compensation plans are in such hodgepodge shape that drastic remedial action is required soon after the purchase has been completed. One acquired company, for example, had five different basic methods of compensating salesmen, referred to as the old plan, and Mark A, B, C, and D. The old plan was the most generous and was enjoyed by the oldest sales employees whose income each year totaled as much as $50,000. More recently employed salesmen were in the four Mark programs and envied "the old-timers who produced less but creamed the till." The acquired company's vice president of sales was 63 years old and had been employed by this company for 38 years. Indeed the various pay plans were his handiwork. The sales vice president was, however, a key executive in assuring the continued financial success of the acquired enterprise, and the acquiring company's president used what he described as "soft hands" in suggesting needed changes. The new point of view of the acquiring management and the gentle insistence of the president that a uniform company plan was required, resulted in substantial changes after a two-year period. A new uniform plan was inaugurated, 21 salesmen out of 40 were replaced, 4 were retired at a new mandatory age limit of 65, 3 were retired for sickness (the Virginia salesman had two heart attacks, could not travel, and made his sales by telephone from his home), and 8 resigned in a group to start a new company. The change in the salesforce was disruptive, but the risks and cost of continuing the old plans were believed to be completely untenable as a basis for new growth and success.

Another marketing integration problem involved the transfer of products between the sales groups of the acquired and the acquirer. In the Tate Company's acquisition of the Wide Company, for example, one of the motivating reasons for the purchase was that the Tate salesmen had excellent contacts with a segment of a national industrial market which bought the kinds of products originated by the Wide Company, a regional marketer in the East. The usual sales meetings were held to introduce Wide products to the salesmen of the Tate Company and they evinced great initial enthusiasm for adding these products to their line. Several months went by with no appreciable increase in the sale of Wide Company products by Tate salesmen, and it was concluded by Tate's top marketing executives that the salesmen were reluctant to jeopardize their sales contacts for Tate's proven existing products with the products of the Wide Company which were less well-known and from the salesman's point of view, unproven.

The Strang Company, too, encountered product line integration problems when it tried to add an item of industrial manufacturing equipment produced by a recently acquired company. The equipment product was related to but slightly different from the industrial products sold by the Strang Company; its customers were also potential purchasers of the newly acquired product. At first the Strang Company's salesmen were afraid of the product and after one year of staff sales effort to familiarize company salesmen with the product's merits, only 8 out of 50 salesmen had sold even one.

The vice president of sales then organized a task force of seven people to identify the marketing problems, to work intensively with supervisors and salesmen, and to push the new product aggressively through the sales group to potential customers. The next year produced a sharp increase in sales of the product, one which had an attractive gross margin. The lesson learned, according to the sales vice president, was that something more than the usual sales meeting was required to get a sales group to take on new although related products. The creation of a special task force to help salesmen understand the new product's advantages and to train salesmen in the technical facts proved an effective solution in this case.

ADMINISTRATION OF CHANGE IN THE ACQUIRED COMPANY

A common representation made during negotiations for the acquisition of a company is, "There will be no changes in your policies and programs. You will continue to operate exactly as you did before. The only difference is that we, rather than others, will own the stock in your enterprise." Unfortunately such a representation is not true. It *cannot* be true. Even the least amount of financial control is a change, and the eventual changes may range from minimum financial control to complete overhaul and reorganization of the acquired operations. Owners and managers considering the sale of their enterprises to others must realize that this is an inevitable result of the transfer of ownership.

The representation of continuing and unimpaired independent operations was described by one acquiring president as "being in the category of substantial honesty. You cannot be completely honest in the negotiations because if you are, nobody will ever sell to you. The best you can do is to be substantially honest and then rely upon faith and wisdom in administering changes to make the acquisition successful, both for the acquirer and for the acquired."

The president of a company that had been acquired stated to a friend who contemplated selling his enterprise to a midwestern company, "No matter what the buying executives say, things will be different. A larger organization must have administrative procedures; otherwise there will be chaos. When the buying executive says 'you will be a separate, autonomous unit, operating just as you are,' it just plain is not possible. You have to tie into the parent company and live according to their rules. To be sure, you may have a short honeymoon, but after that you comply or go."

There were other situations in which the acquirer at the time of acquisition had every intention of continuing the acquired operation essentially as it was managed in the past. The dynamics of change in business, however, led later to recognition that something had to be done if the enterprise was to grow and progress toward its potential, or, in some cases, to survive.

And in other cases, of course, it was apparent to both the acquirer and the acquired that changes must be made soon after the legal amenities for acquisition had been accomplished. Sometimes long-time owners of an enterprise were reluctant to discharge or provide early retirement for key employees who had turned out to be less than effective and an implicit condition of the terms of sale of the company was that the new owners would take remedial action.

The complexities of each business situation are so great and different that it is not possible to derive useful generalizations as to how change should or should not be administered. One problem may require drastic surgical action, another may only need a mild treatment of preventive medicine, and another may require nothing more than periodic checkup over the years.   The description of action taken in the administration of several companies will be helpful, we believe, in suggesting some of the factors to be taken into account.

Some participants in the acquisition process have suggested that when the necessity for change in the acquired organization has been decided upon, immediate action should be taken to make what seem to be the appropriate corrections. If, for example, the acquirer concludes that a vice president of sales is not competent after 40 years of service with the acquired company, no delay should be tolerated in removing him and putting someone on the job who it is hoped will be more effective.   We doubt whether this concept is valid in most cases.   The particular environment within which the drastic action is to be taken may be such that a substantial part of the sales organization may quit if what appears to them to be an unfair executive decision is put into effect.

There are marketing situations where salesmen do in fact control segments of product sales and the loss of the sales organization could do irreparable harm to the acquired company.   In one case the top management of the acquirer, faced with such a problem, fired the head of sales, an old-timer, assuring themselves that "if the salesmen leave, let them — we can build a new organization and they will be sorry they left."   The salesmen did leave, went to work for a competitor, and maintained their hold on old customers.   Three years later the acquiring management still had not been successful in creating a new salesforce or in recapturing the markets lost.   We are not suggesting that no action can or should be taken in cases similar to this, but only that as in most decisions of administration, the risks and losses possible from executive decisions be weighed carefully against possible gain before action is put into effect in the acquired organization.

An interesting administrative problem involving change faced Mr. Mercer, a vice president of the Bates Manufacturing Company. Mr. Mercer and his company's vice president of finance negotiated the acquisition of the Moe Company, a midwestern electronics operation located within a block of an existing division of the Bates Company. The Bates division specialized in machined parts and had an excellent machine shop operated by highly skilled machinists. The division employed about 250 people and included a vice president and general manager, a director of sales, a director of manufacturing, and a director of finance, as well as the usual department and section heads found in high precision machine shops of that size. The newly acquired company was engaged in the development and manufacture of related and complementary products, although with a much smaller machine shop. The award of a large production contract to the Moe Company required additional shop facilities or an extensive program of subcontracting the work. The Moe Company employed 300 people and included the same general organization of key personnel found in the Bates division.

Shortly after the Bates Company acquired the Moe Company, the president of Moe, who had been in ill health, resigned and left for a six months' stay in Europe. Mr. Mercer was asked by the president of the Bates Company to stay at the Moe Company to determine what benefits could be achieved by merging the operations of the Moe Company and the Bates Company division, to reorganize if necessary to accomplish these benefits, and to search for a candidate either within or outside the company to take over the top management of both organizations.

Mr. Mercer studied the activities of the two complementary organizations, talked with key people at both locations, and concluded that considerable benefits could be realized if the two structures were merged into one. Machine shop work could be centered in the old division and assembly work concentrated in the Moe Company, and since the two sales groups called on essentially the same customers, a combined approach might prove to be more effective. In going over the organization structures of the two groups, it was plain to Mr. Mercer, and to the people involved, that for each top position in the combined arrangement, there were two candidates. He tried to evaluate the strengths and weaknesses of all the key people, selected one for each job, and discussed the decision with the person chosen for the top position as well as with the person picked as the assistant. This was accomplished with only apparent surface distress, and within two months after the acquisition of the Moe Company, an announcement was made of the new structure and of the scheduled moves of equipment and people between the two plants. The moves were to take place over a weekend.

Late Friday afternoon as Mr. Mercer walked through the accounting department of the Moe Company where chairs were stacked on desks and files preparatory to moving, he said to several of the girls working on the move, "Won't it be wonderful on Monday to be working together in one place?" One girl with tears in her eyes responded, "Mr. Mercer, you are the only person in the whole wide world who thinks this is a good idea." The moves were made and people found themselves in new surroundings with new working relationships to be established. A month later, an executive from outside the Bates Company was hired to become vice president and general manager of the combined plants. In addition to the usual problems of a new top manager in a new situation, he had all the organizational difficulties implicit in a merged operation such as this. Several key people resigned, production effort diminished, rumors swept through both plants and profits turned to losses, even though each of the two plants had been profitable prior to the combination.

In this particular set of circumstances, the speed with which the unification of two previously independent groups was accomplished was too fast. In retrospect, Mr. Mercer concluded that more effective integration could have been achieved if additional time had been allowed to evaluate carefully the capacities and skills of the key people. The Moe Company's organization was especially sensitive and insecure because not only had they been acquired, but also their chief operating executive had resigned and had been temporarily succeeded by a Bates Company vice president who "knew the division people up the street better than he knew the employees of Moe." The logic and efficiencies to be accomplished by bringing together the two groups were clear, but the administrative manner in which the consolidation was done, together with the speed of combining the two organizations, could have been handled more effectively by the executives of the Bates Company.

Rapid action was taken, also, when a New England company acquired a company in the midwest. The acquired company's sales and profits had declined steadily for eight years, and at the time of purchase substantial losses had been incurred for two successive years. The company was in an industry which could benefit greatly from the technical achievements of the acquirer. Negotiations for purchase from the family that owned the company included the provision that the president would resign and the new owners would provide a successor. He was selected from the staff of the acquiring company and within two months after he assumed top management responsibility, he had:

1. Reduced the cost of the principal raw material purchased by 15%;
2. Fired the executive vice president and the vice president of sales who were actively recruiting company employees to form a new company;
3. With no accounting and financial control, hired one controller, fired him, and hired another to perform the function;
4. Hired a new vice president for sales;

5. Persuaded the chairman of the board, a family owner holdover, to stay away from headquarters;

6. Reduced the number of employees from 650 to 550 and maintained the nonunion status of the employees; and

7. Brought in 17 new men to operate at all levels of management.

The president of the acquiring company stated that here the acquired organization was desperately sick and everyone in the organization knew it was sick. The former owners knew changes had to be made even though under their management they did not have the courage or judgment to face the stress involved in change. Six months after the acquisition the company's gross margin increased from 27% to 33%, and a reasonable, but prospectively higher, rate of return was being realized.

In another sick company, the acquiring management took quite a different tack. The president of the acquired company was described as a "tyrant who surrounded himself with yes-men of little competence." The tyrant characterization of the president was known prior to the purchase, but the capabilities of the other key executives had been obscured by the company's success. During the first year of ownership, the top management got firm impressions of the top five executives and within another year successfully terminated four of the five with no deleterious repercussions on the morale or production of the company. The approach, according to the president of the acquiring company, was to operate the division over a sufficient period so that employees came to recognize for themselves that certain of the key executives were not doing their jobs. When the four vice presidents left, no other employee went with them and the acquiring company president observed that morale and productivity had never been higher.

Perhaps the most significant conclusion which can be

drawn from these cases is that acquiring managements should take enough time to become acquainted with the realities of the situation before taking action. Sensitivity and insecurity will be found in most acquired organizations, and actions taken by the acquirer must be timed to strengthen, not weaken, the operating effectiveness of the group.

The attitudes and motivations of owners who sell their interests in a company and remain on in top management positions can also change, even though the acquiring company does nothing to affect the essential activities of the acquired company. The Preston Company, for example, was owned by two men: Mr. Bart, a highly trained technical executive, and Mr. Cane, a very competent business management executive. Both were in their early forties and had organized and developed the company over a ten-year period into a considerable financial success. In July 1960, needing additional capital to finance their growth and not wanting to have stockholders other than themselves, and also aware that their large personal fortunes were locked into the company, they agreed to sell to a West Coast company for listed securities and to continue to manage the operation as a division of the purchaser. For a few months the arrangement worked very well, but gradually Mr. Bart began to arrive at the office at 10 A.M. and leave at 3 P.M. Weekend trips lengthened from Thursday nights until Tuesday mornings. Mr. Cane sought to protect his partner and friend, but soon even he was disturbed by the lack of productive work by Mr. Bart. Mr. Bart's wife, aware of touchable, tangible wealth for the first time, encouraged a two-month vacation to the Caribbean, where they bought a house, and she influenced her husband to spend more time with the family. The deteriorating condition became known in and outside the organization, and Mr. Howe, president of the acquiring company, went to the Preston Company to determine what should be done. Mr. Howe met with Mr. Bart, discussed the need and desire for his professional contributions, and helped Mr. Bart analyze what he really wanted to do. Mr. Howe stated that Mr. Bart would be most welcome to stay on and work for his $40,000 salary, but that if he did decide to leave, it was important for Mr. Bart and the organization to know the real reasons for leaving. Mr. Bart thought about the problem for five days and then resigned.

Mr. Howe, in this situation, appreciated the implications which might arise if one of two principal owners resigned shortly after having been acquired. He could project and anticipate the questions which might arise among the employees and, in addition, he wanted Mr. Bart to be a friendly resigned executive rather than a vindictive former employee whose statements always seem to seep back to the working group. Mr. Howe handled the matter personally by flying to the city where the Preston Company was located; he tried to persuade Mr. Bart to stay, and then helped him think out for himself what he really wanted to do. This personal interest was recognized by the other former owner, Mr. Cane, and even though Mr. Bart resigned, the relations between the acquired and the acquirer were reinforced by the astute administrative action of Mr. Howe.

Another example of effective administration of the problems resulting from change in the business situation of the acquired companies was found in the Note Company, a large producer of a basic raw material which decided to integrate toward the eventual customer by purchasing fabricators located strategically throughout the country in order to provide local and quick service to customers. When the first eight fabricators were acquired, the management of Note intended to have the head of each company report directly to headquarters with no intervening echelons of regional or district management. The prospect of direct access to the headquarters office appealed to the fabricator owners who relied upon the good faith of the representation.

Later, as more and more fabricating companies were purchased in other parts of the United States, it became apparent to the Note management that 15 subsidiaries could not be managed effectively by one vice president and general manager, Mr. Smith, at the home office. Accordingly, Mr. Smith asked one of the well-known management consulting firms to study the problem and come up with a recommended organization structure. He received the consultant's report recommending a new organizational setup, and aware of the attitudes and feelings of the acquired managements, he selected certain regional and district managers from the heads of the companies acquired, discussed the opportunities with them, and then called a meeting of all managers to raise the problem and state the action to be taken.

The use of consultants in this case gave the solution adopted the benefit of an outside and objective point of view. This approach enabled Mr. Smith to state that he had sought the best professional help available to face the problems, and this, together with the care with which former company presidents from within the company were moved into larger responsibilities, permitted a smooth change. Mr. Smith noted that none of the acquired company managers resigned, even though most of them were sufficiently well off financially to leave and retire.

DEALING WITH KEY PEOPLE

One of the most emotion-filled topics of acquisition we encountered during our study was the problem of dealing with key people in acquired companies who did not meet the standards of performance expected by the managements of the acquirers. Owners of companies who sold out to others frequently launched into lengthy statements about the moral responsibilities of management to care for long-term employees. It was said, "Letting 50- and 55-year old key people out on the streets with limited alternatives for employment is immoral and inconsistent with the ethics of responsible businessmen. Business has a responsibility toward these key people." Acquirers of companies, on the other hand, with no less feeling for the problems involved for the deposed executives, pointed out that if the enterprise was to succeed and grow, their best judgment had to be exercised in the selection of personnel. If it was concluded that Mr. Jones, with 30 years of experience and without useful contributions to make in other areas of the company, could not perform efficiently, then he had to go so that the survival of the whole enterprise would not be jeopardized.

These are very difficult problems for which there are, of course, no quick, easy, and pleasing answers. We observed that some of the owners who sold their companies and withdrew from management were the most articulate about the social responsibilities of businessmen. These same owners, more frequently than not, had owned most or all of the stock of the enterprises sold and had never included their key employees in a compensation plan other than salary. Stock option plans, and stock purchase plans, were unknown to their experience and in some situations no or inadequate retirement plans had been provided. Some of the outspoken critics of the way in which employees were treated are reminiscent of the agnostic older citizens who quickly turn to religion in their declining years. Indeed, some observers on the morality issue involved in terminating older people do so in the comfortable atmosphere of retirement resulting from the proceeds of sale of their companies.

The handling of key personnel in acquired companies in the situations studied varied from the ruthless to the considerate. The managements of some acquiring companies engaged in fraud, misleading representations, and other unsavory conduct both during the negotiations and in the integration process. In one situation, for example, a vice president of the acquiring company stated to Mr. Bell, a vice-president of the company to be acquired, that if they were successful in purchasing the company, the intention was to bring the newly acquired company together with two others in the same business and to make Mr. Bell the top vice president of sales. This was confirmed subsequently by the acquiring company president when he visited the offices as part of the negotiation team. Mr. Bell was not a large stockholder but was a key member of the company's top management. The company to be acquired was largely family-owned and the presidency was held by one member of the family group. In this situation the president discussed the advantages and disadvantages of selling with his top executives and the consensus of judgment was to sell. Negotiations were consummated and the acquirer took over. On the first day of control, Mr. Bell was called in by the new owners and told that he was fired. They gave him 60 days' termination pay, and a pat on the back, and said goodbye.

Unfeeling and needless cruelty was found in another situation. When the Rose Company bought the Star Company in Dallas, the president of the acquired organization, Mr. Stone, who was not a principal stockholder, was given a three-year employment contract at his existing salary of $28,000 a year. Very shortly after the acquisition friction and conflict arose between the two organizations, and the headquarters management decided to put one of their own men in the general manager's position. This was done and Mr. Stone kept his office, his title, and his compensation; he was told that his role would be to serve as a consultant to the new manager. The arrangement was agreeable to Mr. Stone, but he soon discovered that the new manager had taken over completely, employees were forbidden to discuss problems with Mr. Stone, and the only mail he received was personal, having been screened previously in the mail room to avoid his knowing anything about company operations. For a while

Mr. Stone came to the office every working day, but his frustration and isolation soon led him to resignation. In a few management circles, this process was described as operation "freeze out" and while it may have appeal to certain ruthless management personnel, its practice is not condoned among the preponderance of business executives we interviewed during our study.

Other acquiring managements have approached the solution to this problem in quite different ways. In the Donald Company, for example, the former president of the acquired company retired when the sale was made and the acquirer transferred one of its vice presidents, Mr. Pope, to manage the enterprise. Mr. Pope learned that one of the key executives he inherited as treasurer was generally disliked by the organization and made no substantial contributions. Mr. Pope decided that he would not make an abrupt decision and discharge the treasurer, but rather would give him a number of special and important projects to do. Later the treasurer was asked to take over responsibility for a related but ailing section. At the end of six months, Mr. Pope concluded that since the treasurer had done nothing on the assigned projects and had done little more than check the salaries of the people in the section assigned, termination was the only remaining alternative. But the treasurer was given opportunities to show whether his work attitude and performance would change under a new president.

In the Schmid Company, the president, Mr. Hobe negotiated the purchase of a midwestern company during which he discovered that the operation could be managed best by a young assistant general manager. The president and substantial owner wanted to retire but the problem was what to do about the general manager, Mr. Hale, about 55 years old and formerly a practicing attorney. Mr. Hale and his wife had lived in the small midwestern city for ten years, their children were in college or married, and there were no especial ties which bound them to that vicinity. Mr. Hobe discussed alternatives with Mr. Hale and offered him the opportunity to move to Los Angeles to work in Mr. Hobe's new division as director of administration. The chance to move to Southern California, plus the experience of working in a large and growing company, appealed to Mr. Hale and shortly after the sale was approved, Mr. and Mrs. Hale went to Los Angeles. At the time of our interview, Mr. Hale had been on the job almost a year and Mr. Hobe stated that he was doing a superb job, not only in helping to manage the company acquired but also in participating in the acquisition of other companies.

Sometimes the unpleasantness of terminating key people is softened by recognition by the affected executives that they are not performing according to the new owners' expectations. A division manager of a large food company, Mr. Nash, stated that except for one executive who had been fired for out and out dishonesty, he had been required to terminate only two other executives among the dozens employed by the companies acquired in recent years. The two other executives were brothers and sons of the founder of the acquired company, and as time passed it became evident that they could not handle their jobs. One brother was 64 years old and the other 61. Mr. Nash decided to discuss early retirement with them and telephoned that he would arrive at their plant the following morning. He walked into the office where the two brothers had desks side by side and as he sat down facing their desks, he noticed a copy of a new magazine opened to a story headed, "How to Fire Executives Gracefully." Mr. Nash, after a brief uneasy moment, revealed the purpose of his visit and the two executives seemed greatly relieved to learn that they could retire early. The separation was amicable and, as Mr. Nash reported, "almost jovial."

As in the case of all problems of change in acquired companies, an awareness of the circumstances and a complete understanding of the implications and consequences should precede administrative action to accomplish changes in key executives. We found many companies which had been acquired where the history of operations was a story of a strong family living and growing together. The president of one enterprise said that he knew the names of his 250 employees, department head meetings were held once a week where all major company problems were discussed, a company-wide profit-sharing plan resulted typically in at least one month's bonus for everyone at the end of the year, and if anyone spoiled a batch in the manufacturing process, it became common knowledge throughout the plant and it was not likely to happen again. The management of the acquirer coming into such an environment must recognize the individual's security which arises out of his informal working relationships. Action taken with regard to one executive which seems precipitous or unfair is interpreted by the group as a threat and danger to their position and security. "If it can happen to Joe, it can happen to me." Changes in executive personnel can be made, but they can best be made when the acquiring management has a full appreciation of the social group with which they are dealing.

Changing Benefit Plans

Another problem of change in the acquired company was found in the area of employee benefit plans. Many small and medium-sized companies, particularly those which are owned by members of a family or by a few entrepreneurs, have salary, bonus, expense account, and other perquisites far more generous than usually are found in larger acquiring organizations. The explanation generally given is that these extras are required in order to hold the employees. In a few situations we learned of companies with sales commission compensation plans which permitted each of the dozen salesmen to earn $60,000 to $90,000 a year. A substantial part of the going concern value of these companies was in their marketing success, and any proposal to reduce the salesmen's earnings, either during negotiations or after acquisition, met with violent opposition from the salesmen. The three owners of one midwestern company, for example, all in their sixties and anxious to sell their enterprise, have been unable to find a purchaser because of the high sales commissions they paid. This single obstacle has often stopped discussions at a very early stage of negotiations.

Some owners and managers, sometimes only part-time managers, have provided very generous salary and other benefits for themselves. One company owned by two of the founders and the widow of a third founder, provided salaries of $70,000 a year for the two active founders and $40,000 a year for the widow even though she appeared at the office only on rare occasions. High salaries, company-owned Cadillacs, company-paid vacation trips, company yachts and airplanes, were not uncommon. The owner of an East Coast company was reluctant to sell his business unless his avocation of climbing mountains throughout the world during four months of each year would be permitted by the acquirer and at company expense. Indeed, one acquiring management learned after its purchase that the acquired company maintained two girls in a comfortable apartment in New Orleans.

Another form of employee benefit was the bonus plan. In some companies a cash bonus was paid at the end of the year, frequently related to profits and return on investment which amounted to one or two months' wage or salary. Profits over the years were sufficient to make the payments possible and employees came to think of the extra payment as a fixed part of their incomes. Many employees had the anticipated cash payment spent or committed long before its receipt.

The experiences of acquiring managements in dealing with exorbitant employee benefit plans that we encountered indicate clearly that the problems can be handled much more effectively before the acquisition rather than after. The existence of the elements of benefit programs is usually determinable during the evaluation and negotiation stage and should be part of the terms of the agreement. In one company, with an out-of-line cash bonus plan for all employees, a condition of the purchase was that the acquired management would negotiate and conclude an agreement with the union for the abolition of the bonus. The acquirer here was quite prepared to withdraw from considering the acquisition if this condition was not met. The union did agree to a new contract without the bonus plan, but the risk remains for the acquirer when the contract is reopened on its second anniversary.

A major concern of some large acquiring company managements is that the acquisition of even a small company with what they believe to be an undesirable employee benefit provision will be the crack through which the benefit will be extended throughout the whole company. The president of one active acquiring company said that "somehow the best and most expensive elements of each acquisition benefit plan gets into the over-all employee benefit program."

If, however, an acquirer does purchase a company with a known, out-of-line, but accepted, cash bonus plan for example, the problem of administering a subsequent change must be handled with considerable administrative skill. The Park Company, to illustrate, purchased a company in the San Francisco area. The acquisition was the first of about 20 during a seven-year period. The San Francisco enterprise, owned substantially by one man, had a generous cash bonus plan extending to all employees. Management members of the acquirer were aware of the bonus provision, but decided that the desirability of the company and its area of product activity outweighed the problems inherent in the bonus provision. Subsequent acquisitions were made of companies which did not have bonus plans, and these, together with the San Francisco company and internally developed divisions, constituted the total Park Company organization. The existence of the generous bonus plan at San Francisco became well known among all company employees. They commented, "How can I get transferred to San Francisco? We work just as hard as they do, how come they get two months' extra pay while all we get is a turkey at Christmas?"

Changing the San Francisco division plan quickly could not have been done without real risks of jeopardizing the profitability of its operations. Four years after the acquisition of the San Francisco company, the president of the Park Company employed a pension plan consultant who came up with a substitute plan which could be initiated not only in the northern California division, but also in the other divisions as well. Meetings were held with small groups of supervisors who in turn presented the proposed changes to their subordinates. Five years after the acquisition, the new pension plan was installed and the cash bonus abolished. The president of Park said that it would have been "absolutely impossible to abolish the San Francisco bonus plan outright and it would have been financial insanity to apply the plan to all divisions. But we were able to come up with something substantially equivalent. You cannot take away benefits without something real in return."

Any business operation requires administrative attention. And in a newly acquired company it is especially needful, particularly during the early weeks and months of adapting to new owner relationships. Doubts and concerns do exist in the acquired group and neglect by the acquirer compounds these fears. The assumption cannot be made that the acquired organization will naturally and automatically continue to perform as it did in the past.

The administration of changes in the acquired organization should be done with recognition that the manner in which the changes are made characterize the management attitudes and policies of the acquirer. Ruthless and devious methods were found to be ineffective and acquirers who employed such devices almost always regretted the actions taken. Some changes must be made, of course, and the primary goal is not to keep everyone happy. This is impossible. But it is possible to perform the integration phase of an acquisition according to its definition, "Harmonious coordination of behavior and personality with one's environment," and we add, at a profit.

*   *   *   *   *

In this report we have attempted to discuss some of the management problems included in the acquisition of one company by another. We recognize that the process of acquisition, like the process of administration, cannot be broken into mechanical steps. But the chapter headings selected provided convenient sections for an orderly discussion of the subject. The problem areas studied and reported upon seemed to cover the major and common concerns of managements and owners involved in acquisition.

Our report may be disappointing to those who are looking for easy answers to complex top management problems. It must be remembered that the acquisition of one company by another is a unique experience and each acquisition includes a unique bundle of problems. We sincerely hope that our findings will be helpful to owners and managers of both buyers and sellers as they seek solutions to management problems of corporate acquisitions.